IMAGES
of America

MARITIME MARIN

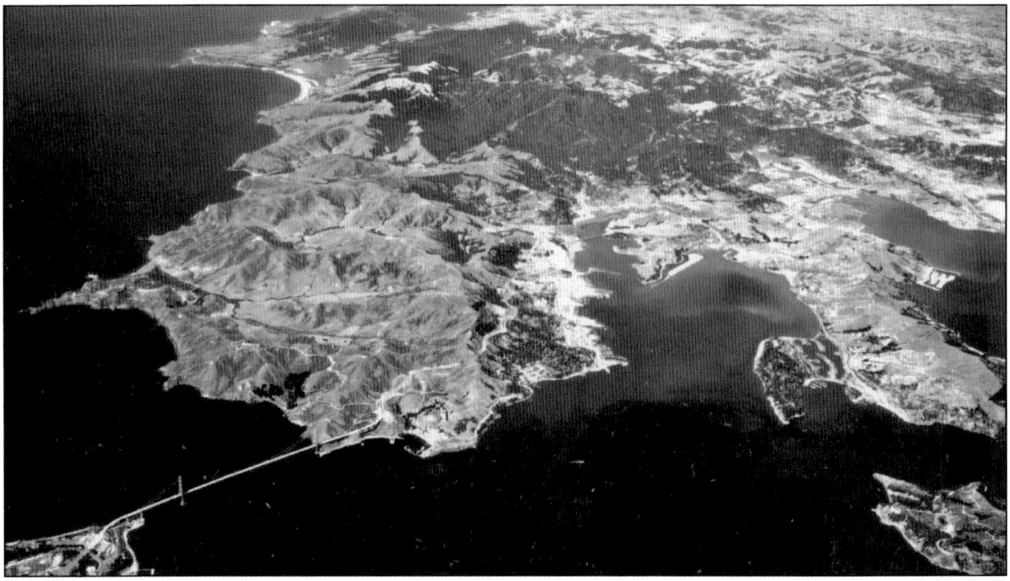

Marin County is connected to San Francisco, one of the world's great cities, by an engineering marvel—the Golden Gate Bridge. (Courtesy Marin History Museum.)

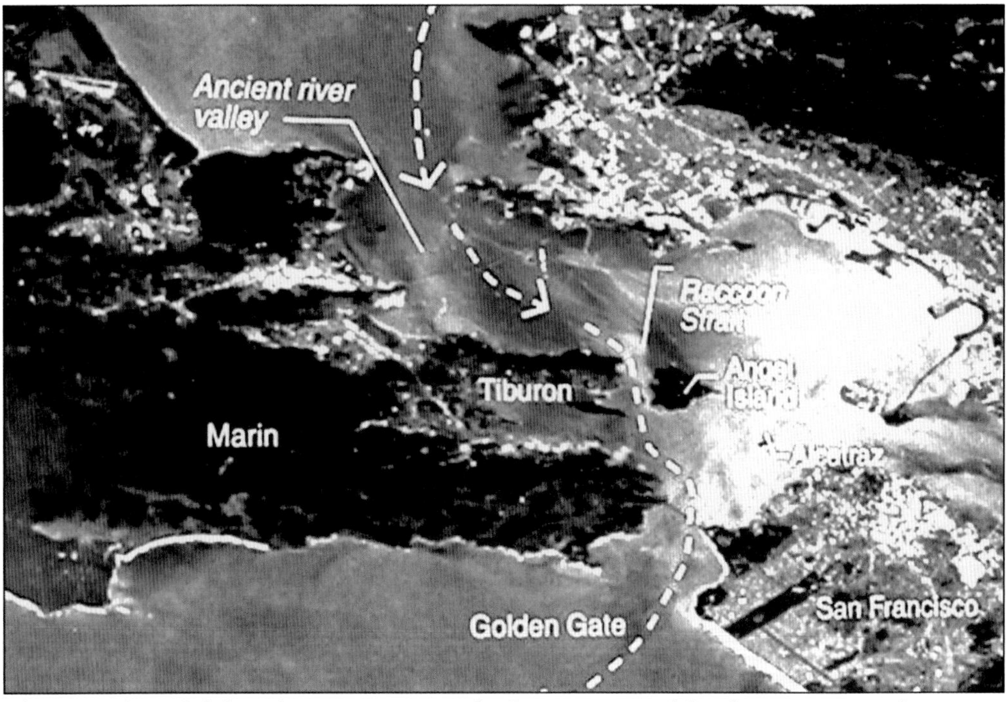

The waters from California's two great rivers, the Sacramento and San Joaquin, create the estuary known as San Francisco Bay. They flow through Suisun Bay and San Pablo Bay and then through Raccoon Strait, between the Tiburon Peninsula and Angel Island, then around the Marin Headlands and out the Golden Gate to the Pacific Ocean. (Courtesy Angel Island Association.)

ON THE COVER: Sailing ships stocked up on wood and water while awaiting cargo in Richardson Bay. (Courtesy San Francisco Maritime National Historical Park.)

IMAGES
of America

MARITIME MARIN

Branwell Fanning

ARCADIA
PUBLISHING

ISBN 978-0-7385-5904-9

Published by Arcadia Publishing
Charleston, South Carolina

Printed in the United States of America

Library of Congress Catalog Card Number: 2008924120

For all general information contact Arcadia Publishing at:
Telephone 843-853-2070
Fax 843-853-0044
E-mail sales@arcadiapublishing.com
For customer service and orders:
Toll-Free 1-888-313-2665

Visit us on the Internet at www.arcadiapublishing.com

Jose de Canizares, chief pilot of the San Carlos,
leader of the exploring parties, and maker of the first maps
of the Marin shoreline, named bays, islands, and prominent land features
after saints, captains, and governors, but nothing after himself.

Contents

ACKNOWLEDGMENTS

I developed a love of the sea and ships as a young boy when we spent our summers at my grandmother's house on the waterfront in Salem, Massachusetts. Because of either age or the Depression, many "old salts" were on the beach, and we boys would gather and listen to tales of the sea by men who had actually sailed before the mast. Often the tales would end with our gathering around a battered sea chest while our tale spinner fished around until he came up with an old key he swore he took from the captain's cabin on the battleship *Maine* when he help raise it in Havana harbor.

Of course, these tales were all true, so I would be remiss if I did not acknowledge their contribution to this tale of another county by the sea far away. And then there is Tom Speckman, my partner in rebuilding an old wooden sailboat. He taught me all I would ever need to know about marine carpentry and sailing a 47-foot yawl without a motor. When I discovered a nest of wooden boats in Sausalito, I felt right at home.

Unless otherwise specified, all images are courtesy of the author.

Other material used in preparing *Maritime Marin*:

Submerged Cultural Resources Assessment, prepared for the Golden Gate National Recreation Area (GGNRA), Point Reyes National Seashore, and Gulf of the Farallones National Marine Sanctuary

The History of the Greater San Francisco Bay Region, Lawrence Kinnaird, Ph.D.

San Francisco National Maritime Historic Park

Broken Shore—The Marin Peninsula, Arthur Quinn

Natural History of the Islands of California, Allen A. Schoenherr and Robert Feldmeth.

The Hidden Treasures of San Francisco Bay, Anderson and George.

A Natural History of San Francisco Bay, Schoenherr.

Chief Marin, Betty Goerke

Island in Time, The Point Reyes Peninsula, Harold Gilliam

New Guardians for the Golden Gate, Amy Meyer

The *Marin Independent Journal*

The Bay Institute

The Belvedere Tiburon Landmarks Society Archives

Chris Morrison, keeper of the Morrison Family Collection

As always, thanks to my wife, Carolyn Fanning, who not only caulked the seams on my old wooden boat but edited and re-edited the copy for this and my other literary efforts.

INTRODUCTION

Marin County could be compared to a ship, with the stern firmly anchored in the wine country of Northern California, the bow at the Golden Gate, the starboard (right) side at the Pacific Coast line, and the port side fronts on San Francisco Bay. The 50-mile-long Pacific Coast is dominated by several huge state and national parks with a few scattered villages and popular beaches. The urbanized areas of Marin County are on the bay side. Also in Marin are several of the bay's islands, including the largest—Angel Island.

During the last ice age, the Pacific Coast was 30 miles farther west, out beyond the Farallon Islands. The present bay was a large valley with a huge river flowing through a gap in the coastal mountain range. The river also cut through the Tiburon Peninsula, creating a gorge that is now the deepest part of the bay. As the ice melted and the oceans rose more than 300 feet, the shoreline crept closer to the mountains until finally the tides were flowing back into the valley, filling it completely. The rising ocean waters also turned several low hills into the Farallon Islands.

The bay was much larger at that time. It covers 546 square miles today, down from 787 square miles when the Spaniards first arrived in 1775. Hydraulic mining during the Gold Rush flushed millions of tons of silt down the rivers to cover the wetlands on the edge of the bay, as well as fill much of its deeper parts. More of the wetlands were lost to land development and public health concerns about mosquito-born diseases. However, it is still the largest estuary on the Pacific Coast, draining a watershed that includes the Sierra Nevada Mountains and the Sacramento and San Joaquin Rivers. The San Francisco Bay estuary consists of five or six bays. Marin fronts on San Pablo Bay and part of central San Francisco Bay. Richardson Bay is entirely in Marin, as is Tomales Bay out on the Pacific Coast.

The two great rivers meet and form a delta before the water enters the bay and begins to flow down the Marin shore. This torrent of freshwater (minus the millions of acre feet shipped to Southern California) combines with the saltwater from the ocean pouring in through the Golden Gate twice a day on eight-foot tides. The brackish water supports a complex web of aquatic life. From plankton to salmon to sea lions, the Marin shore is teeming with wildlife.

On Marin's Pacific side, the great white sharks have their breeding grounds at Tomales Bay, and California grey whales visit twice a year on their annual migration to and from Baja. It was here that Francis Drake, not yet knighted, careened the *Golden Hind* for repairs in 1579 and the Spanish galleon *San Agustin* was wrecked in 1595. These were the first European contacts with the native people, who called themselves Miwok.

The Miwoks lived a simple existence. Acorns picked off the ground under the forest of oak trees covering Marin provided a staple food source supplemented by deer, elk, and bear meat, and fish and shellfish from the ocean and bays. There were several linguistic branches of the tribe living in Marin when the first permanent settlers arrived after 1775. The dense forests isolated the settlements except by water. The bay and ocean became the freeways for communication between each Marin settlement and the rest of the tribes in the Bay Area. Boats made by bundling reeds together were the vehicles operated by skilled boatmen, who were also leaders in their villages.

The county was named for one leader, called "El Marinero" by the Spaniards and "Chief Marin" by the Americans.

The immense forests of oaks and redwoods were the first targets of early settlers. Sawmills arrived by sea, and lumber was shipped out the same way, mostly to build San Francisco, a growing settlement across the bay. As the trees along the coast were cut, railroads were extended into the interior and up the coast to get to more lumber. Ferry terminals were added at the southern end, and Ross Landing, several miles up Corte Madera Creek, became the busiest seaport in California. Specially constructed lumber schooners plied the dangerous Pacific Coast, requiring the construction of lighthouses and lifesaving stations.

The relative isolation of Angel Island made it a logical choice for a quarantine station to protect the population from infectious diseases arriving on passengers from Asia. An immigration station, also on Angel Island, has been controversial ever since and is now being restored as a monument to those immigrants whose welcome was not equal to those arriving at Ellis Island on the East Coast.

While never as robust an industry as in the neighboring cities of San Francisco and Oakland, the building of ships and boats has a long history in Marin. Marine craftsmen on both Marin coasts have been noted for their construction and repair of workboats and fine yachts. Several of the largest ferries ever built were launched in Marin, and local shipyards provided 93 ships to the U.S. Navy and maritime fleet in World War II.

The only skirmish between the Mexicans and the Americanos, leading to California's independence, was fought in Marin, and Marin has hosted navy and army facilities dating back to the Civil War. Because of its strategic location commanding the entrance to the bay, coast artillery batteries on the north side of the Golden Gate and on Angel Island were manned for a century. From muzzle loaders to Nike missiles, installations in Marin have guarded the bay and its cities.

Antisubmarine nets made in Marin guarded ports from Seattle, Washington, to Sydney, Australia, in World War II. Crews to manage floating drydocks accompanying the fleet were trained at a special school in Marin. Three-hundred thousand soldiers passed through the army posts on Angel Island en route to the Pacific battlefields. Almost all of these huge installations became county, state, or federal parks, or scientific research centers by the end of the 20th century.

While 10,000 ships a year pass through the Golden Gate en route to other destinations in the bay/river complex, lacking the continental rail connections of Oakland or the deep-water port of San Francisco, Marin's maritime development has been low-key, which is just the way its people want it. The beaches of West Marin fill up on sunny days; the harbors on the bay side are jammed with yachts; and the restaurants along the waterfront on both sides are enjoyed by locals as well as visitors.

San Francisco Bay is not just a name on a map. It has meant freedom, hope, beauty, fun, commerce to the world, and home to those who have been fortunate enough to live along the shores of Marin.

One

Roadless Marin

Marin stretches about 50 miles from north to south. Its long shoreline has frontage on San Pablo Bay and the north and central sections of San Francisco Bay. Smaller offshoots are Richardson and San Rafael Bays, and Belvedere, Ayala, and Horseshoe Coves. On the Pacific Coast are Tomales Bay, Drakes Bay, Bolinas Bay, Drake's Estero, and Bodega Bay (shared with Sonoma County). Marin's majestic redwoods provided wonderful shade in the hot summers, but their dark understory made land travel almost impossible. The land was laced by rivers and streams flowing down the sides of Mount Tamalpais, which were sources of food and freshwater. The 600 or so sites that have been identified as Miwok settlements have been near the bays and waterways. The local Miwok Indians maintained communication between nearby villages by footpaths, but travel to neighboring tribes around the bay required boats that were made of reeds. When the Spanish arrived in Marin, they found vast forests of redwood trees interspersed with oaks. The clear-cutting of these great forests resulted in the destruction of most of the rivers as the top soil washed off the hillsides. Mexico took over from the Spanish and parceled out the land into great ranchos. The grantees of the land, who were mostly from the British Isles, went into two main businesses—cattle and lumber. Both required reliable transportation. Businessmen in Marin needed roads to get to their ports. Gradually, wagon trails were cut out of the forest, followed by railroads. Their terminals became the important ferry ports of today—Sausalito, Tiburon, and Larkspur. At that time, Ross Landing, where the College of Marin is located today, was the busiest port in California.

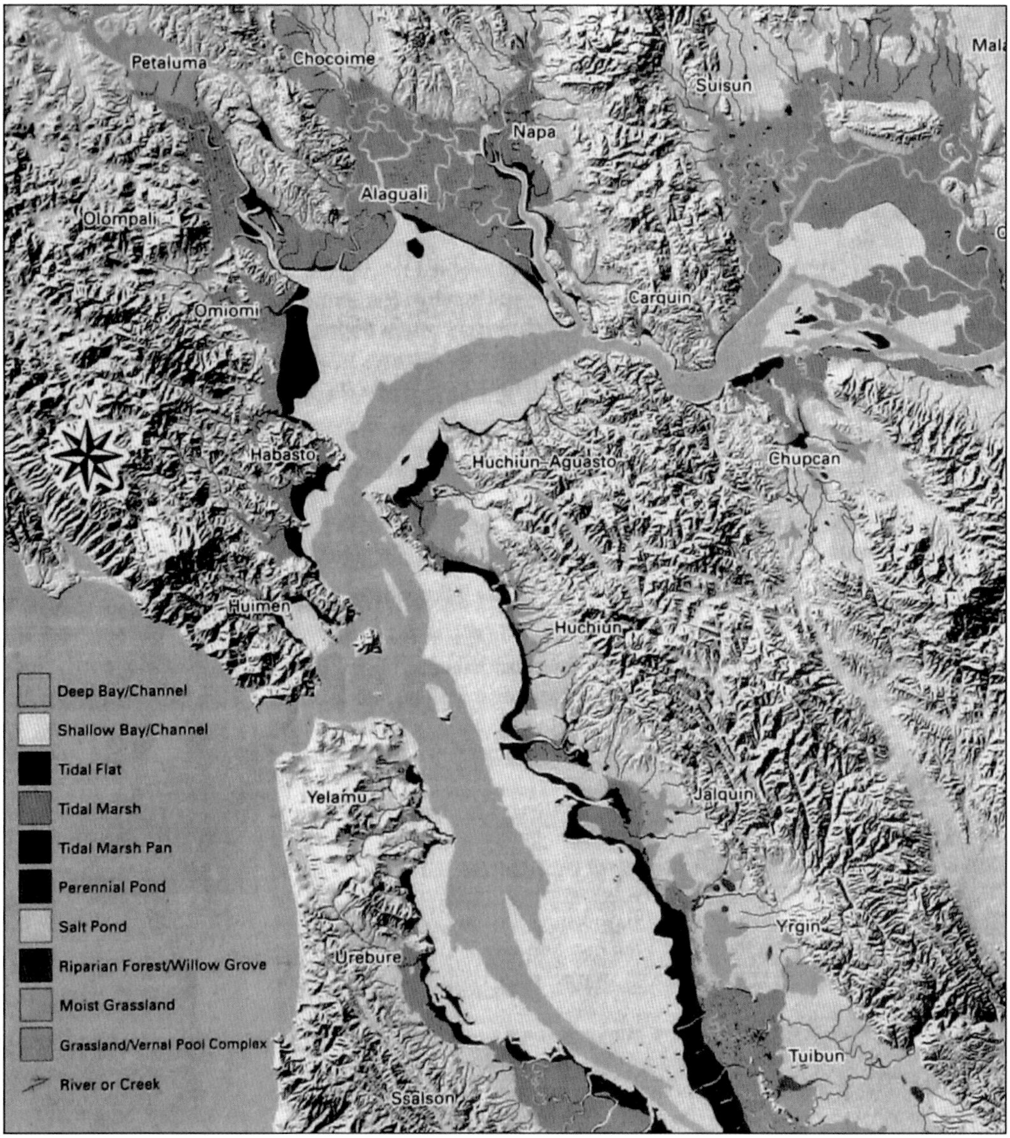

Ninety-seven percent of the forest, which once covered the hills and valleys of Marin, were cut for lumber and to clear the land for farms and ranches. The siltation following the cutting of the forests and the sediment washed down by the hydraulic mining in the Gold Rush country reduced the size of the San Francisco Bay estuary subject to tidal action from 787 square miles to 548. The former deep water lost to the estuary is pictured in white in this image from the San Francisco Bay Conservation and Development Commission.

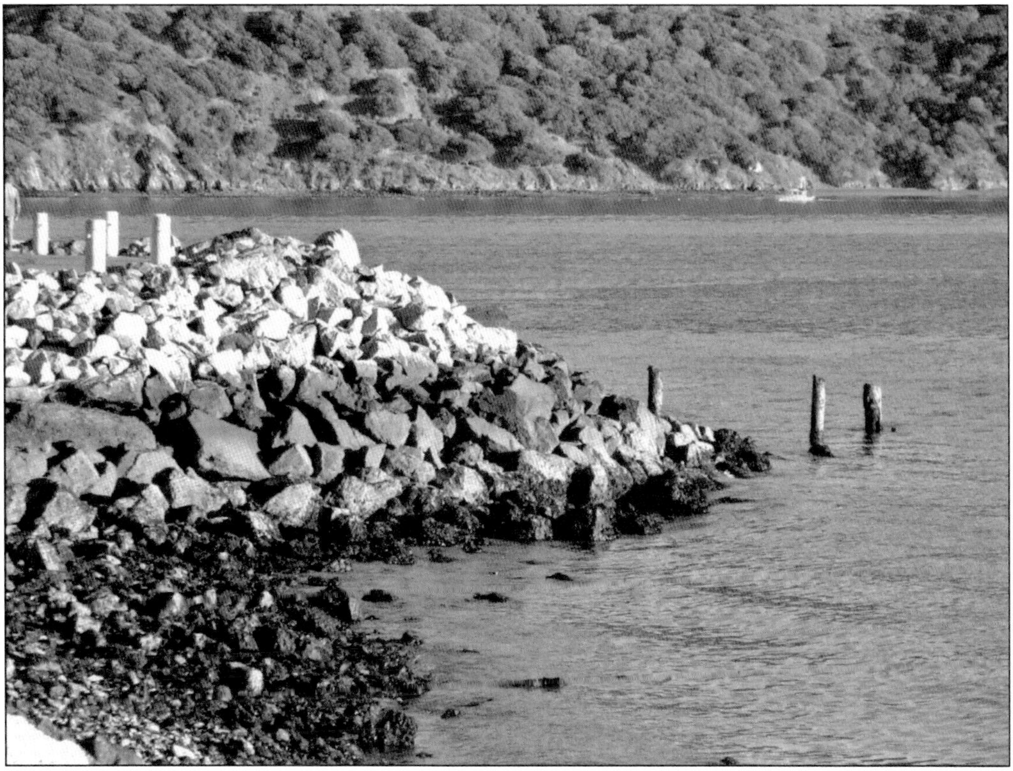

Twice a day, with each change of the tide, the ocean floods in and out. Raccoon Strait rises and falls six to eight feet, as seen in the dark band in this photograph of the shoreline. Combining the tidal surge with the flow from the rivers produces a dangerous current that all mariners treat with caution. The mingling of freshwater and saltwater creates a unique ecosystem.

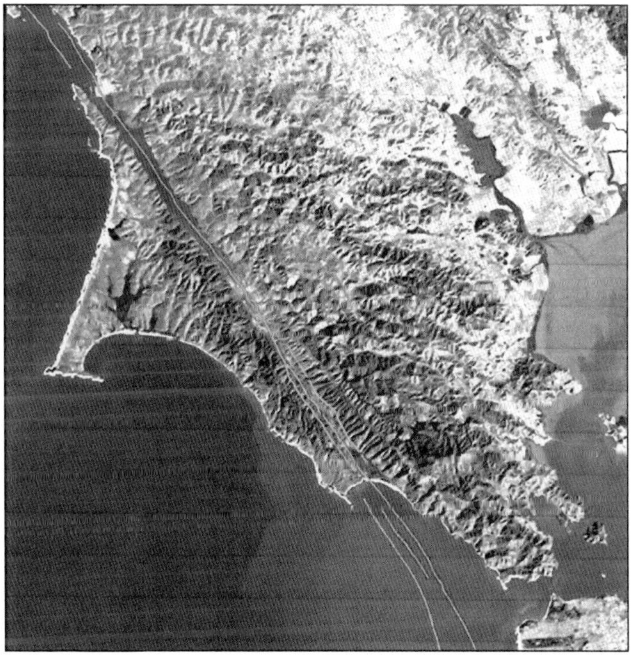

In a satellite view of Marin, it is easy to see the effects of the San Andreas Fault. The fault creates the lagoons at Bolinas and Tomales Bay. The land to the west of the fault is moving north in relation to the rest of the county.

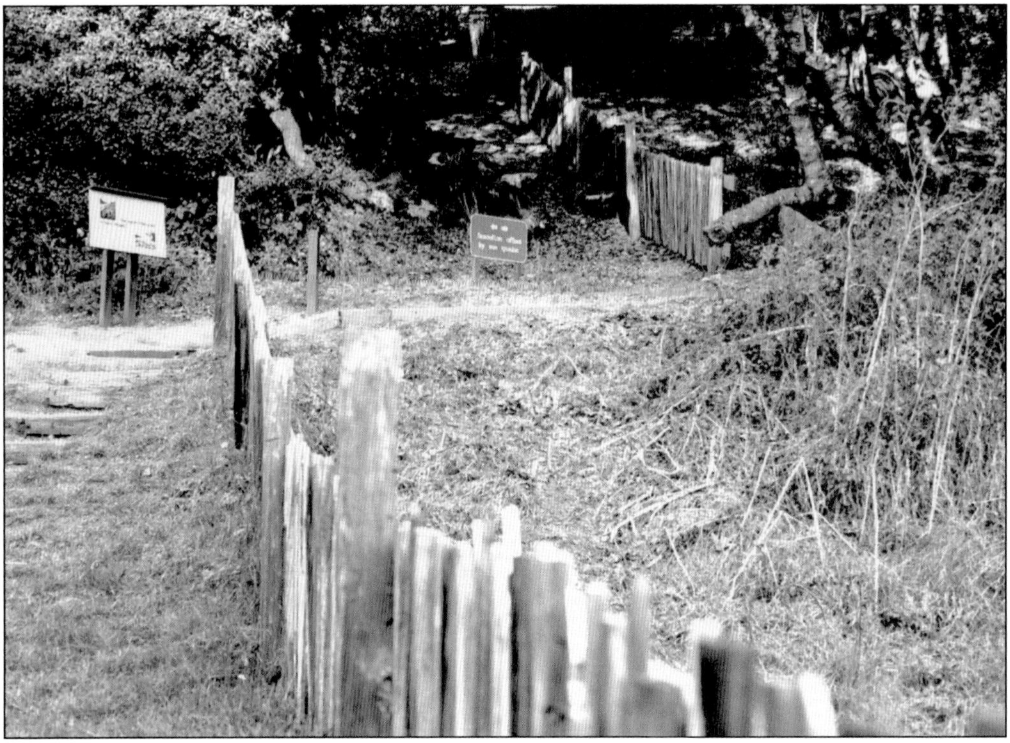

The 1906 earthquake that devastated San Francisco was centered in the Olema Valley near Tomales Bay. Roads and fences along the fault line shifted 20 feet, as seen in this photograph. Bishop pines, which thrive in granite, are on the west side of the fault line while redwoods are on the east. Scientists say that 25 million years ago, Point Reyes was 200 to 300 miles to the south of its present position.

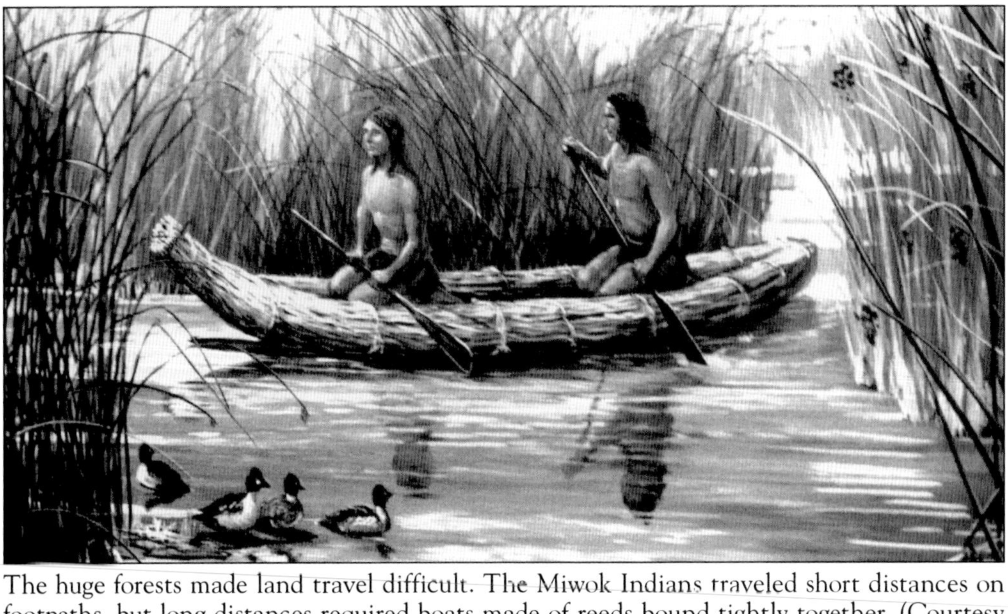

The huge forests made land travel difficult. The Miwok Indians traveled short distances on footpaths, but long distances required boats made of reeds bound tightly together. (Courtesy San Francisco Bay Model.)

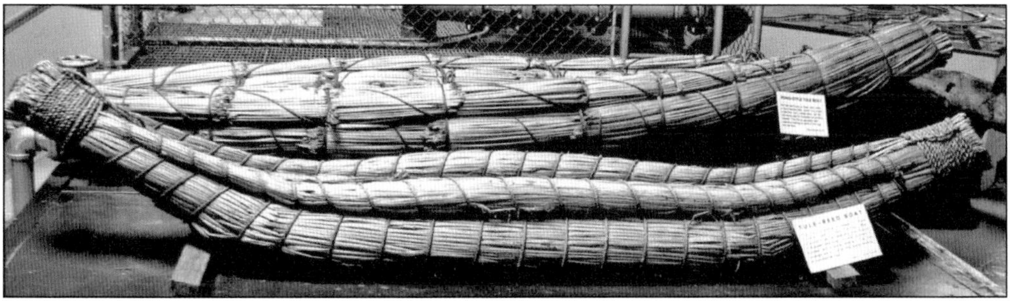

These reed boats are on display at the Bay Model in Sausalito. They were seaworthy for four or five hours before becoming waterlogged. In spite of living in a great forest, the Miwoks never developed dugout canoes.

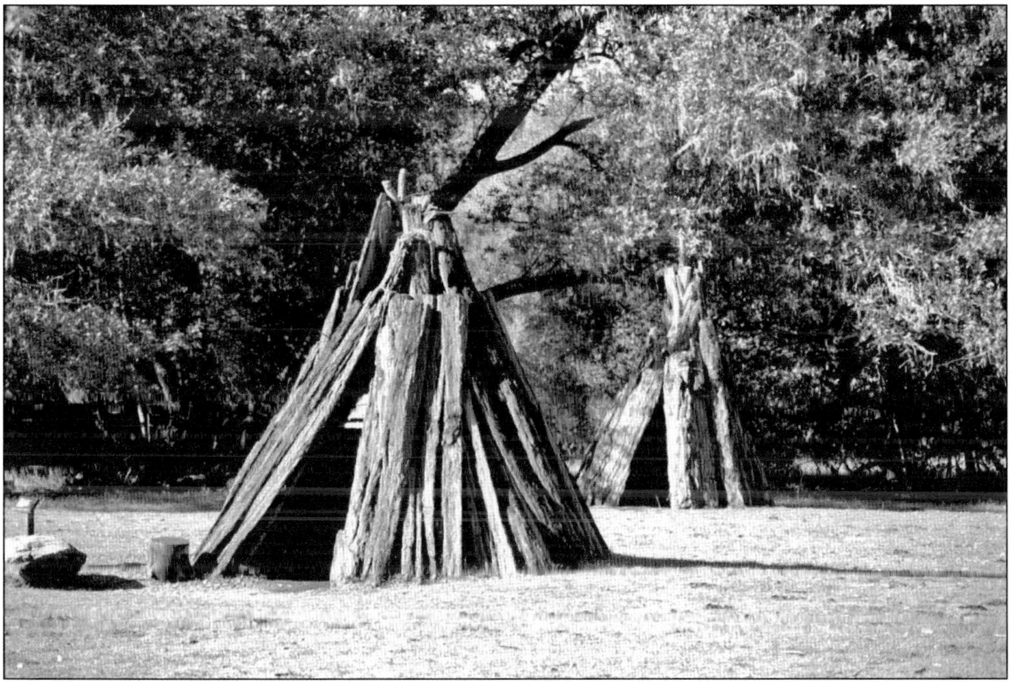

A Miwok village has been recreated by descendants of the local tribes at Point Reyes. Several generations would live in one of these huts, which were covered with long strips of bark from the forests.

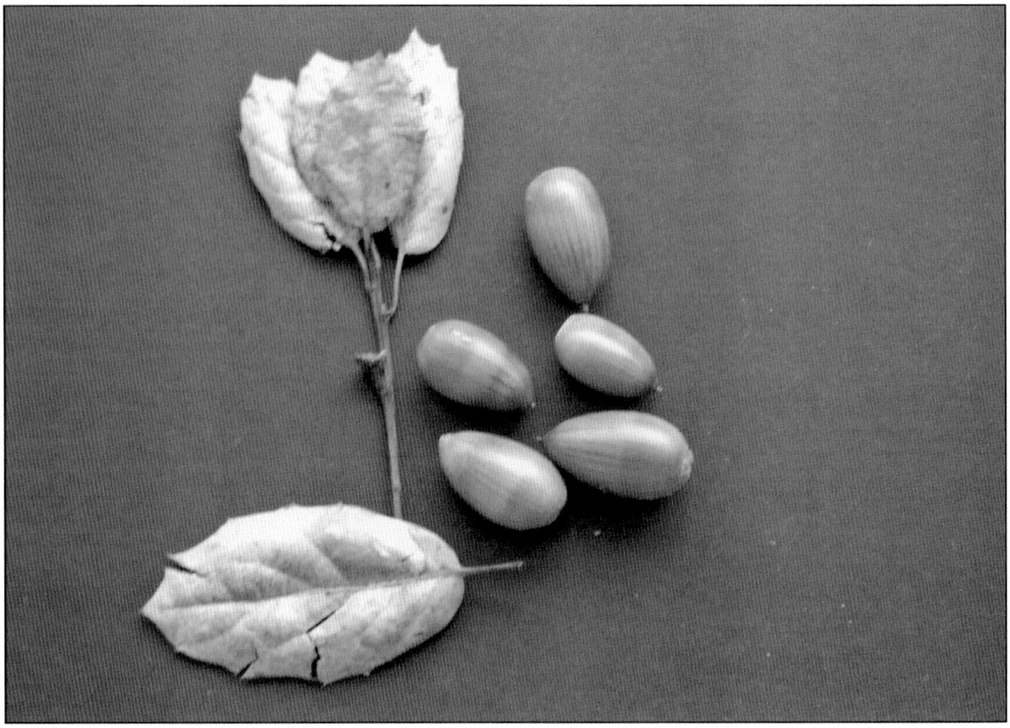

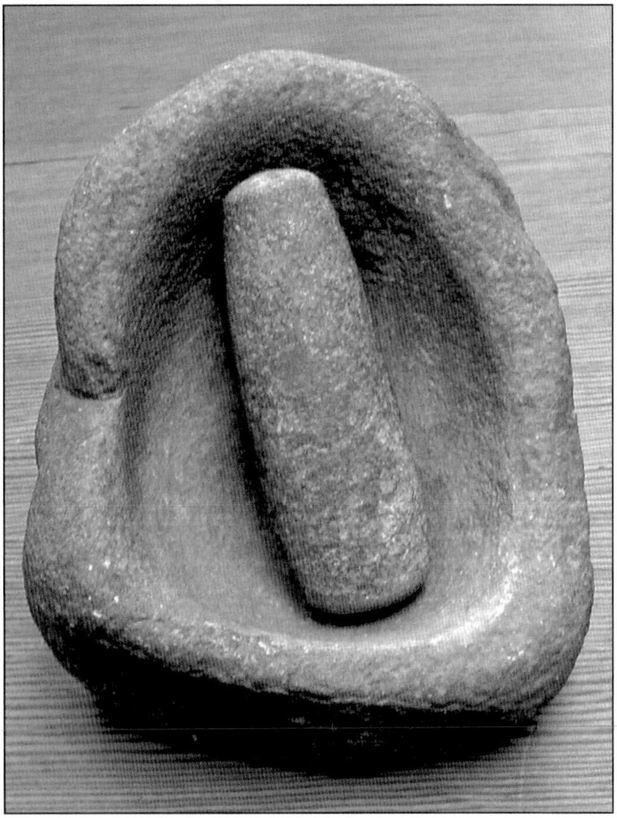

Oak trees were also a part of the great forests and were considered personal property by the tribesmen; the trees could be passed on to following generations. Acorns were a staple in the Miwok diet. After the acorns were collected and the nuts cracked, they were leached in water to remove tannins and then ground to a mush.

Mortars, such as this one found near the bay on the Tiburon Peninsula, were used to prepare the acorns. The acorns provided carbohydrates, fats, fiber, and protein in the Miwok diet and were easily stored from season to season. Shellfish were also an important part of their diet and were one reason that most villages were located near the bays or ocean. Huge shellfish mounds mark their settlements.

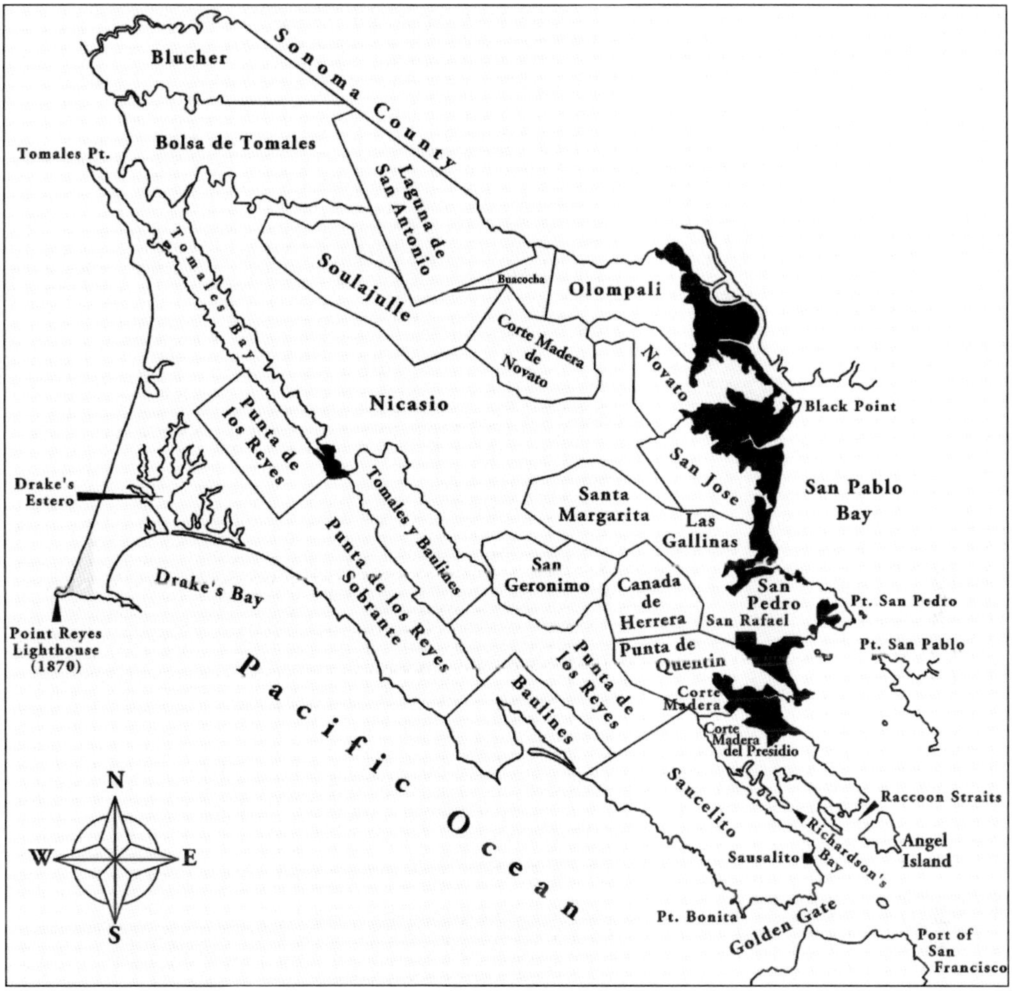

During Spanish rule, the land was administered by the padres at the missions. Following the Mexican revolt, the government in Mexico City realized that it had little chance of hanging on to its empire in Alta California, so the government started a program that granted huge parcels to friends and others who had supported it. This map shows the original division of what would become Marin County. Several of these ranchos were as large as 40,000 or 50,000 acres. Many of the grantees were from the British Isles who had been, or became, Catholic and who could speak Spanish. John Reed, from Ireland, and Englishman William Richardson shared most of southern Marin. California became independent of Mexico in 1848 and joined the United States in 1850. The United States recognized most of the land grants, and a period of consolidation of the ranchos, particularly in West Marin, began.

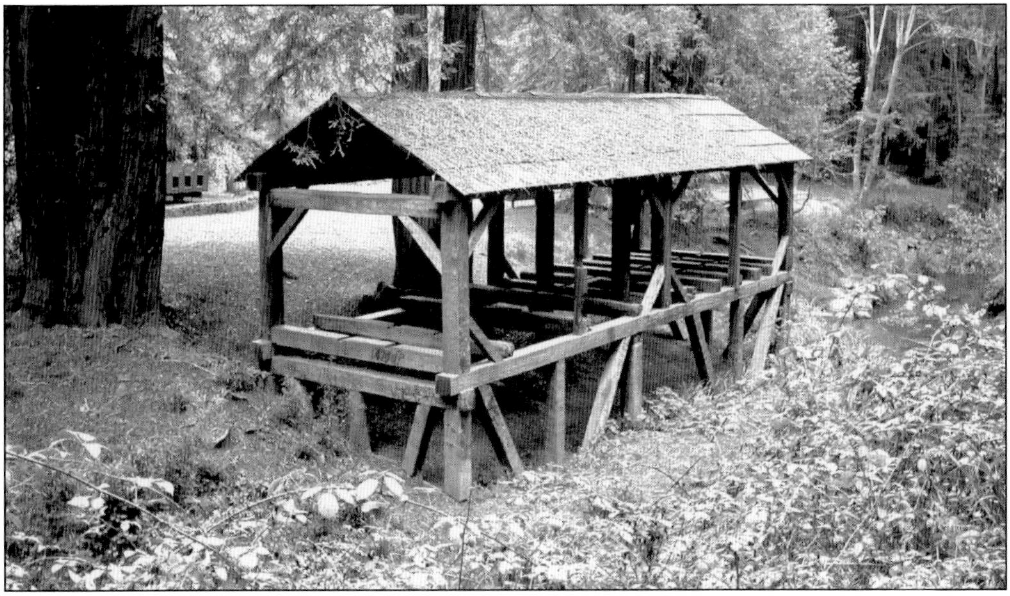

John Reed received the land grant known as Rancho Corte Madera del Presidio. Its 8,000 acres included the modern cities of Belvedere, Tiburon, Mill Valley, Corte Madera, and Larkspur. Reed opened a sawmill in Mill Valley as soon as the equipment arrived from Europe. Oxen hauled the huge redwood logs to the mill and the lumber to ports for shipment, mostly to the new, growing city that would become San Francisco.

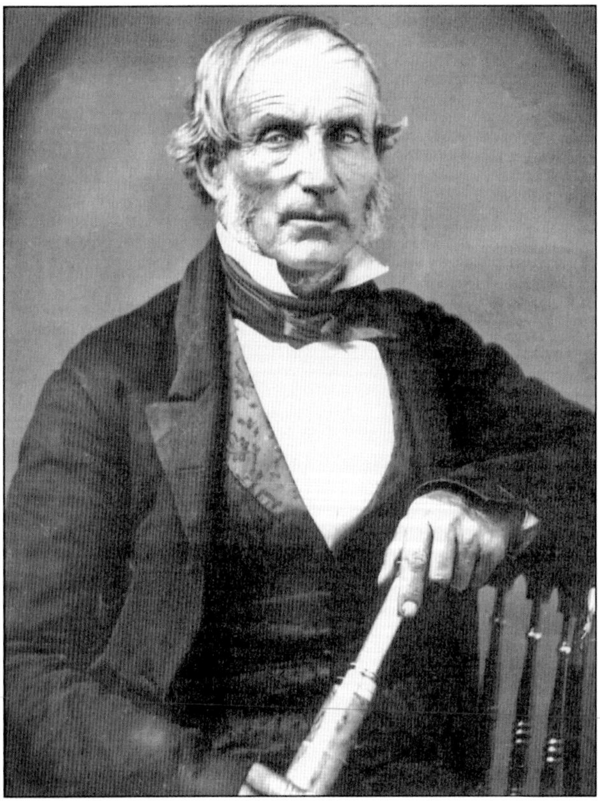

Capt. William Richardson was given almost 20,000 acres, which included the modern city of Sausalito, part of Mill Valley, Stinson Beach, the Headlands, and much of Mount Tamalpais. Unlike John Reed, Richardson was a speculator who lost most of his land. He did make the original layout of a small town called Yerba Buena by the Mexicans and San Francisco by the Americanos, where he was also captain of the port. Richardson Bay carries his name.

Two

The Age of Sail

Marin's Pacific Coast is alternately one of the most beautiful locations on earth and one of absolute terror. The spectacular outcropping of rocks attracts artists and photographers but has also claimed more than 100 ships and the lives of at least 1,000 mariners. A sailing vessel at the mercy of the winds, tides, and vicious currents found entering the Golden Gate a hazardous venture. A gale could blow ships upon the beach; if becalmed, the currents could drag them onto the rocky coast. The Manila galleons, Spain's treasure fleet, road the trade wind across the Pacific from the Orient, making landfall along Marin's coast. The captain of one of them, the *San Agustin*, was ordered to seek a safe harbor on this coast, but a storm blew the ship ashore. The surviving crew made it to Mexico in small boats.

The first several explorations of San Francisco Bay came overland from Monterey in the 1760s. Because they had no boats with them, the Golden Gate and the Strait of Carquinez prevented these explorers from proceeding farther north. The Spanish authorities determined that the southern shore of San Francisco Bay would be the northern boundary of their new empire. The chain of missions would begin in San Diego and end in San Francisco. It was not until 1775 that the first ship captain ventured cautiously through the fog-bound Golden Gate and headed straight for Marin. The *San Carlos* spent about a month anchored in a sheltered cove on Angel Island while the first real exploration of the bay was undertaken. The first settlers also arrived, not by sea, but overland from Mexico. In 1817, the Franciscan padres extended the missions to include Marin with the founding of Mission San Rafael, officially just a branch of Mission Dolores in San Francisco. The 1830s were the beginning of a rush of commercial shipping from overseas and the East Coast to the Bay Area, but Marin lacked deepwater ports or transcontinental railroad terminals, so the area did not benefit from the increase. The whaling fleets came to Marin for the winter, and codfish packing was a major industry, but Marin's maritime industry in the age of sail was built around serving Northern California with lumber, dairy products, and recreation.

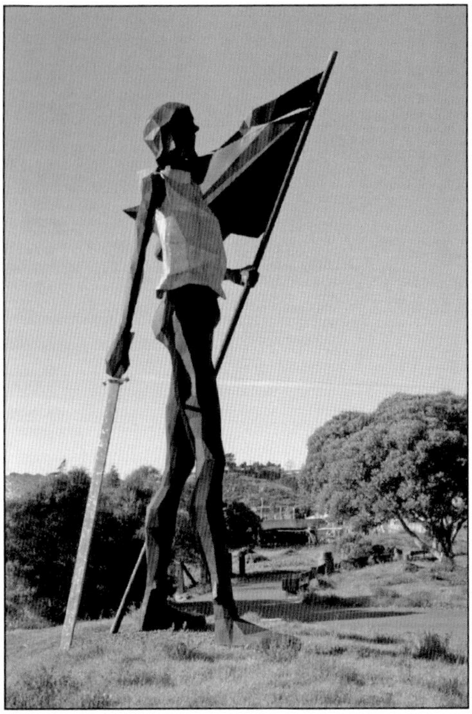

The first European visitor to Marin, as far as is known, was the swashbuckling English pirate Francis Drake, not yet knighted, who came in 1579 for more than a month. The white cliffs of Point Reyes reminded him so much of his home in England that he named his discovery New Albion. His visit is memorialized by this statue on Sir Francis Drake Boulevard, the primary east-west road in Marin.

Francis Drake cruised the Pacific Coast of South and Central America in search of Spanish gold. After looting and burning Panama, his ship, the *Golden Hind* (model below), finally became so loaded with his pirate's haul that Drake decided to head home to England. The Spanish fleet blocked the way he had come, so he decided to head west across the Pacific. But first, he needed to repair, and he careened his ship at Point Reyes.

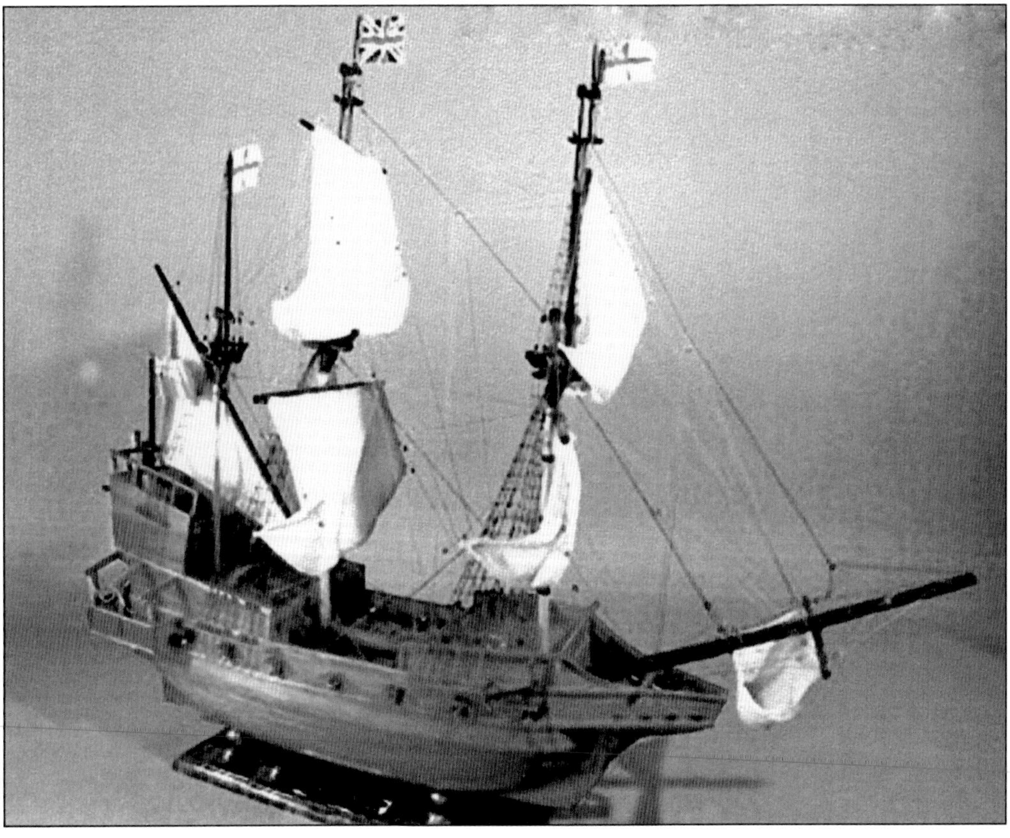

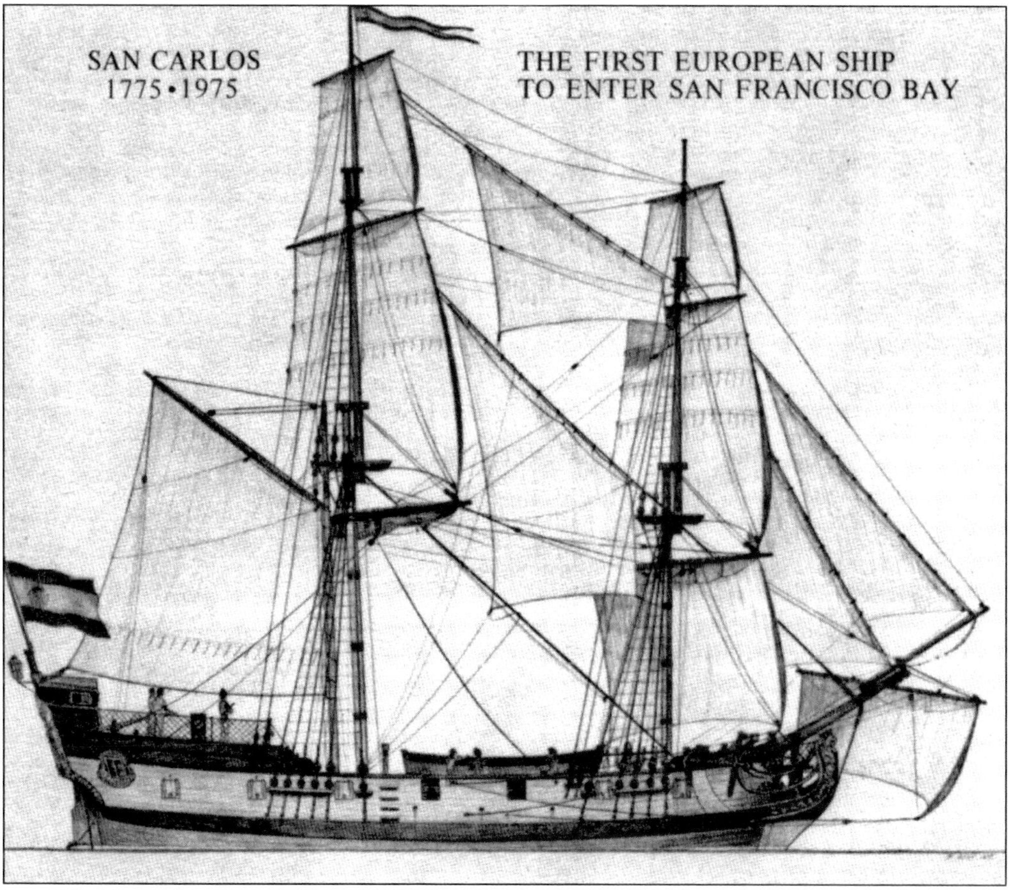

In 1775, while the American Revolution was commencing on the East Coast, the Mexican commandant ordered Lt. Juan Manuel Ayala to explore the large body of water discovered by several overland expeditions. Ayala anchored his ship, the *San Carlos*, in a cove on Angel Island while his pilot and sailing master, Jose Canizares, mapped the bay. The *San Carlos* became the supply ship between Mexico, Monterey, and San Francisco until driven ashore in a storm and wrecked in 1797. (Courtesy the Landmarks Society.)

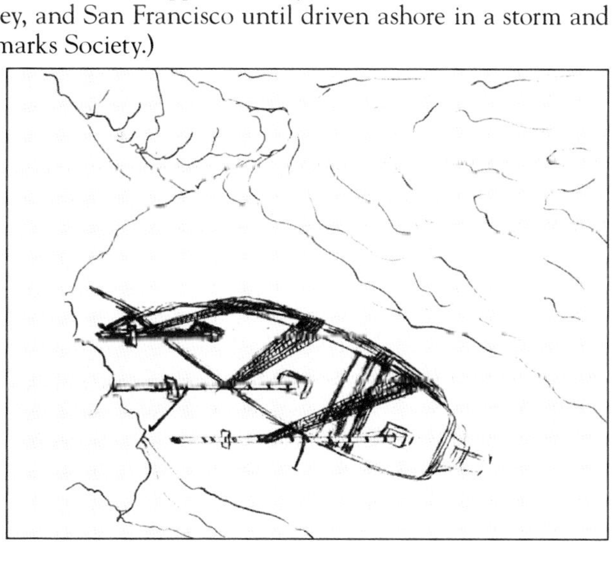

One of the next ships to visit the bay was also in distress. The British warship HMS *Racoon* was severely damaged trying to enter the Columbia River and could not make it back to England. The ship was careened in the same cove where Ayala had anchored, and repairs were completed. The now-seaworthy vessel left for home, leaving its name on the strait, although the spelling was altered to Raccoon, like the animal.

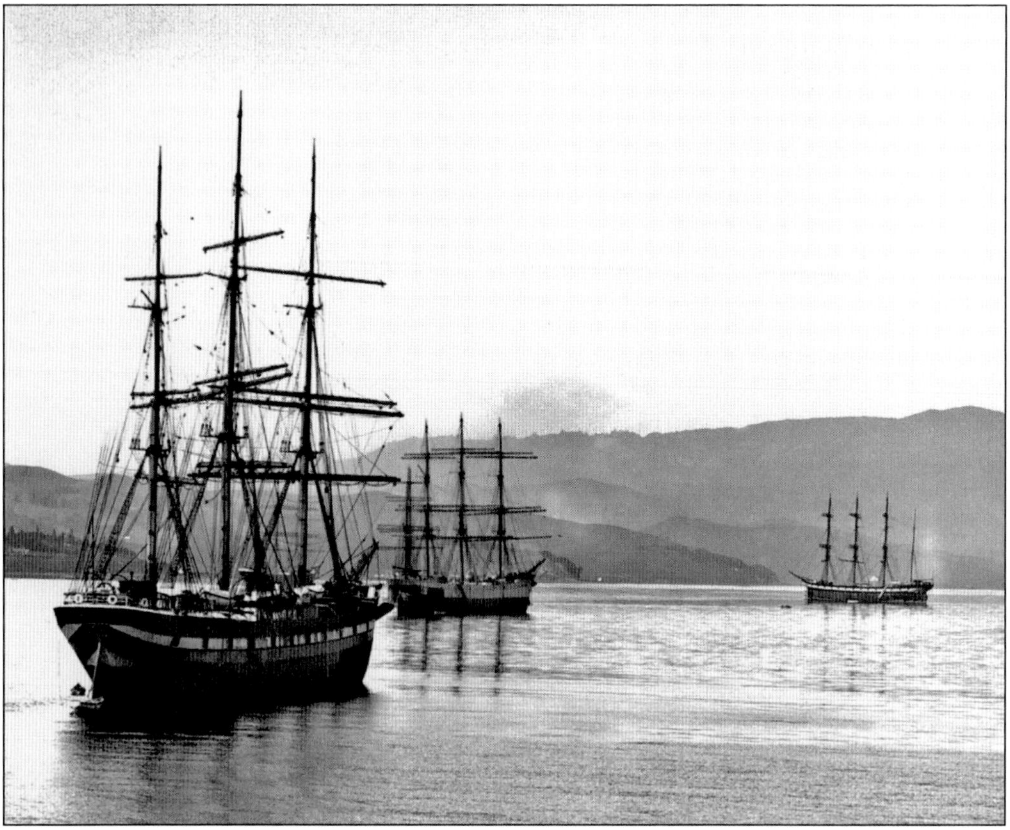

In 1836, Richard Henry Dana, aboard the *Alert*, entered San Francisco Bay on his epic two-year voyage before the mast. Dana saw a single Russian ship at anchor and no other. "Not a sail came or went during our whole stay," which lasted about five weeks. Twenty-four years later, Dana returned and was amazed that "clipper ships of the largest size lay at anchor in the stream," and from his window he could see "wharves and harbor with their thousand ton clipper ships, more than London or Liverpool." Angel Island, where Dana had obtained a year's worth of firewood on his first voyage, was now "clean shorn of trees." (Both, courtesy San Francisco Maritime National Historical Park.)

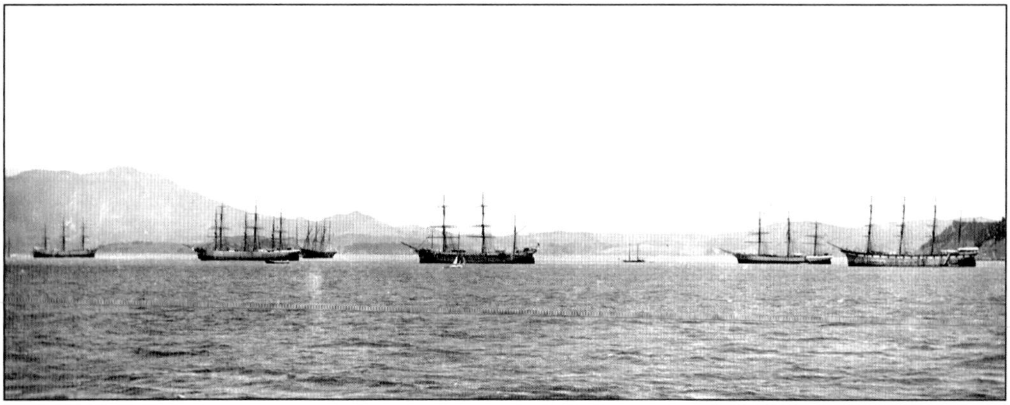

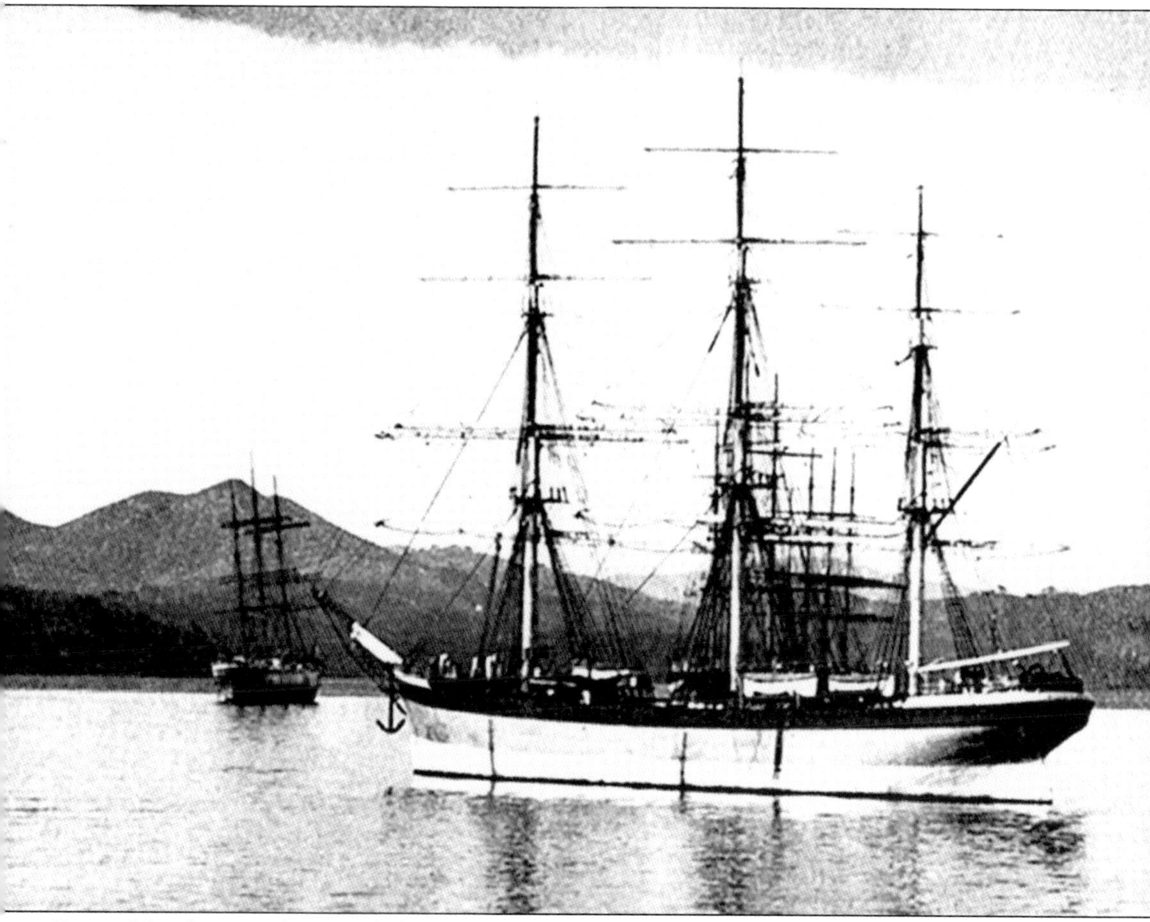

Scenes like the one above and those pictured opposite in Richardson Bay were like the ones Richard Henry Dana might have been describing, with whalers, grain ships, lumber schooners, and cargo carriers of all types waiting for sailing orders. (Courtesy San Francisco Maritime National Historical Park.)

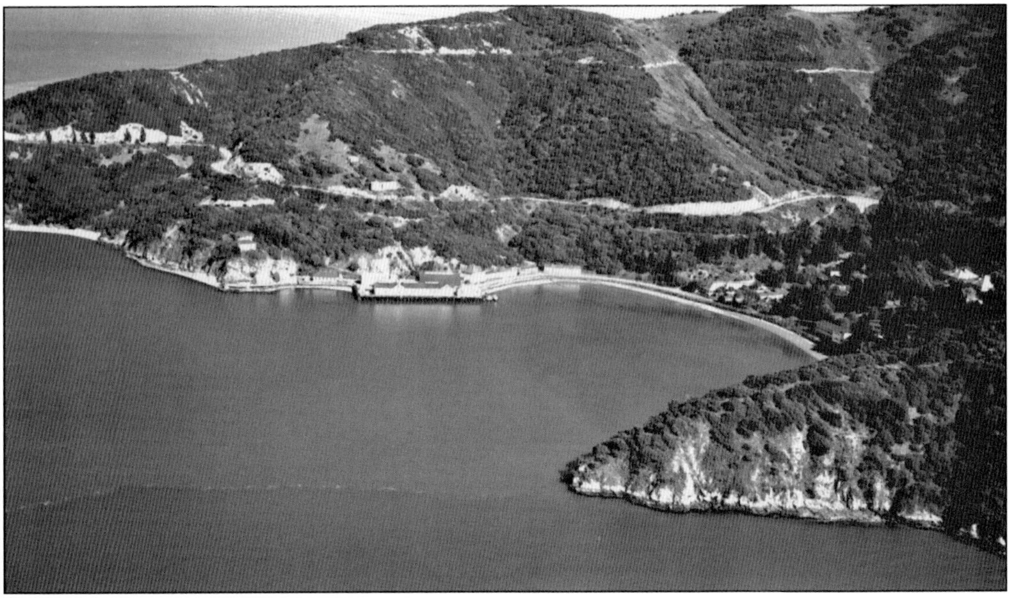

The cove on Angel Island was the safe haven for the earliest explorers. The *San Carlos* stayed for several weeks while its sailing master, José de Cañizares, in one of the *San Carlos*'s small boats, made the first charts of the bay. The island was first called Our Lady of the Angels, but it soon became known as Wood Island by the sailors who filled their firewood bins before departing on long voyages. The cove was eventually named for Lt. Juan Manuel Ayala. (Courtesy the Landmarks Society.)

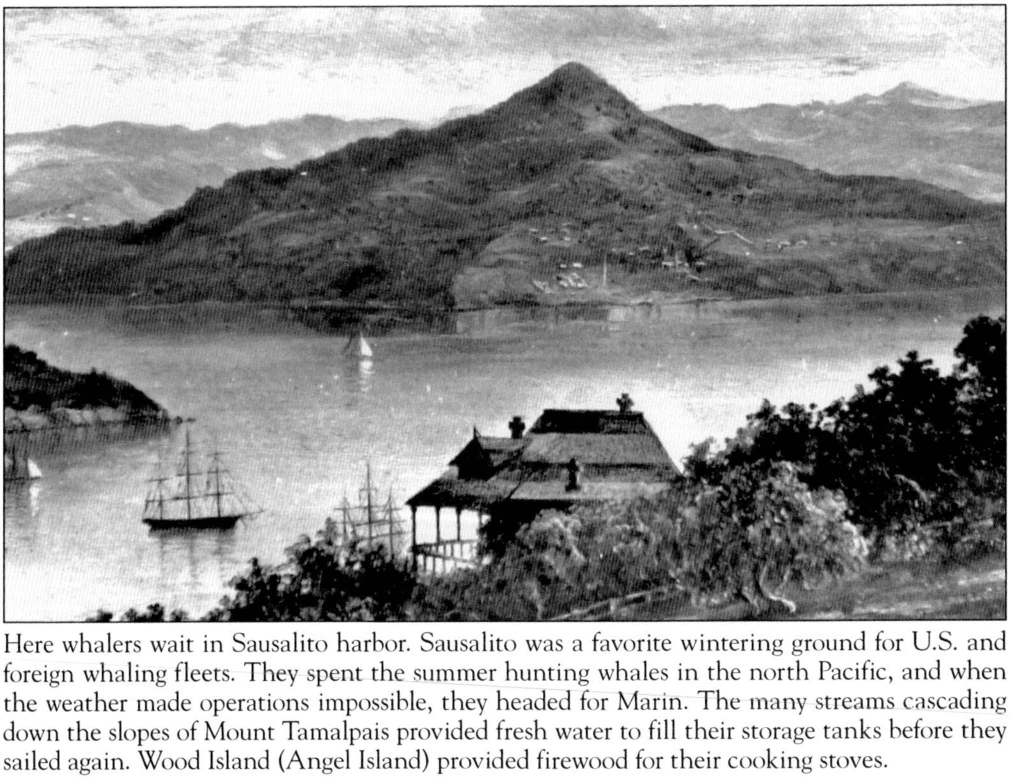

Here whalers wait in Sausalito harbor. Sausalito was a favorite wintering ground for U.S. and foreign whaling fleets. They spent the summer hunting whales in the north Pacific, and when the weather made operations impossible, they headed for Marin. The many streams cascading down the slopes of Mount Tamalpais provided fresh water to fill their storage tanks before they sailed again. Wood Island (Angel Island) provided firewood for their cooking stoves.

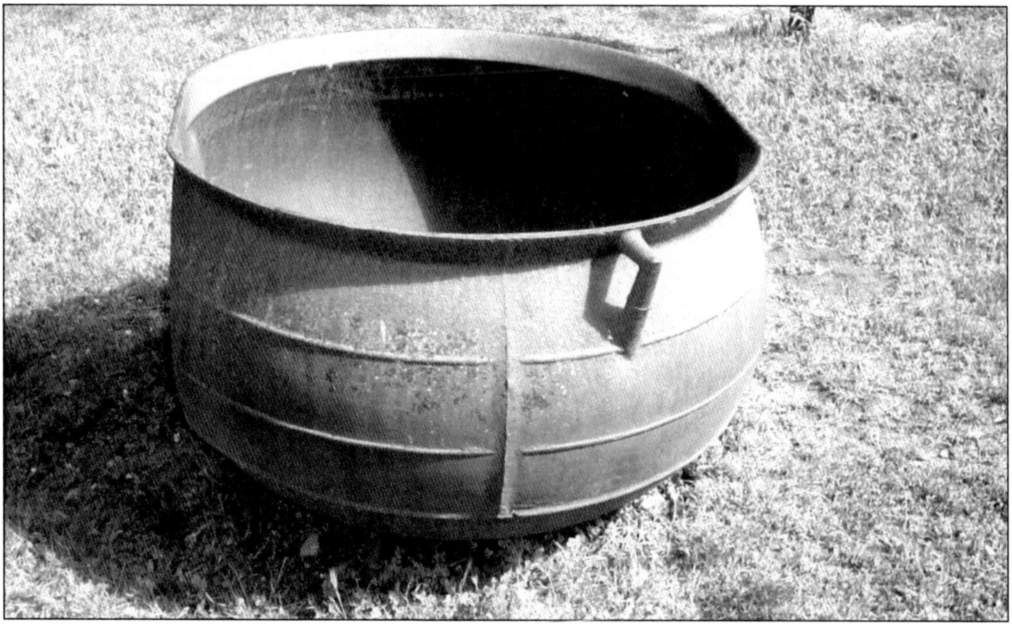

Salvaged from the whaling days is this try pot, used to render the oil from blubber aboard a whaler. On early Marin ranches, tallow and hides were the moneymakers, not milk or beef. Tallow was rendered in this try pot before being packed in barrels and shipped to Mexico. After further refining in Mexico, it went to the East Coast or to China to be made into candles.

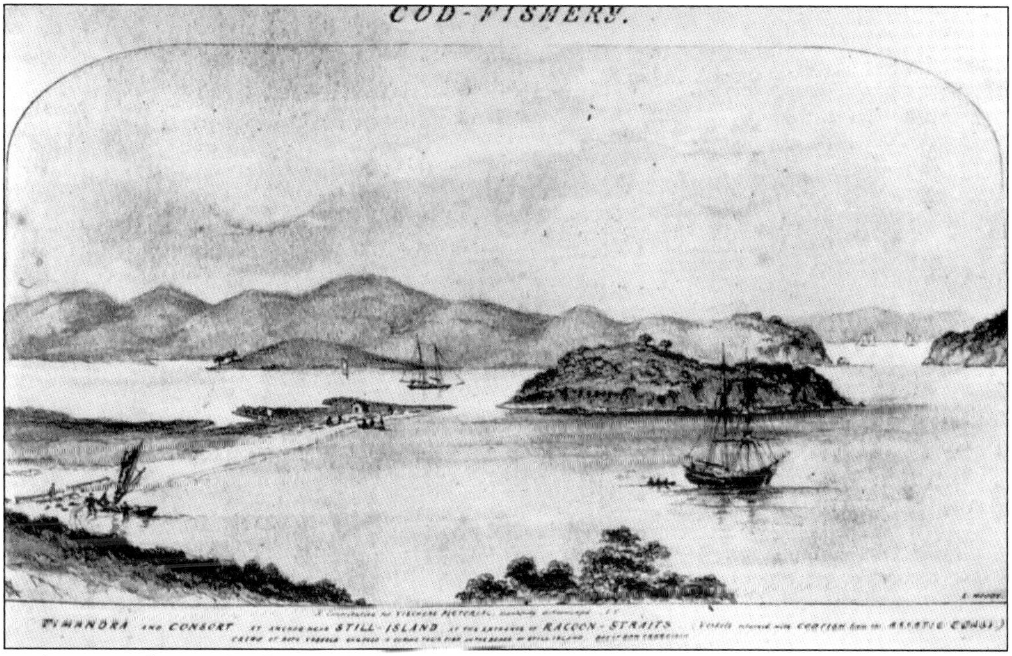

In the 1860s, large schools of codfish were discovered in the Bering Sea near Alaska. More were found in the Sea of Okhotsk near Siberia. Soon hundreds of vessels headed to the north Pacific waters every spring, returning to Marin loaded with cod. This sketch shows ships filled with cod landing near Beach Road in Belvedere. The codfish packing plant, which was located here, had as many as 100 Chinese workers at one time.

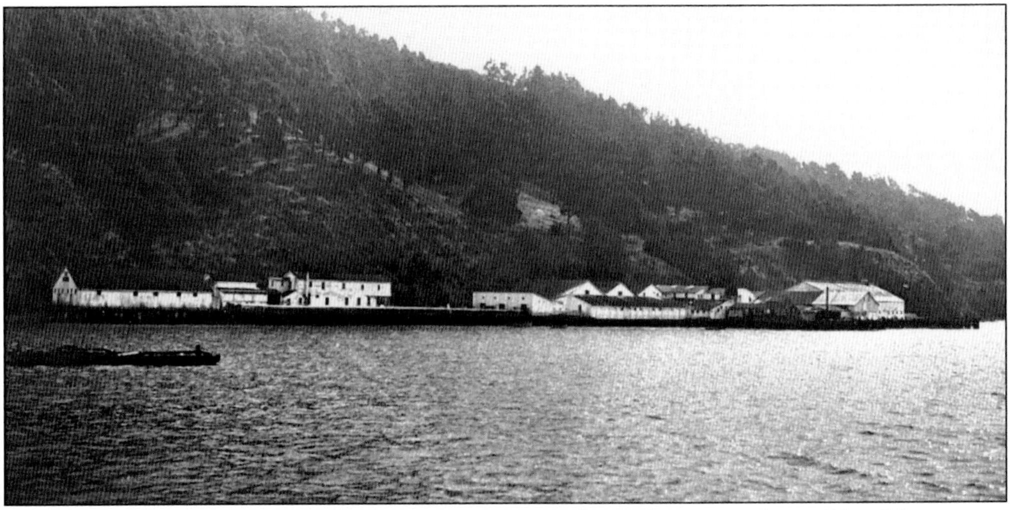

The Union Fish Company had a large warehouse, wharf, drying yards, and bunkhouses on tidelands that became West Shore Road in Belvedere. The company operated until 1937, when most of the buildings were destroyed by fire. Homes in this location were selling for $3 million and up in 2008. (Courtesy the Landmarks Society.)

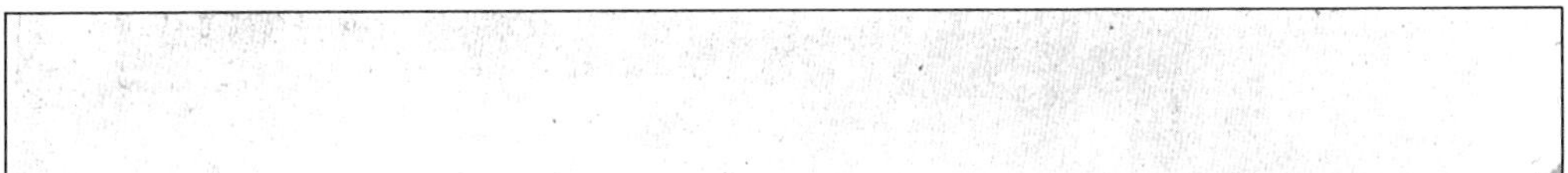

Fish-drying racks at the Union Fish Company codfish packing plant are pictured here. Workers lived right at the plant, and on Friday and Saturday nights, they joined with the ranch hands, railroad workers, and sailors to enliven Main Street in Tiburon. The company Lynde and Hough owned another large codfish cannery that was located where the Romberg Tiburon Environmental Research Center is today. (Courtesy the Landmarks Society.)

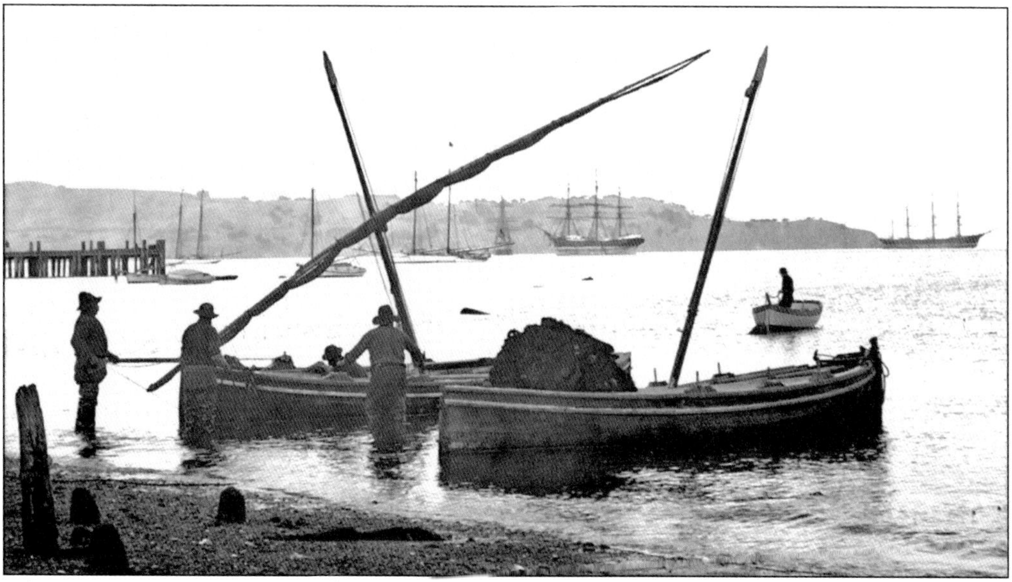

Feluccas, usually associated with the protected waters of the Nile River and the Red Sea, were favorites of these Italian fishermen, seen readying their craft at Sausalito. The fleet of lateen-rigged feluccas was called *silene* by southern Italian immigrants. They were small and light with an angled mast raked forward and a large triangular sail hanging from a two-piece yard. (Courtesy San Francisco Maritime National Historical Park.)

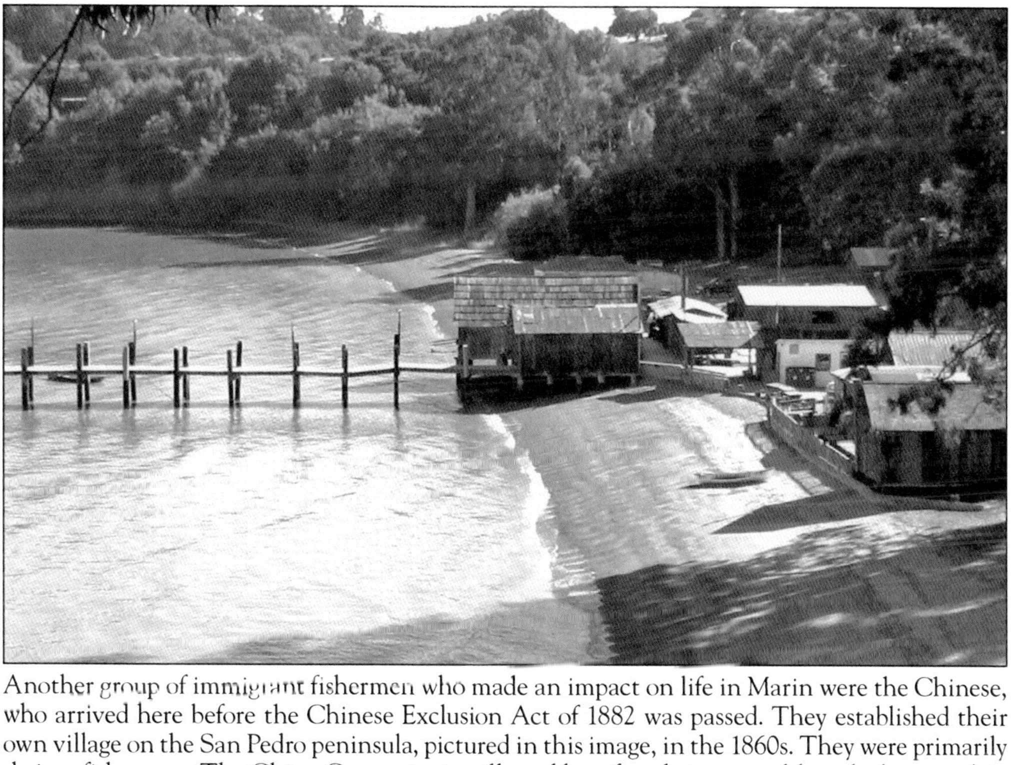

Another group of immigrant fishermen who made an impact on life in Marin were the Chinese, who arrived here before the Chinese Exclusion Act of 1882 was passed. They established their own village on the San Pedro peninsula, pictured in this image, in the 1860s. They were primarily shrimp fishermen. The China Camp pier is still used by a few shrimpers, although their catch is usually sold as bait.

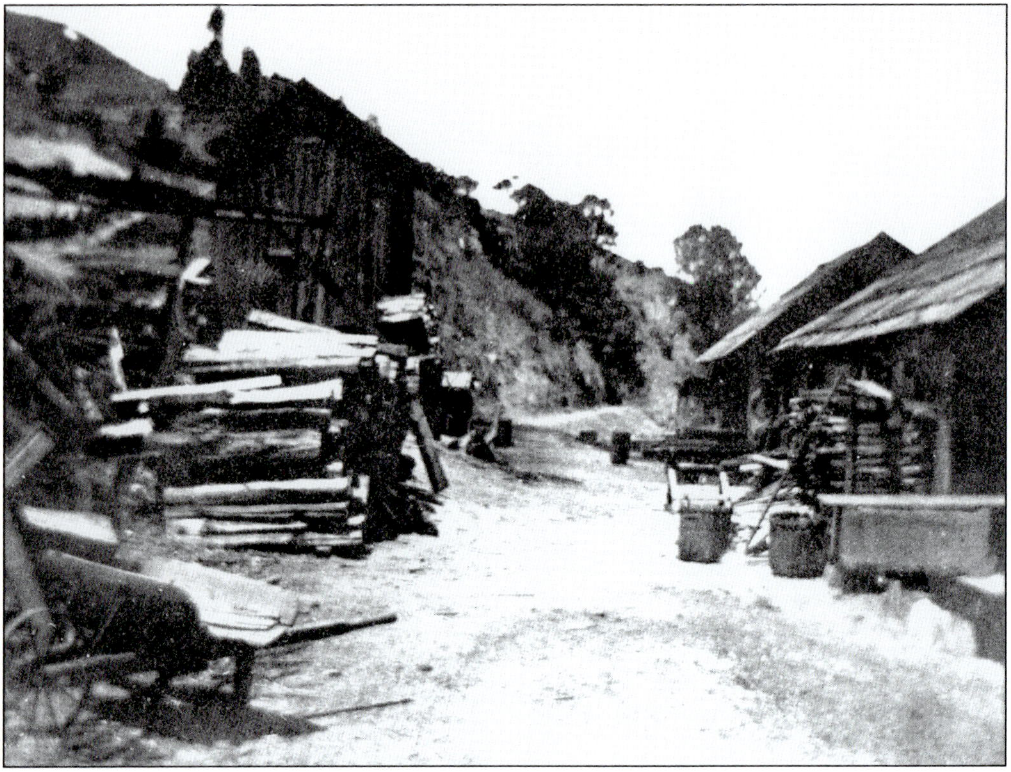

In the 1880s, five hundred people lived in China Camp. Most were from Canton and stayed pretty much to themselves, not necessarily by choice. The shrimp they caught were air dried on racks and shipped throughout the United States and to China. China Camp is now part of a 1,600-acre state park preserving the name and the remaining buildings. (Courtesy San Francisco Maritime National Historical Park.)

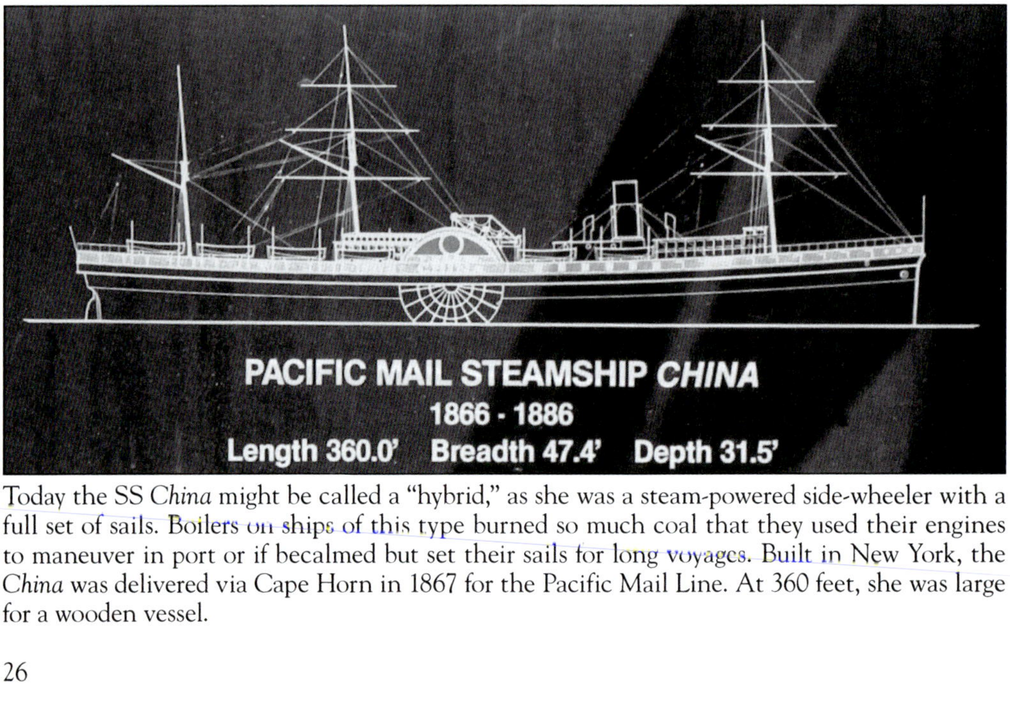

Today the SS *China* might be called a "hybrid," as she was a steam-powered side-wheeler with a full set of sails. Boilers on ships of this type burned so much coal that they used their engines to maneuver in port or if becalmed but set their sails for long voyages. Built in New York, the *China* was delivered via Cape Horn in 1867 for the Pacific Mail Line. At 360 feet, she was large for a wooden vessel.

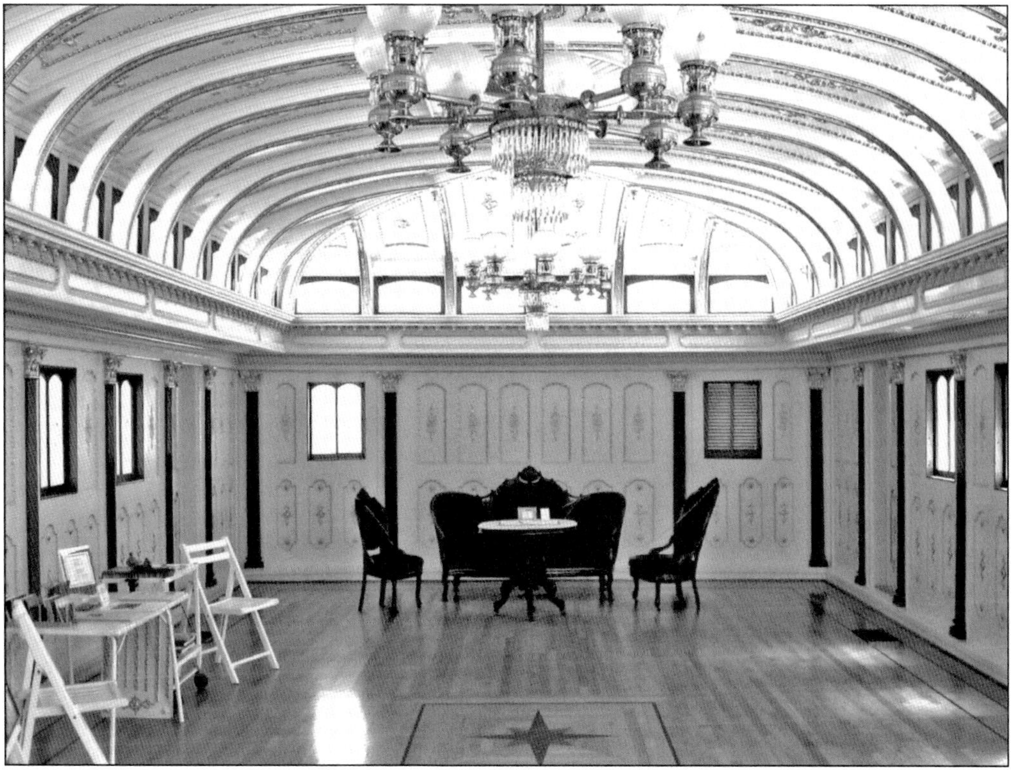

The *China* made 30 round-trip voyages to the Orient before being burned and salvaged at the Tiburon ship crematorium in 1879. Iron ships with propellers had replaced the graceful clipper ships and leisurely side-wheelers on the high seas. The *China*'s beautiful social cabin was saved and is open to the public on the Belvedere shore.

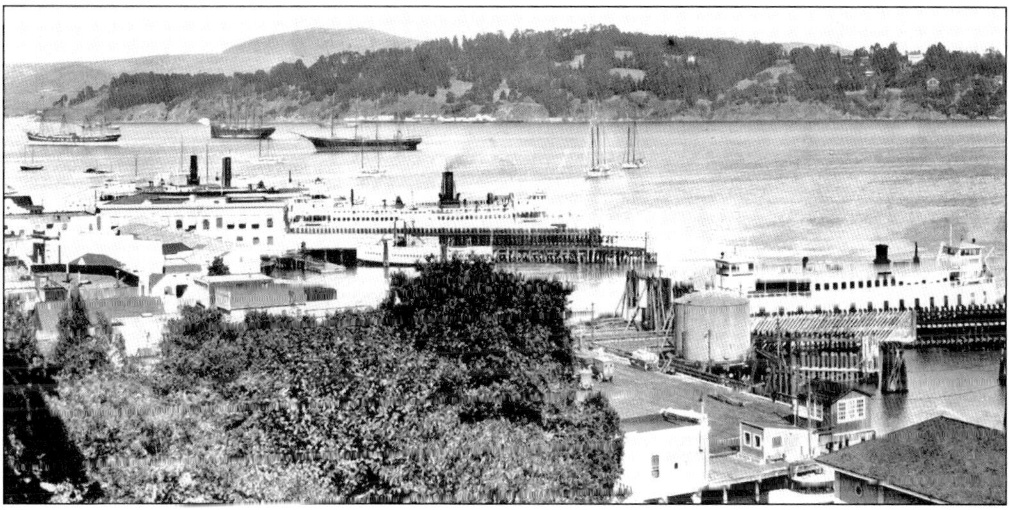

The harbor at Sausalito was a busy place as the age of sail neared its end. Sailing ships waiting to unload or to take on cargo filled Richardson Bay, while new fancy ferries were loading passengers for the trip to San Francisco. Both Sausalito and Tiburon combined rail terminals with ferry service. Sausalito concentrated on passenger service, while Tiburon specialized in freight handling. (Courtesy San Francisco Maritime National Historical Park.)

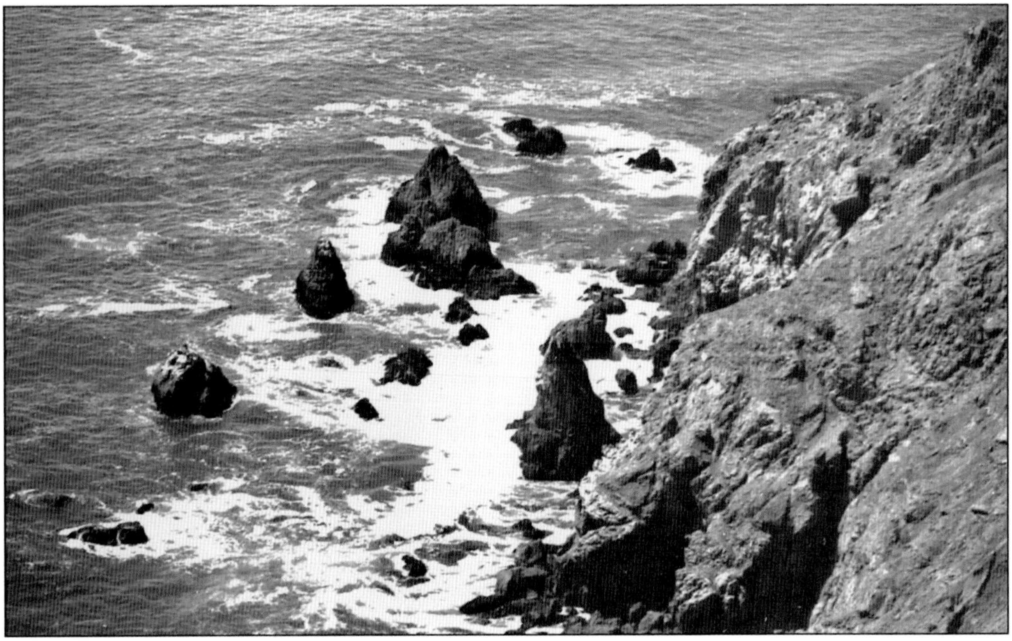

Like the toothy jaws of a hungry shark, the rock-bound coast of Marin waits for its next victim. It was not easy maneuvering a large, heavily loaded vessel depending on the vagaries of the wind for power, in the dark of night, or in the heavy fogs for which the Pacific Coast is noted. Many a skilled captain lost the battle and his ship.

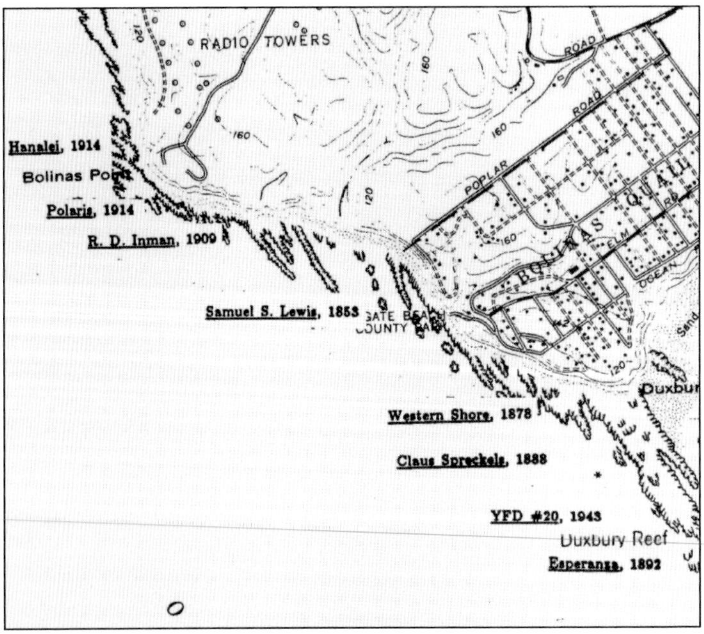

The harbor at Bolinas was one of the earlier destinations on the Pacific side of Marin. While it looks safe and serene today, it claimed its share of victims in early sailing days. More than a dozen ships ended up on the rocks off Bolinas Harbor. Generally, both the ship and its cargo were total losses. With a water temperature of 50 degrees, there was usually a large loss of life as well. Duxbury Reef just outside the harbor mouth claimed the most victims. (Courtesy Bolinas Museum.)

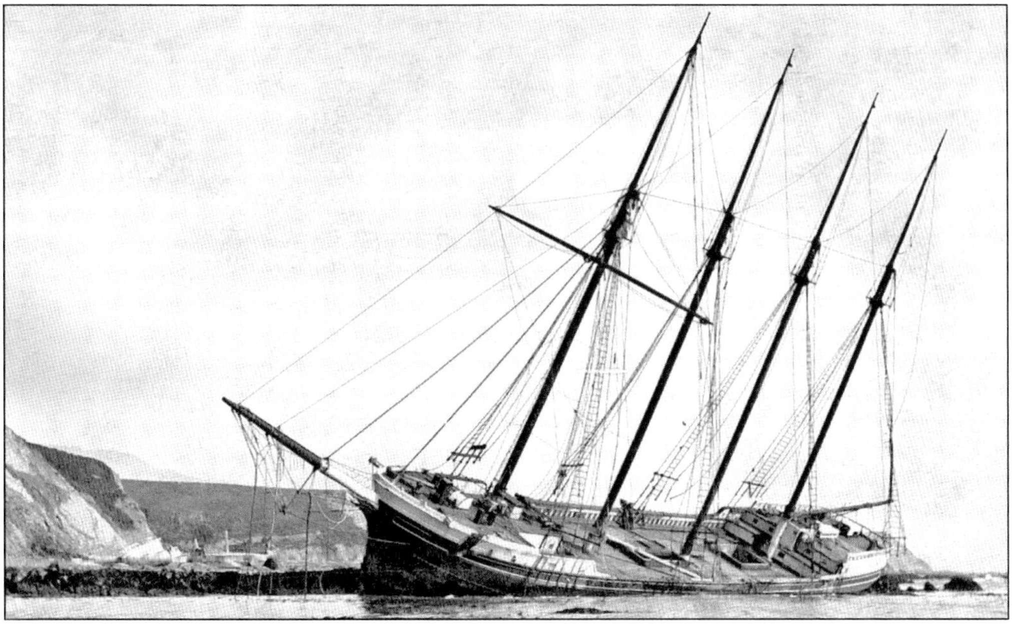

The four-masted schooner *Polaris* sits aground on Duxbury Reef in 1914. Helpless in the gale-force winds, she was driven ashore and left high and dry by a receding tide. Salvers stripped the ship before her remains were washed away by another storm. "The vessel was ground to splinters . . . scattered, mashed, and pulverized. The ship herself lined the shore—a breakwater of matchwood" was the description in the local newspaper. (Courtesy San Francisco Maritime National Historical Park.)

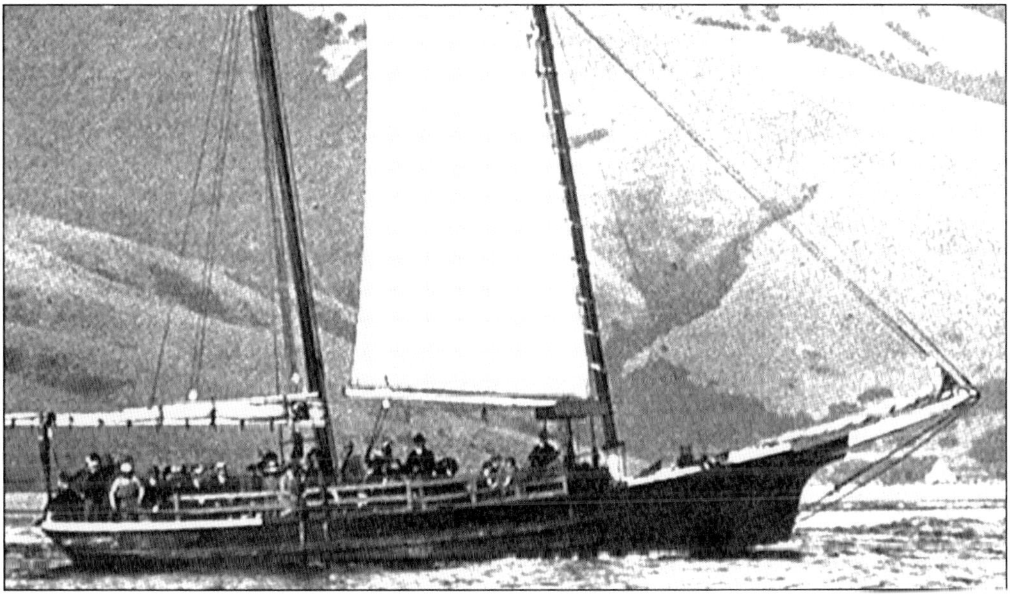

As roads improved, there was less demand for schooners, such as the *Jennie Griffin* (above). The last schooner to service Bolinas was *The Owl*, owned by Capt. Louis Petar. She carried everything, including passengers, dairy and farm products, live hogs, mail, and all kinds of supplies between Bolinas and San Francisco. Captain Petar and engineer Arthur Bourne also used her to carry supplies to the community on the Farallon Islands and the lighthouse at Point Reyes. (Courtesy Bolinas Museum.)

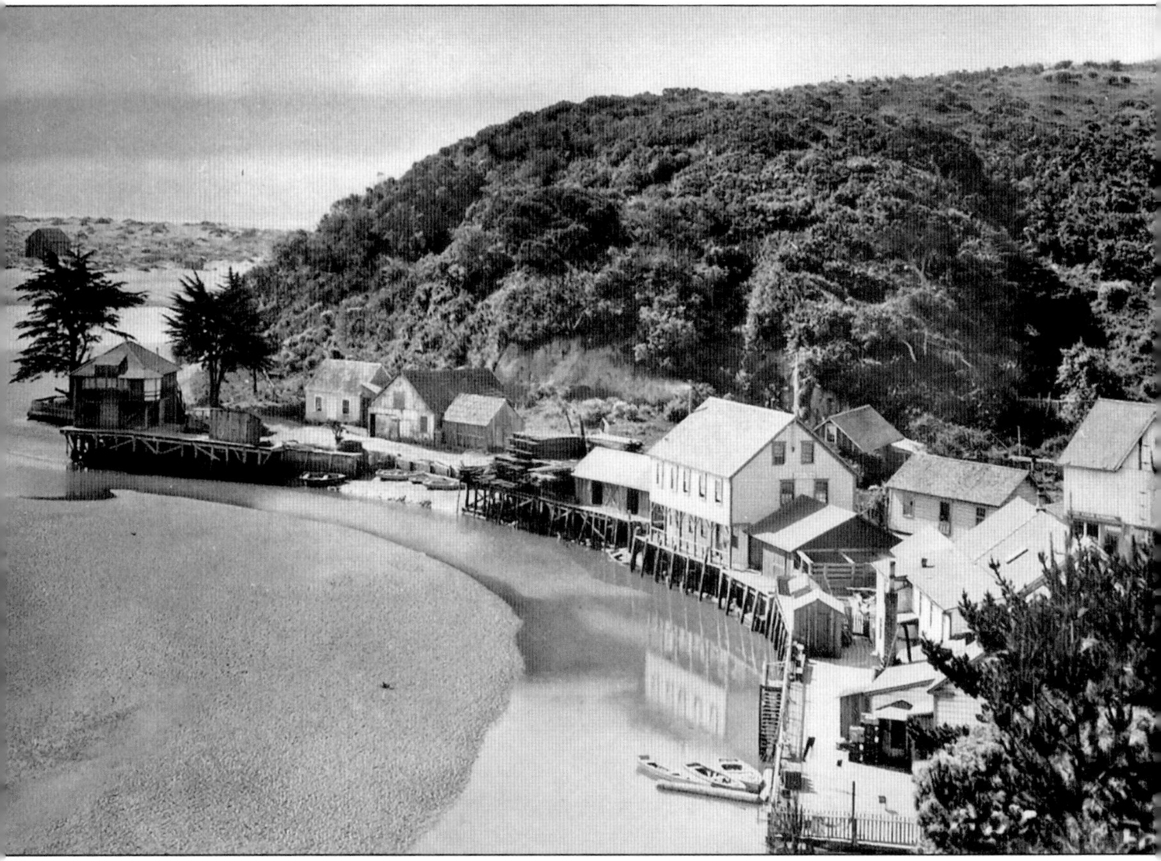

Many of the first settlers in Bolinas were schooner captains. When they brought their schooners into the Bolinas Lagoon to pick up lumber, paper from the mill, and dairy products for San Franciscans, they saw fertile land in a beautiful setting. Many set up homesteads and started producing dairy products, meat, fish, hay for horses, firewood, and lumber. The economy of West Marin depended on the schooner traffic from Bolinas. Three hundred ships entered the lagoon in July and August 1883. (Courtesy Bolinas Museum.)

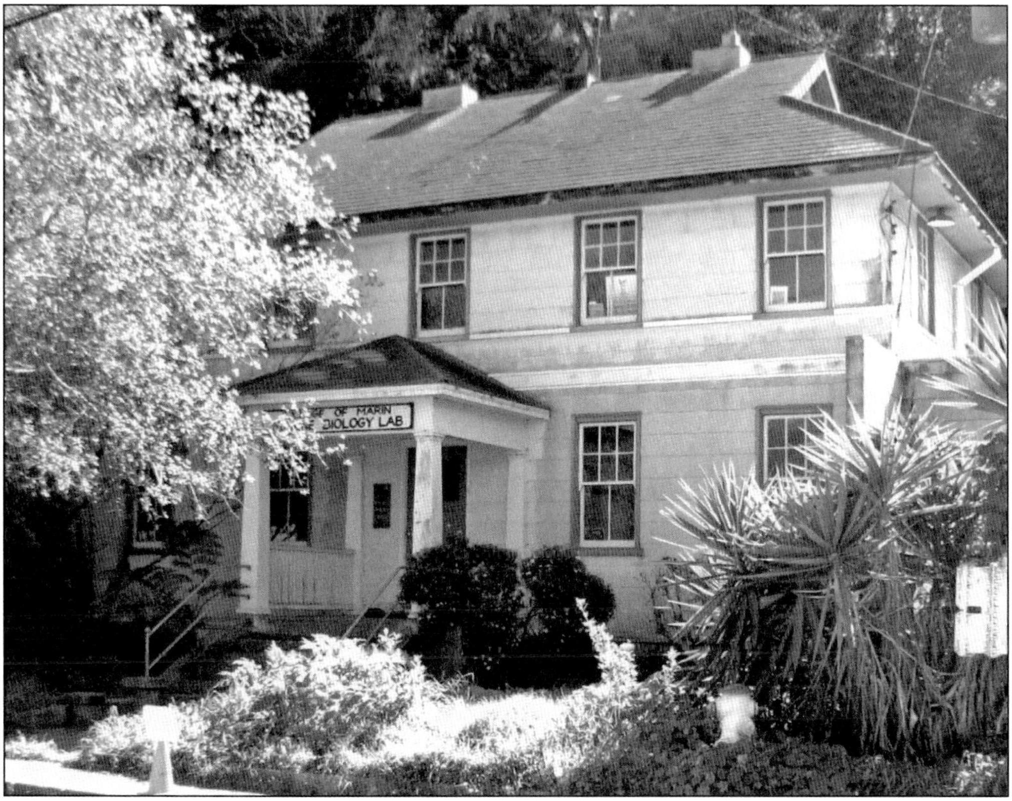

So many ships were wrecked trying to enter Bolinas Lagoon or on Duxbury Reef just outside the entrance that a lifesaving station was built on Wharf Road. After the *Hanalei* wrecked and lost most of its 30 crewmembers and 27 passengers, a new U.S. Coast Guard station was built in Bolinas with a lookout tower on the mesa. Built in 1915, it was closed after World War II when siltation made maneuvering U.S. Coast Guard vessels impossible.

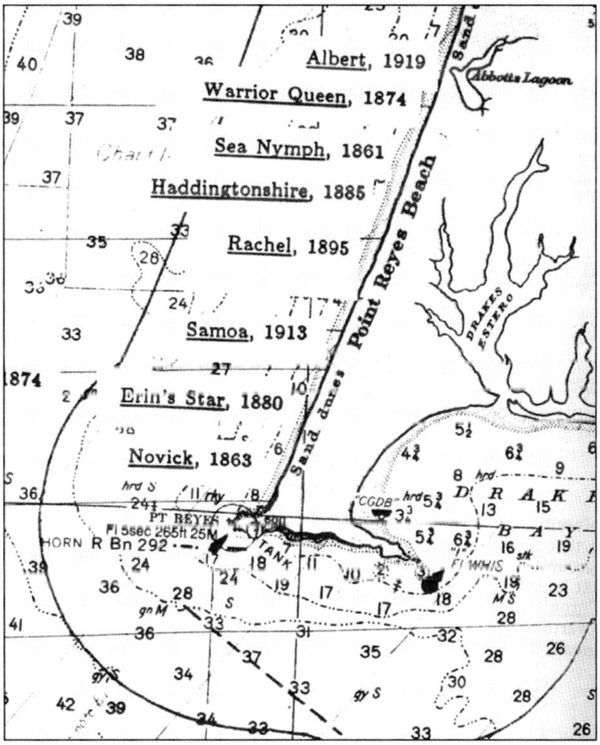

The navigators of sailing ships found it especially difficult to round Point Reyes. The hulks of many fine ships, square-riggers, and iron bottoms can be found off the treacherous rocks at Point Reyes Beach (often called Ten Mile Beach), including the *Albert* and the *Samoa*. (Courtesy San Francisco Maritime National Historical Park.)

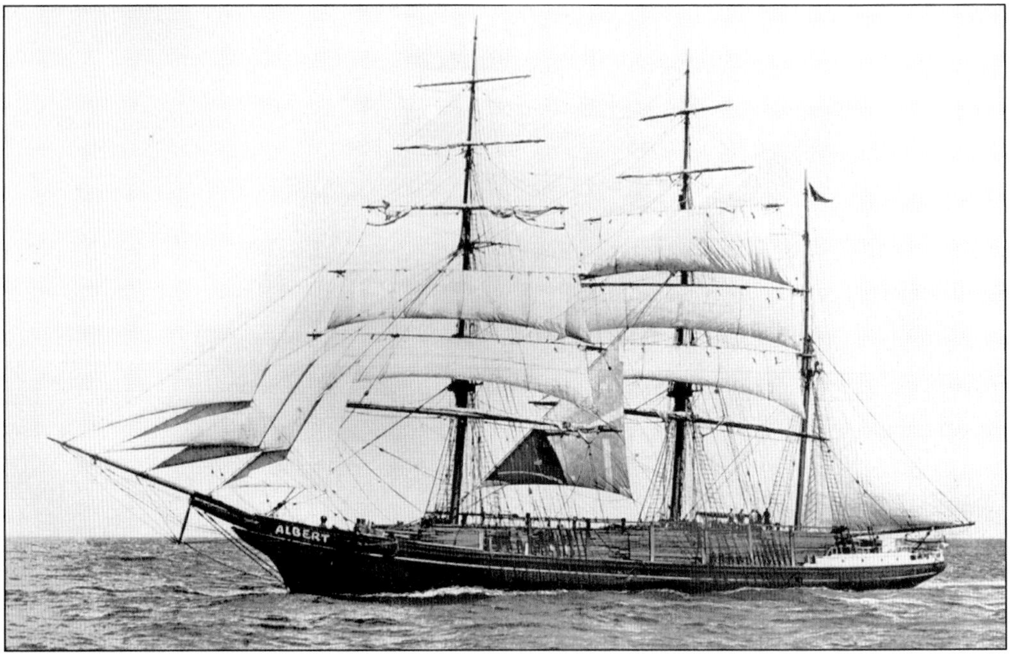

The bark *Albert*, built in 1890, sailed from New Zealand in 1919. In a combination of fog and light winds, she went aground off Point Reyes. She broke in two and disappeared. The passengers and crew, with the exception of the captain, were rescued by the Point Reyes lifesaving station using a breeches buoy. The *Albert* was one of the last full-rigged ships still operating in these waters. Note the deck load of lumber. (Courtesy San Francisco Maritime National Historical Park.)

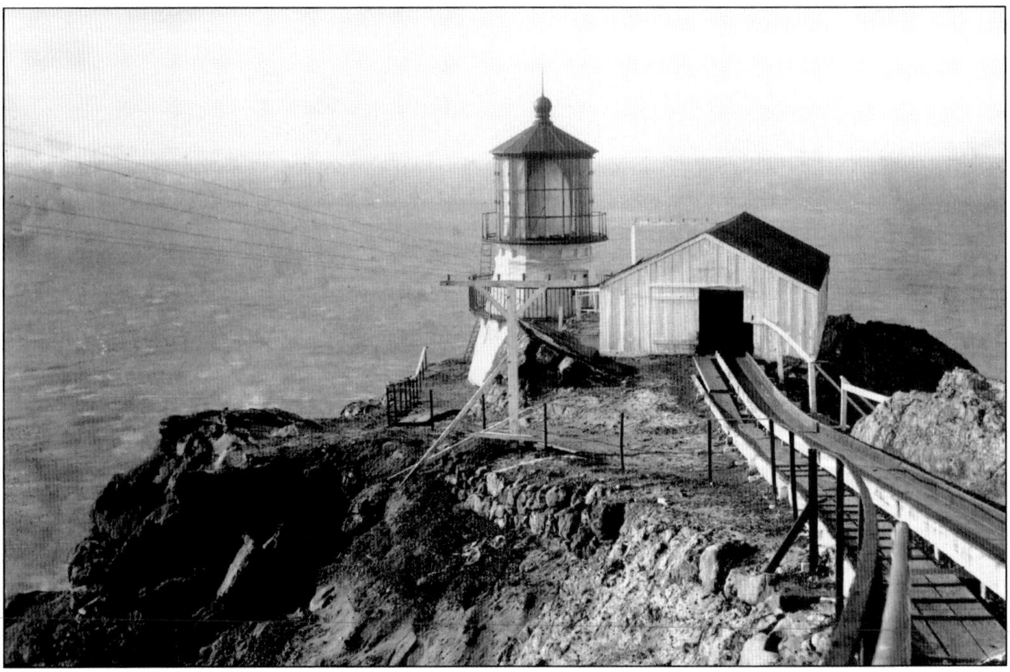

The Point Reyes Lighthouse has a 3-ton lens that was made in Paris of 1,000 pieces of glass. The 120,000-candlepower light could be seen 24 miles at sea. (Courtesy Marin History Museum.)

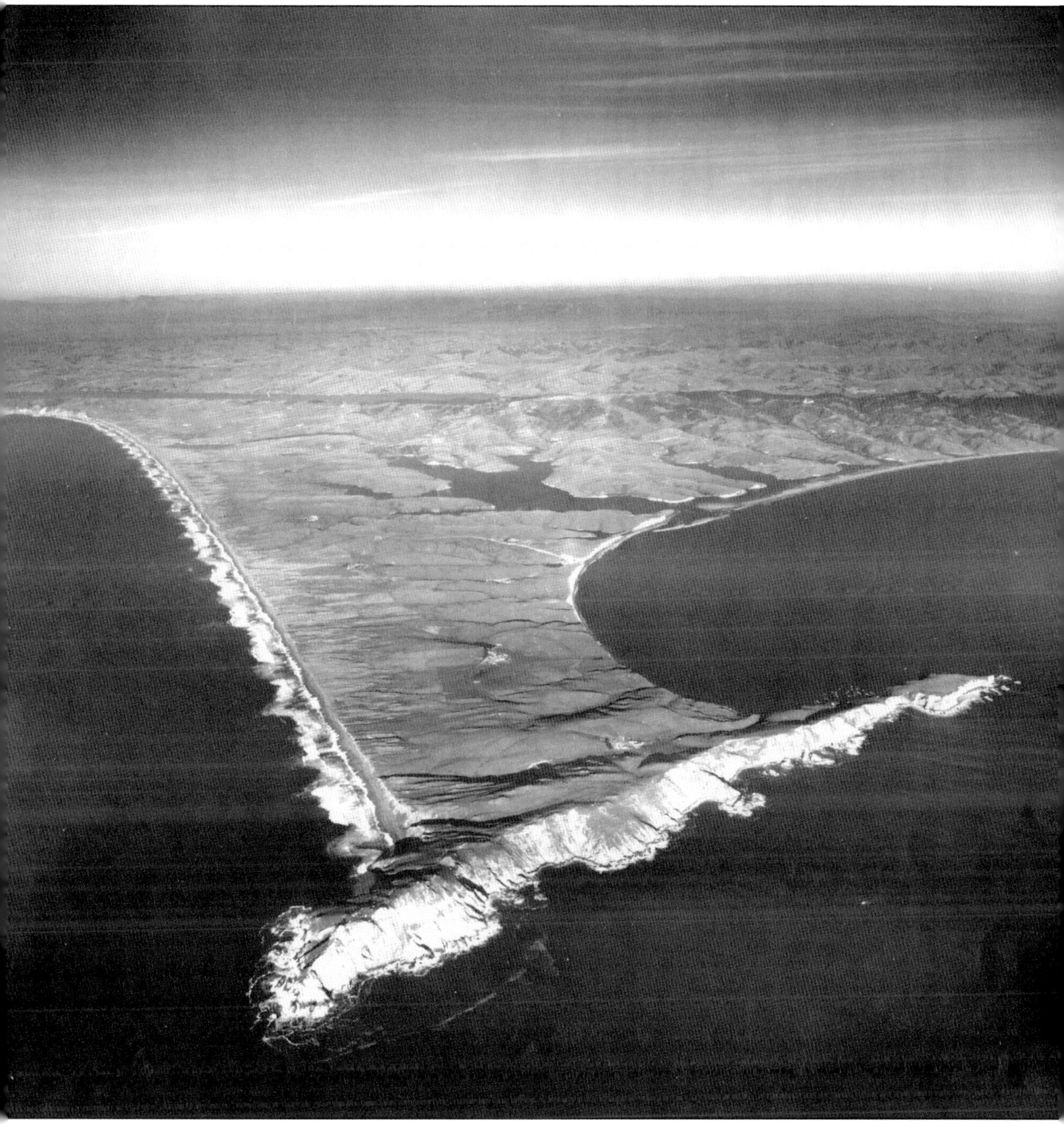

The number of ships wrecked on the Pacific Coast of Marin grew to such alarming proportions that in 1848 a lifesaving station was installed. Lifeboats, powered by oars in the early days, meant backbreaking work in stormy seas, but the men had to get lines out to the stranded ships. If breeches buoys could not be used, they had to get survivors into their lifeboats and then make repeated trips to the nearest beach. In 1870, a lighthouse was placed on the western most tip of the Point Reyes Peninsula. In 1915, the U.S. Lifesaving Service was combined with the U.S. Revenue Cutter Service to form the U.S. Coast Guard. The U.S. Lifesaving Service's motto, "You have to go out, you don't have to come back," was adopted by the coast guard. The U.S. Lighthouse Service, also known as the Bureau of Lighthouses, operated the lighthouses until 1939, when they also became part of the coast guard. In this aerial view of Point Reyes is Ten Mile Beach, Drakes Bay, and Drakes Estero. (Courtesy Marin History Museum.)

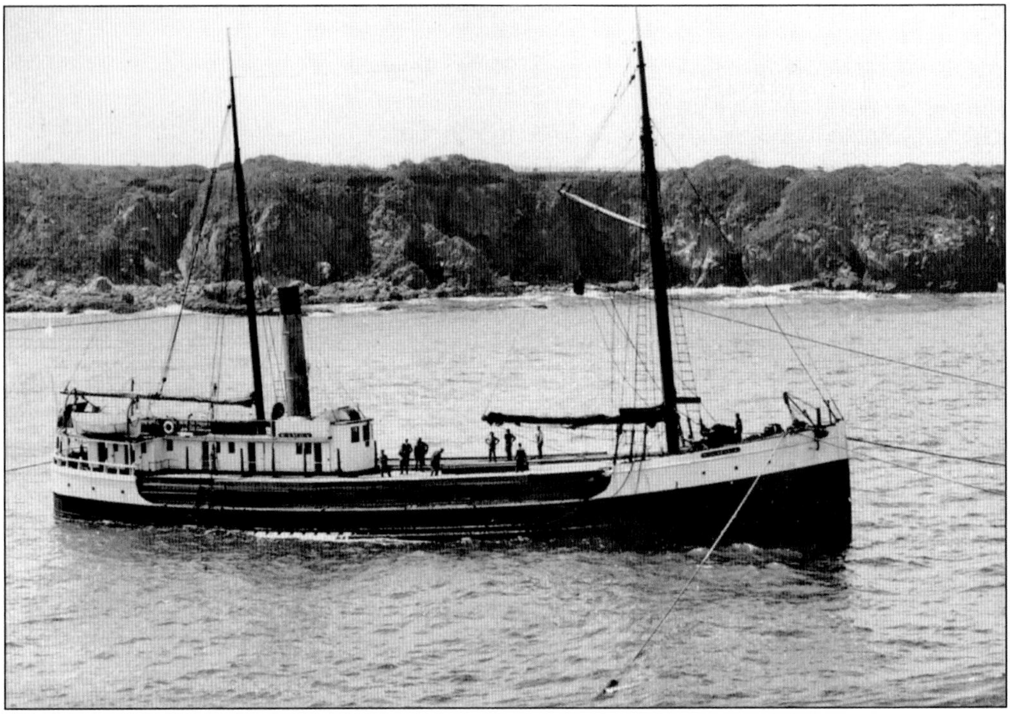

The *Samoa* was a typical coastal steam schooner in the lumber trade. Built in 1898 in San Francisco, she could carry 450,000 board feet of lumber and 23 cabin passengers, plus 10 in steerage. She went aground in a fog at Point Reyes in 1913. The ship disappeared beneath the sands of Ten Mile Beach, also known as Point Reyes Beach. (Courtesy San Francisco Maritime National Historical Park.)

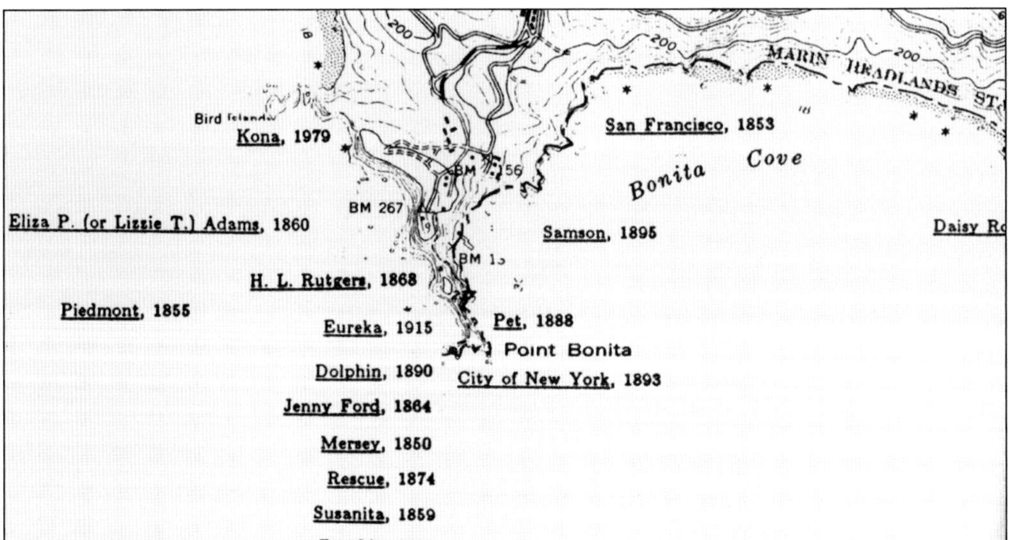

The catalog of shipwrecks at the Golden Gate is quite lengthy. Rounding Point Bonita was difficult even on good days. When the weather turned nasty or night descended, the rocky shoreline won new victims.

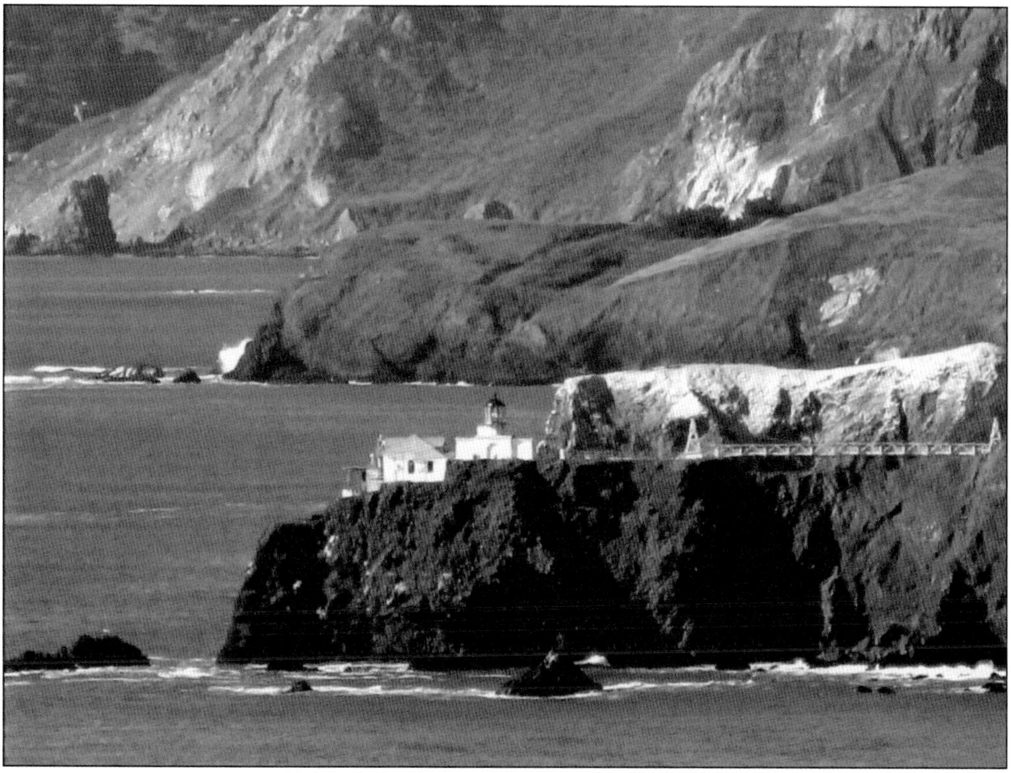

For two centuries, mariners avoided the Golden Gate, but when they found it, they still had trouble getting past Point Bonita guarding the entrance. A beacon installed high on the cliffs above the Marin side proved ineffective in bad weather, when it was needed the most. This lighthouse was built low on the coast to shine its light under the fog.

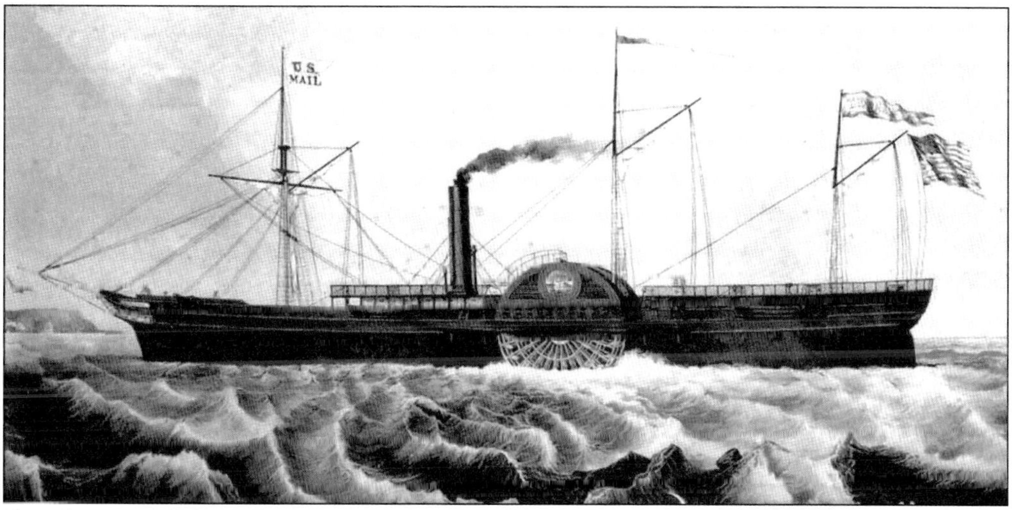

One shipwreck left its name on Marin's map. The SS *Tennessee* was built in New York in 1848 and came via Cape Horn to be one of the finest ships in Pacific Mail Steamship Company's fleet on the Panama run. She was an elegant wooden side-wheeler, 211 feet long, with two decks and three masts. She carried 200 cabin passengers and 350 in steerage. (Photograph by Cathy Forbes; courtesy Stephen J. and Jeremy W. Potash collection.)

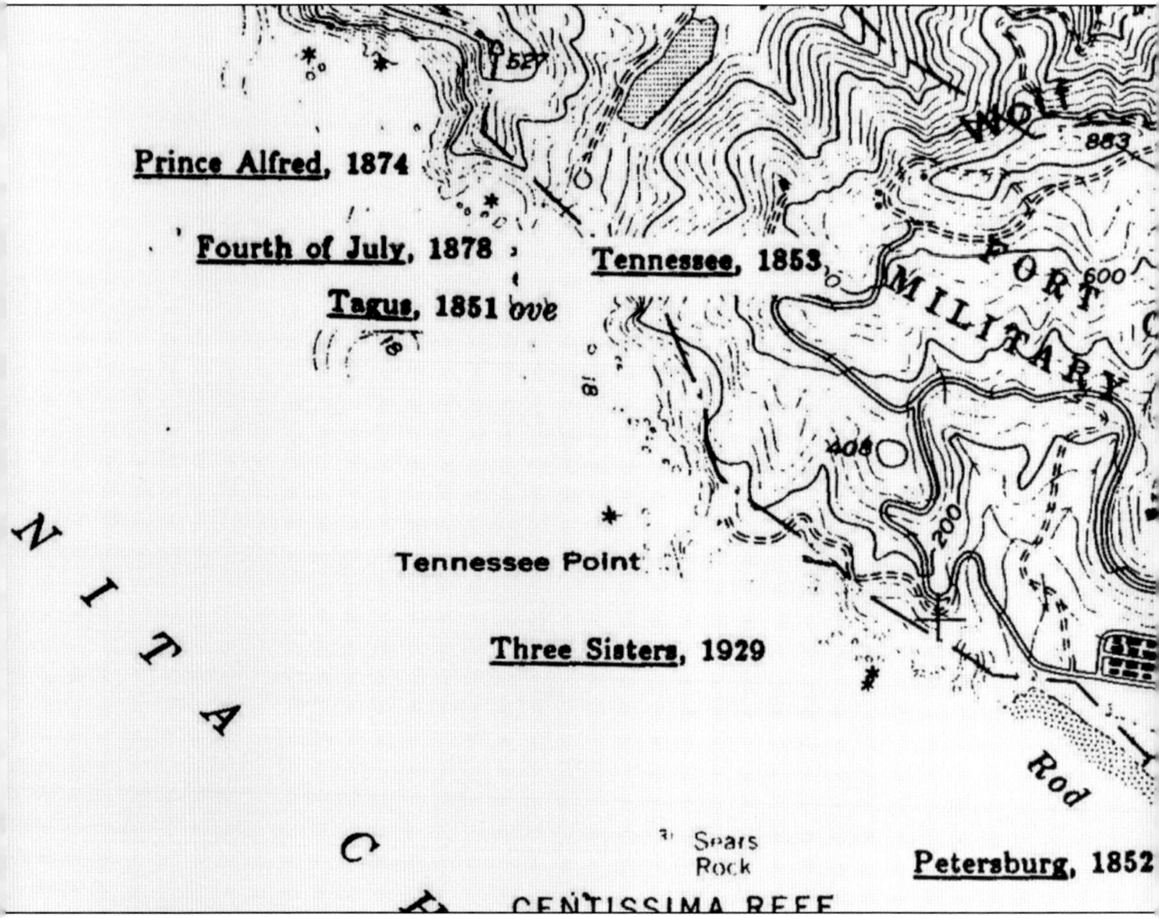

The *Tennessee* brought thousands of fortune seekers to San Francisco during the Gold Rush, but in 1853, at the end of a 14-day run from Panama, which included a stop in Acapulco for coal, the *Tennessee* ran into a thick fog and tried to make it through the Golden Gate by "dead reckoning." Instead she ran gently onto the beach. All passengers, baggage, and mail, including 70,000 letters, were saved, but the ship was a total loss. The area is now known as Tennessee Cove, which can be reached via Tennessee Valley Road, following Tennessee Valley Creek to Tennessee Point and Tennessee Beach.

Three

The Pacific Coast

Marin's coastal highway can easily compete with Italy's Amalfi Drive for sheer beauty, but it also has few peers for danger. The persistence of fog around the Golden Gate had caused early explorers to miss the entrance to the bay for 200 years. Once these explorers challenged the Golden Gate, their primitive navigation equipment and lack of control in the vicious currents often led to disaster. Today sunbathers relax on the long stretches of sandy beaches while their toddlers gleefully splash in the shallow water, but only the bravest or most foolhardy adventure far offshore where the great white shark lurks.

The entire 100-square-mile Point Reyes peninsula and surrounding territory was owned by Oscar and James Shafter, transplanted Vermont attorneys. They and other inheritors of the large West Marin land grants had resisted selling to settlers, so vast areas of the coast were still available in the 1960s to be combined with the large military installations to create the Point Reyes National Seashore and the Golden Gate National Recreation Area.

By the mid 1800s, tourism, ranching, and aquaculture became the main industries. Railroads extended to West Marin to serve the lumber mills, and dairy ranches were busy on the weekends, bringing picnickers and hikers to the coast. Aquaculture farms on Point Reyes and in Tomales Bay are still producing millions of oysters and clams each year, and dairy ranching is Marin's largest industry. In a rich, carefully controlled fishing ground off Marin's Pacific shore lies an area of almost 6,000 square miles of marine sanctuaries, home to 36 species of marine animals, 164 species of birds, and five species of sea turtles. Fishing is not a major Marin County industry, as most commercial fishing boats are based elsewhere. The California gray whales spend their summers in Alaska and their winters in Baja. This 10,000-mile migration brings them close to Point Reyes twice a year. These animals are the size of six elephants with two blowholes that can spout up to 15 feet high. They have become a major tourist draw, with whale watching from the end of the Point Reyes peninsula or from tour boats that venture out to observe the mammals.

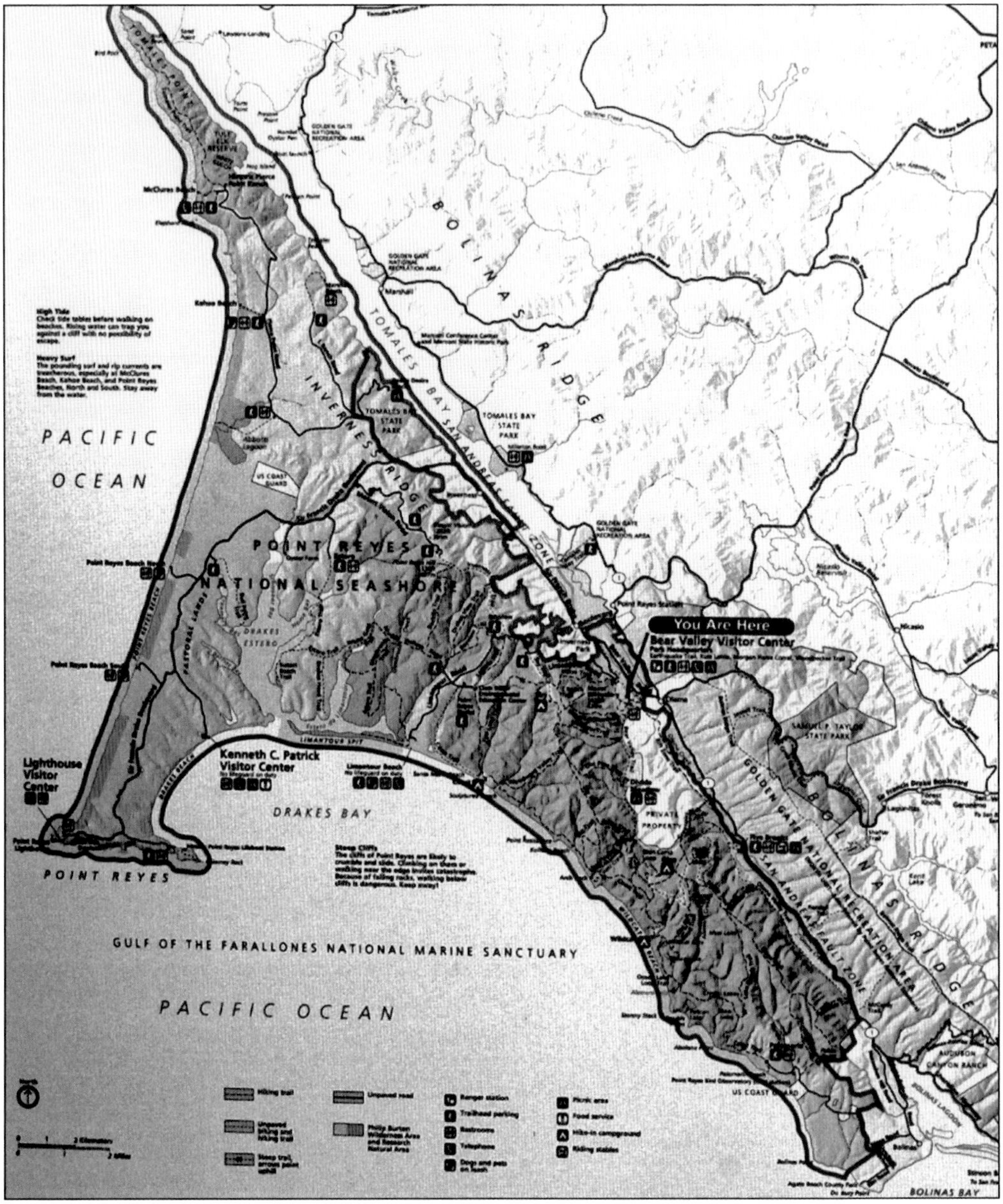

Point Reyes, the final resting place for numerous ships and their unlucky passengers and crew, was the first seashore designated as a national park. The federal government purchased the dairies that had been operating there since the mid-1800s but assured their continued operation by leasing them back to the former owners. The Golden Gate National Recreation Area, known locally as the GGNRA, is an assemblage of state and federal parks. Included in the 120,000-acre Marin segment are Point Reyes National Seashore, Samuel P. Taylor State Park, Mount Tamalpais State Park, the watershed of the Marin Municipal Water District, Muir Woods National Monument, the Marin Headlands, Angel Island State Park, and several smaller parks.

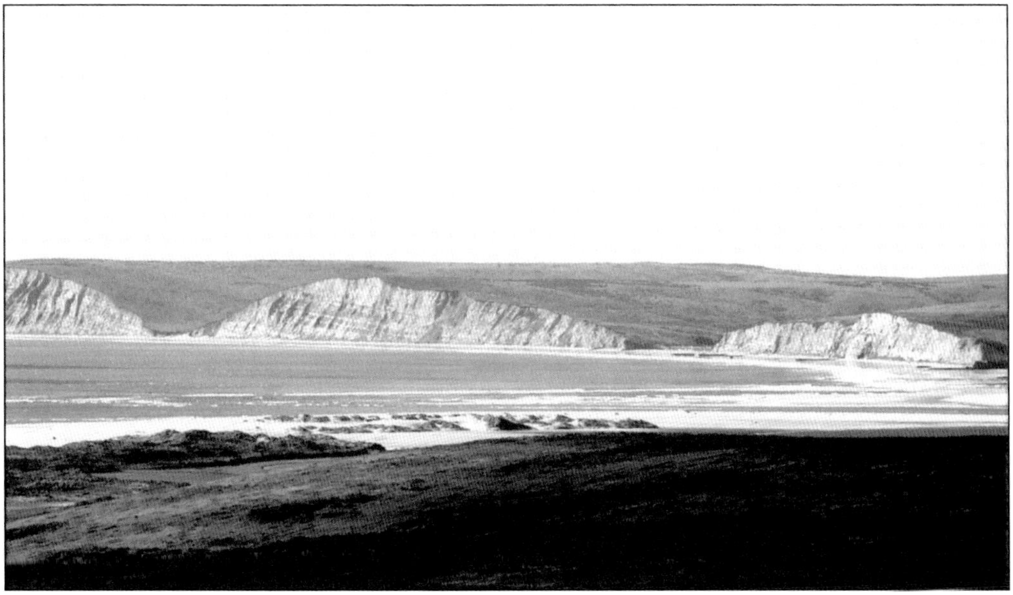

It is not difficult for anyone who has ever seen the White Cliffs of Dover in England to understand why Francis Drake named his landing spot on the Point Reyes peninsula "Nova Albion." Drake built a small fort and unloaded the *Golden Hind* while his crew completed repairs. He did not need the fort because he found the natives friendly.

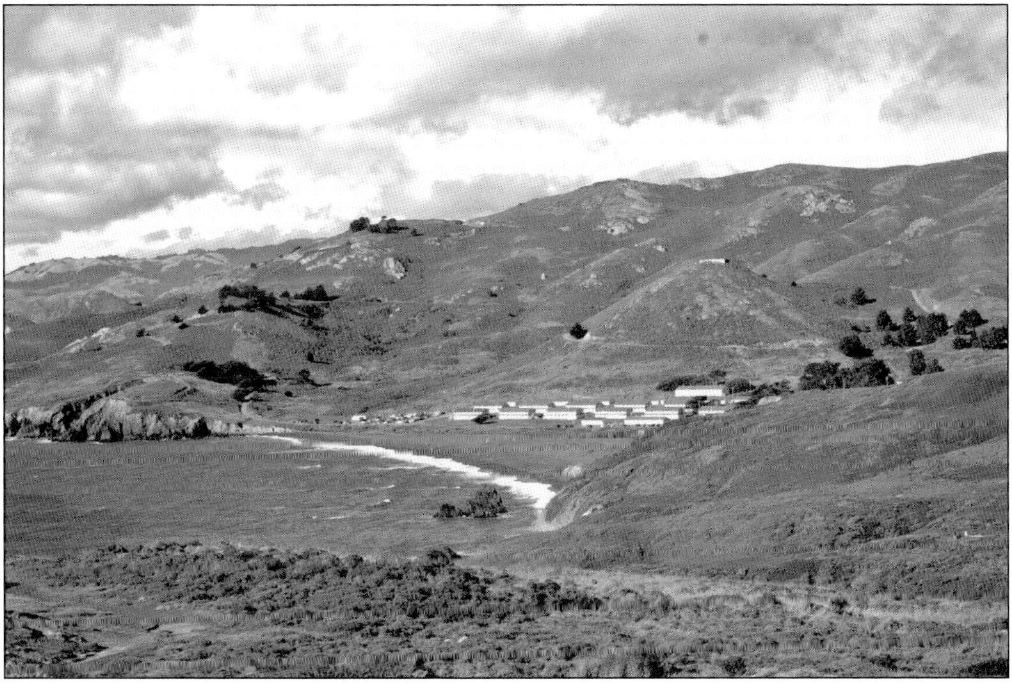

The GGNRA and the Point Reyes National Seashore contain a wide variety of recreational opportunities. A greenbelt stretching from the Golden Gate to Tomales Point, some of the parks are mostly wild land with few trails, while others have paved parking and overnight accommodations. The rebuilt Fort Baker in the headlands is designed to be a conference center, as is Fort Cronkhite (above), both former coast defense installations.

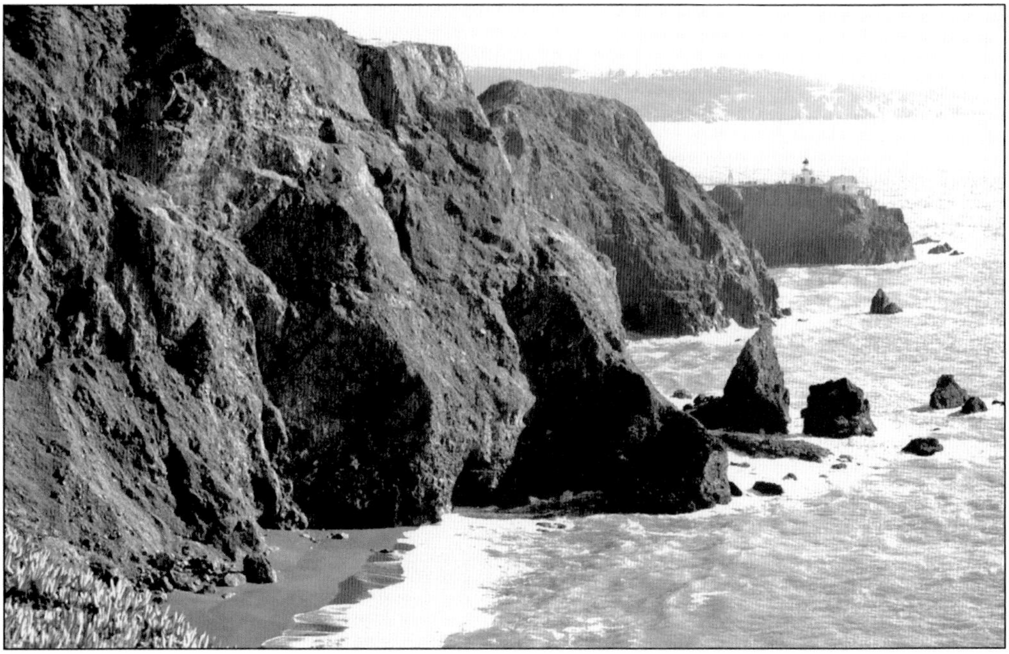

Point Bonita, guardian of the entrance to the Golden Gate, was fogbound much of the year. Its beacon was set low to the water and without a tower so that its light would show under the fog. Equipped with a high-powered lens and a fog bell, it probably did save a number of San Francisco–bound vessels but not all.

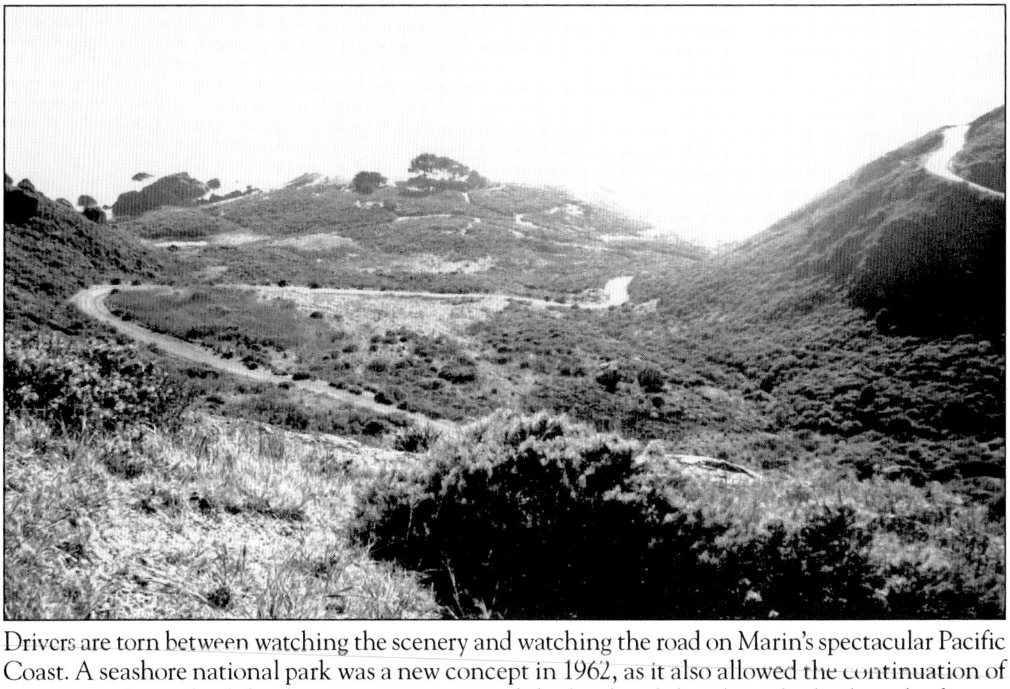

Drivers are torn between watching the scenery and watching the road on Marin's spectacular Pacific Coast. A seashore national park was a new concept in 1962, as it also allowed the continuation of private ranches. The federal government acquired the land and then leased it back to the former owners for a period of years. Leases, which are about expire, foment the usual controversy between those who want the land to become wilderness and those who want the dairies to continue.

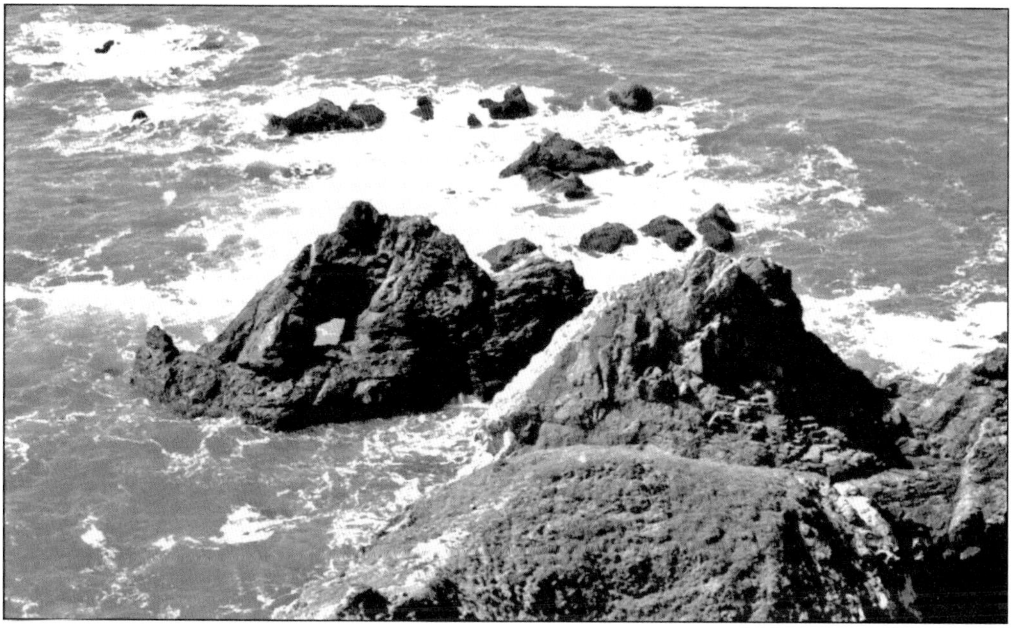

Rock outcroppings, separated from the mainland, provide an attractive roosting location for seabirds. There are 33 endangered species in the GGNRA, including fish, wildlife, and plants. As the prevailing north wind moves over the surface of the ocean, it draws up great volumes of nutrient-rich water from the depths. This attracts hoards of hungry animals above, under, and on the surface.

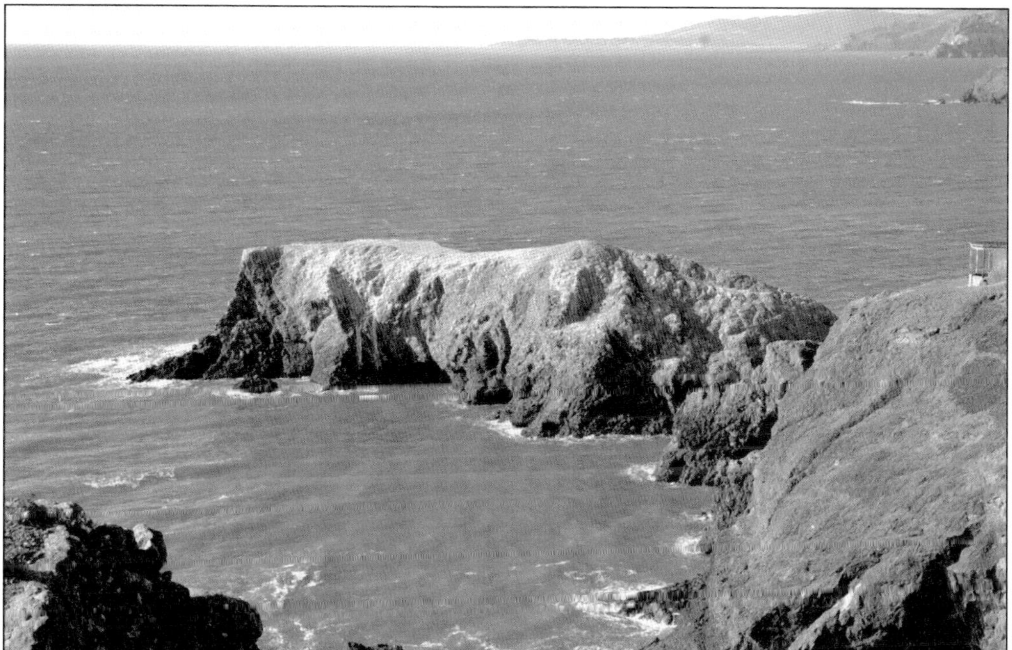

Birds, seals, and sea lions flock to the area to feed on the fish. In 1960, the Audubon Society identified 164 species of birds on the Point Reyes peninsula alone. Bird Rock provides a natural sanctuary for nesting birds that is safe from predatory land animals.

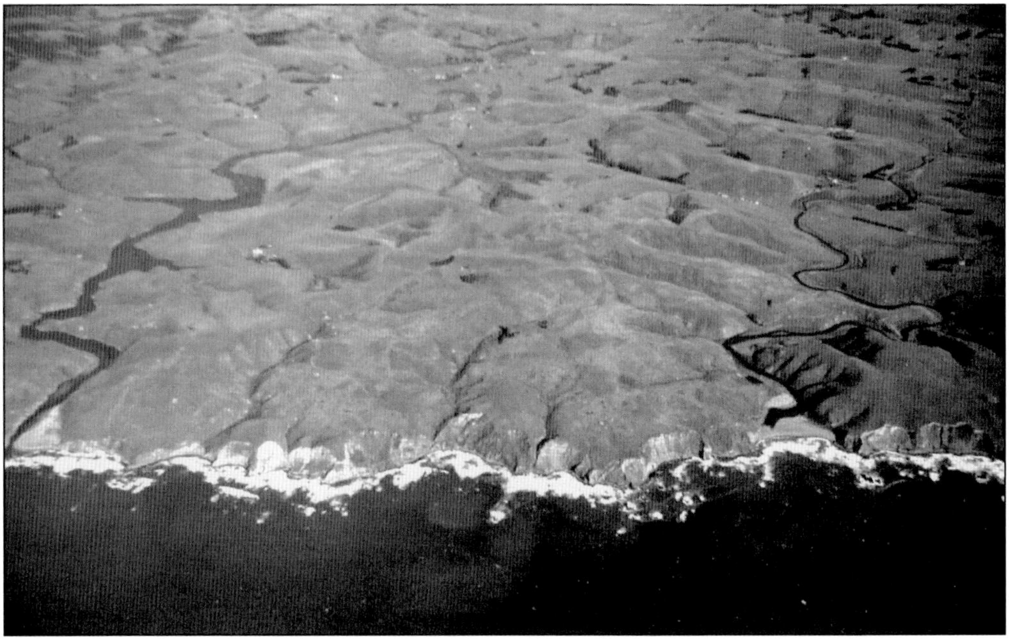

Two esteros—Americano, on the left in this view of the northwest corner of Marin, and San Antonio on the right—provide valuable habitat in an area where few rivers flow into the ocean. Estero Americano is also the boundary between Marin and Sonoma Counties.

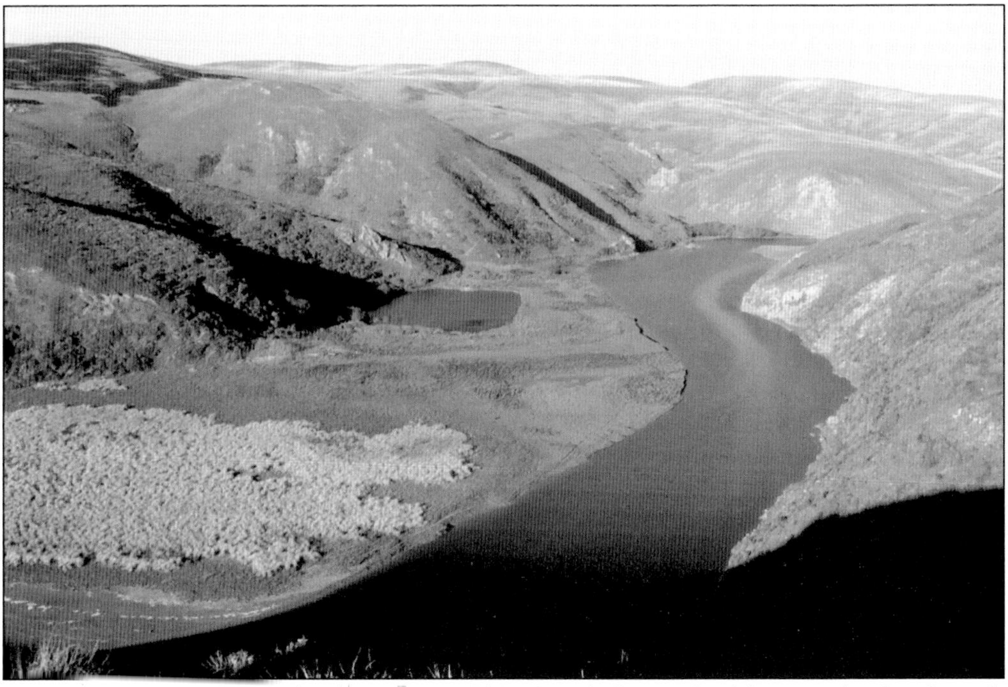

Estero San Antonio, known locally as Stempel Creek, only flows inland for several miles, through ranch land. Early settlers planted potatoes and other crops until the land was exhausted. They then tried dairy ranching for several generations, but changing health laws made this unprofitable. Some are still raising cattle, but most are raising lambs for market.

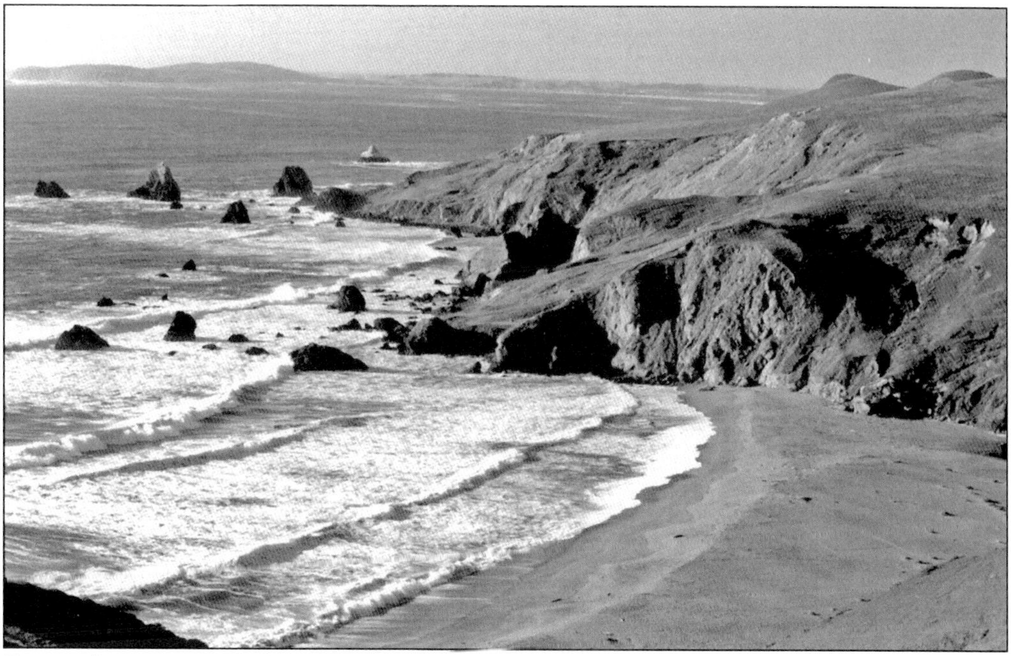

During the summer months, the mouths of the esteros close, creating a broad, sandy beach. These beaches are surrounded by private ranches and are never open to the public.

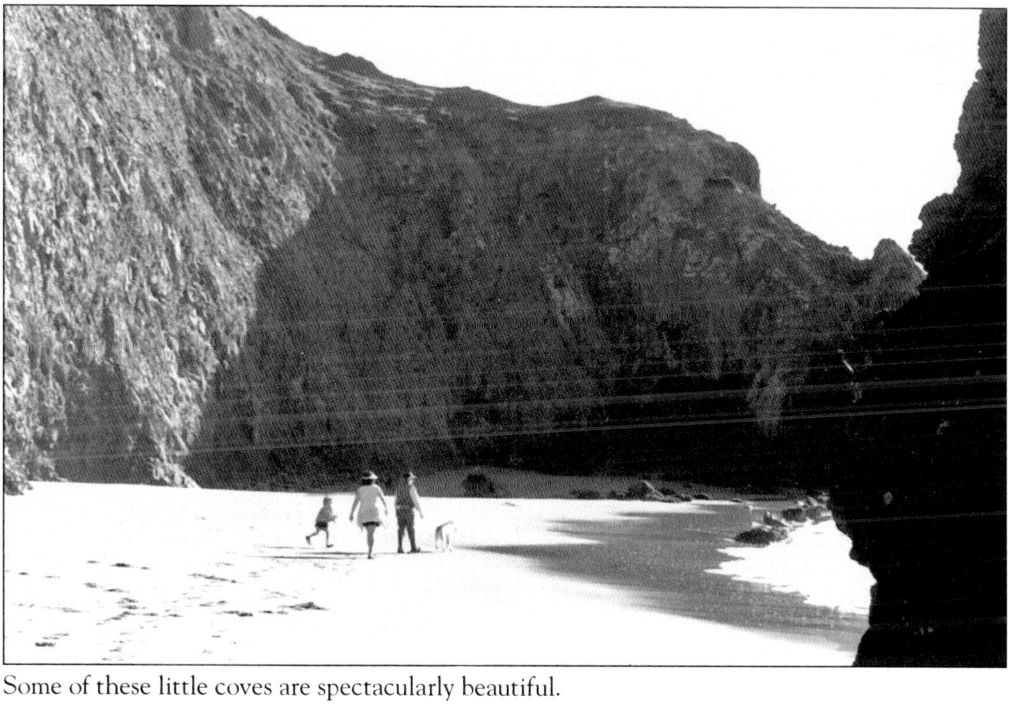

Some of these little coves are spectacularly beautiful.

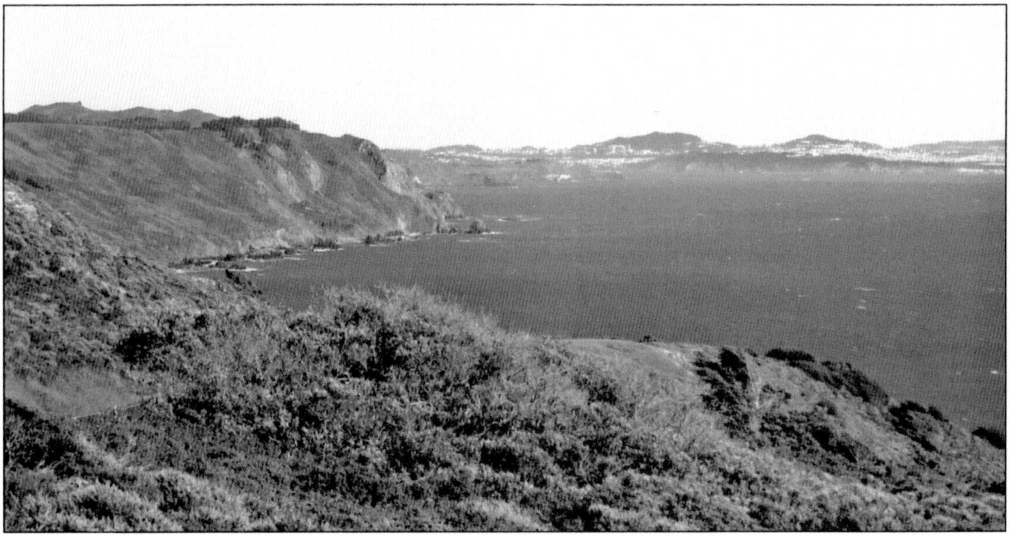

Most of the Pacific coastline in Marin has become part of the GGNRA. The majority of the rest is in private hands, but the Marin Agricultural Land Trust (MALT) has purchased the development rights to more than 90,000 acres, assuring permanent open space for Marin's future.

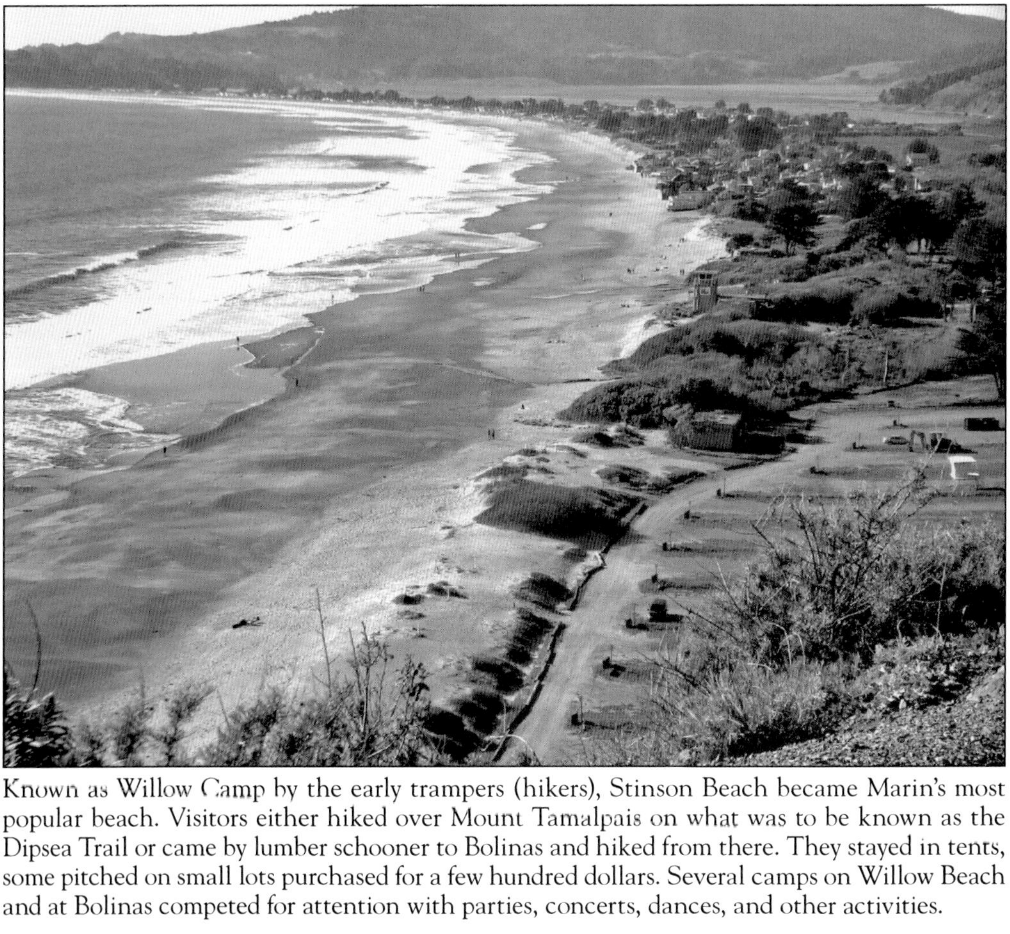

Known as Willow Camp by the early trampers (hikers), Stinson Beach became Marin's most popular beach. Visitors either hiked over Mount Tamalpais on what was to be known as the Dipsea Trail or came by lumber schooner to Bolinas and hiked from there. They stayed in tents, some pitched on small lots purchased for a few hundred dollars. Several camps on Willow Beach and at Bolinas competed for attention with parties, concerts, dances, and other activities.

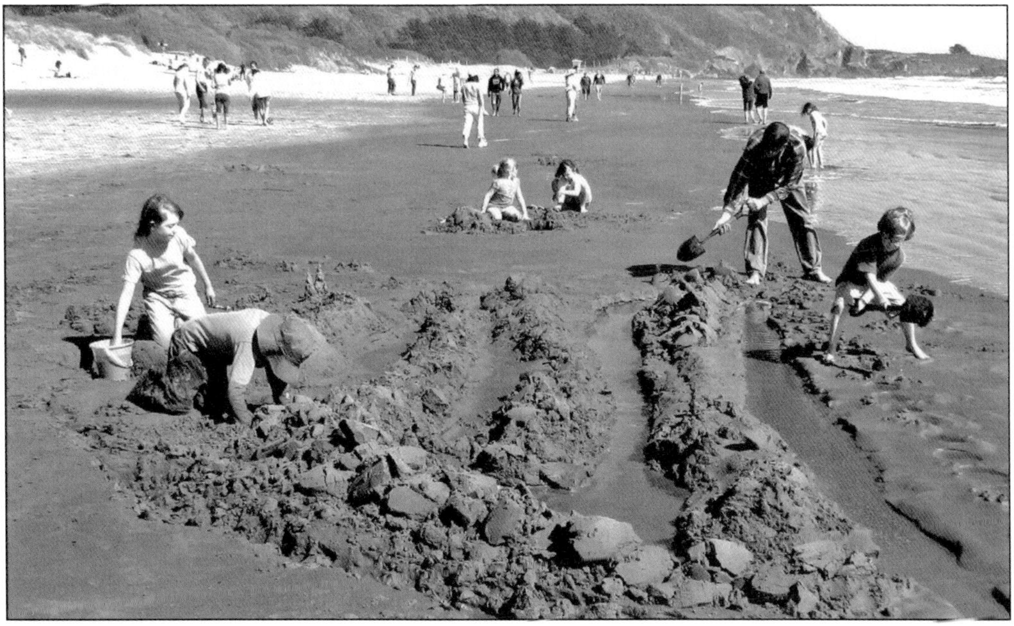

By 1879, there were 20 family tents set up in the sand that would become Stinson Beach. The tents, mounted on platforms, were rented to holiday seekers. There were bonfires on the beach at night and organized games and songfests. Easkoot's Beach, Camp Upton, and Willow Camp competed for vacationers on the 3.5-mile-long beach. There is plenty of beach for these young engineers to design their canal systems.

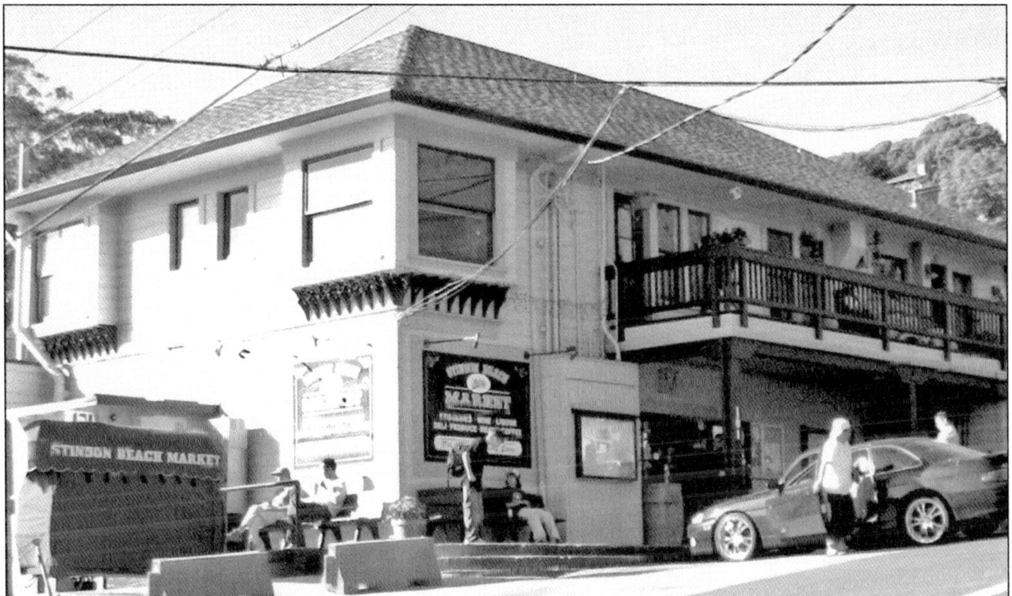

The first real hotel in Stinson Beach was built in 1906 as a rooming house. A year later, it became the Hotel Airey and cottages, and by popular demand, the town grocery store. It is still the favorite gathering point for locals and tourists alike, although it is no longer a hotel. Stinson Beach and Bolinas are like islands in the midst of the Golden Gate National Recreation Area. Most of the homes and business are privately owned, and the beach is controlled by the State of California.

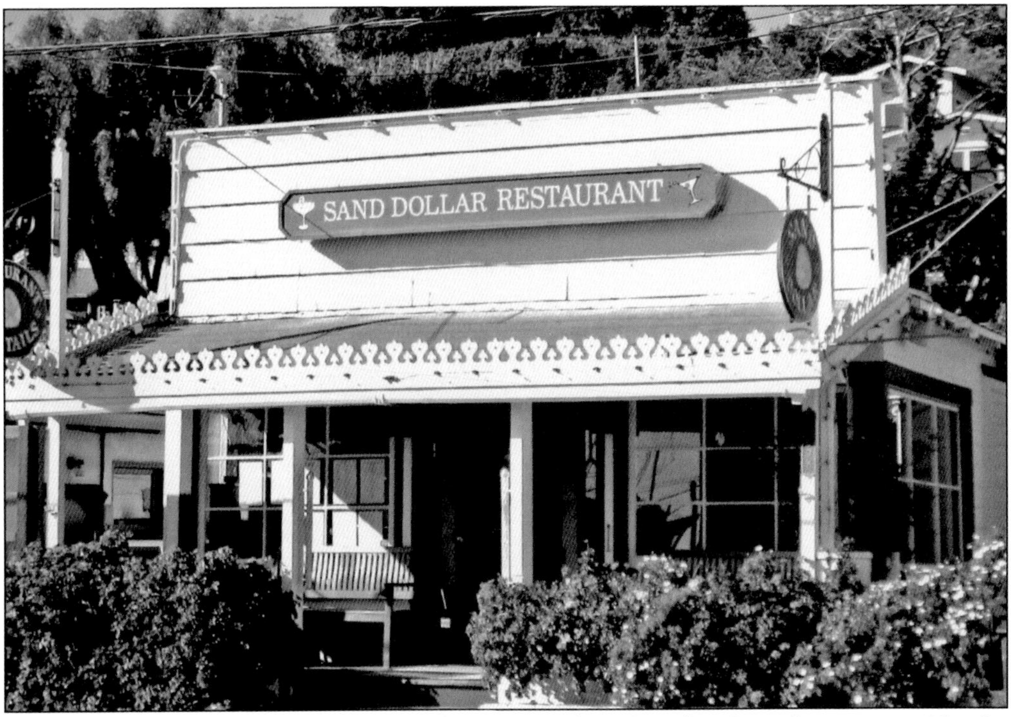

Once a wagon trail became Shoreline Highway, a number of small cafés and restaurants like the Sand Dollar Restaurant sprang up along its path through Stinson Beach. Tent camps gave way to permanent housing, and a sand spit on the edge of town became Seadrift, a gated community of multimillion-dollar homes.

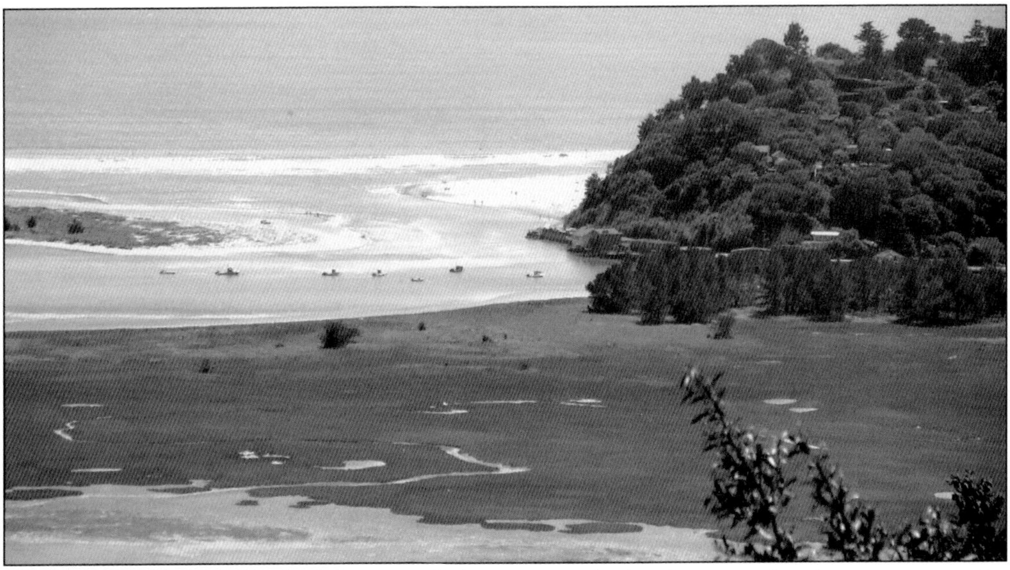

The oldest settlement on the coast is at Bolinas, once the headquarters for the sea otter trade. In the 1852 census, two-thirds of the 323 adults living in Marin lived in Bolinas Township. The lumber schooners out of Bolinas were the main communication link from the coast to the rest of the world. Today the reclusive population is comfortable living on the edge of the San Andreas Fault, which runs through the Bolinas Lagoon.

Lumber was the big seller, and between 1850 and 1900, a dozen schooners were built in Bolinas Lagoon to transport lumber to San Francisco. The lumber schooners could carry hundreds of thousands of board feet of lumber, tons of hides and tallow, and up to 200 passengers for the short but rough trip to San Francisco. During Prohibition, Mexican and Canadian ships would anchor just offshore and let the rumrunners pick up their supplies. (Courtesy Bolinas Museum.)

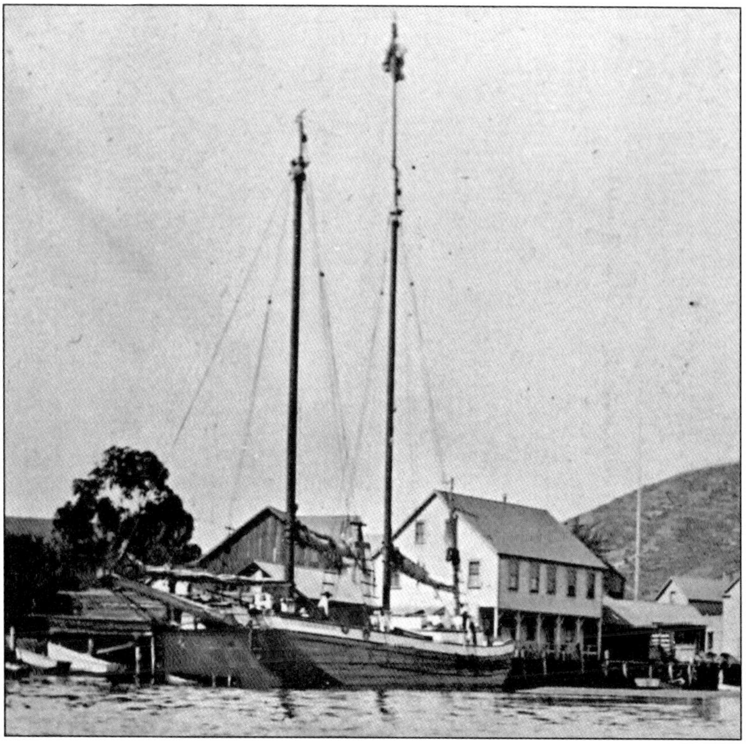

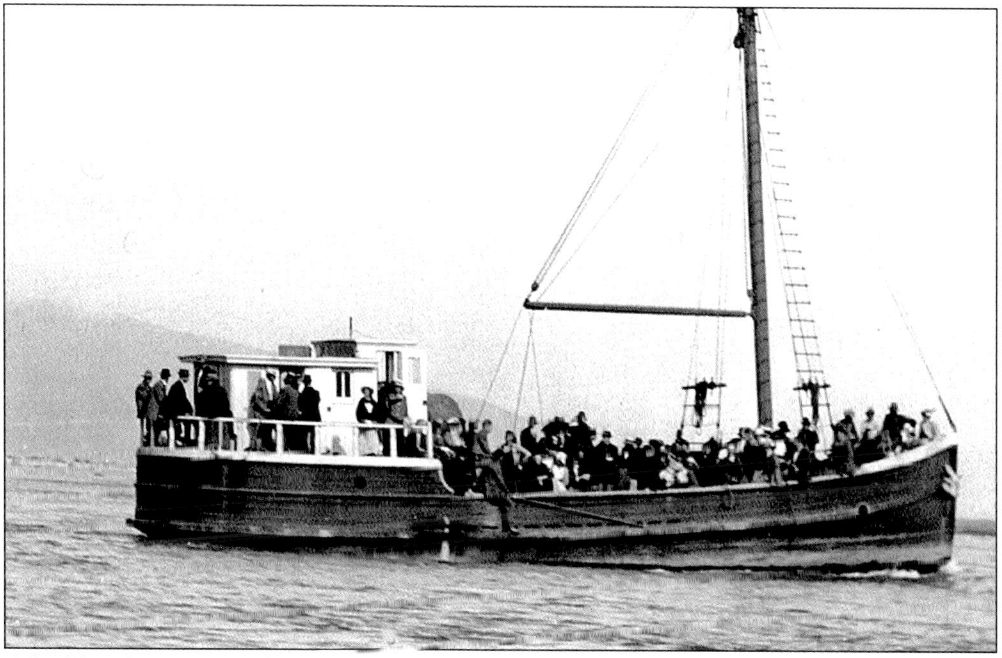

A building boom in Bolinas fizzled out when five thousand 20-by-100-foot lots did not sell at $69.50 in a newspaper promotion. However, when the railroad planned an extension down Mount Tamalpais to end in Bolinas, several hotels, rooming houses, and taverns sprang up. Soon there were churches and schools, and in 1879, the Druids Hall opened. The lumber schooner *The Owl* transported hundreds of passengers on a trip to San Francisco. (Courtesy Bolinas Museum.)

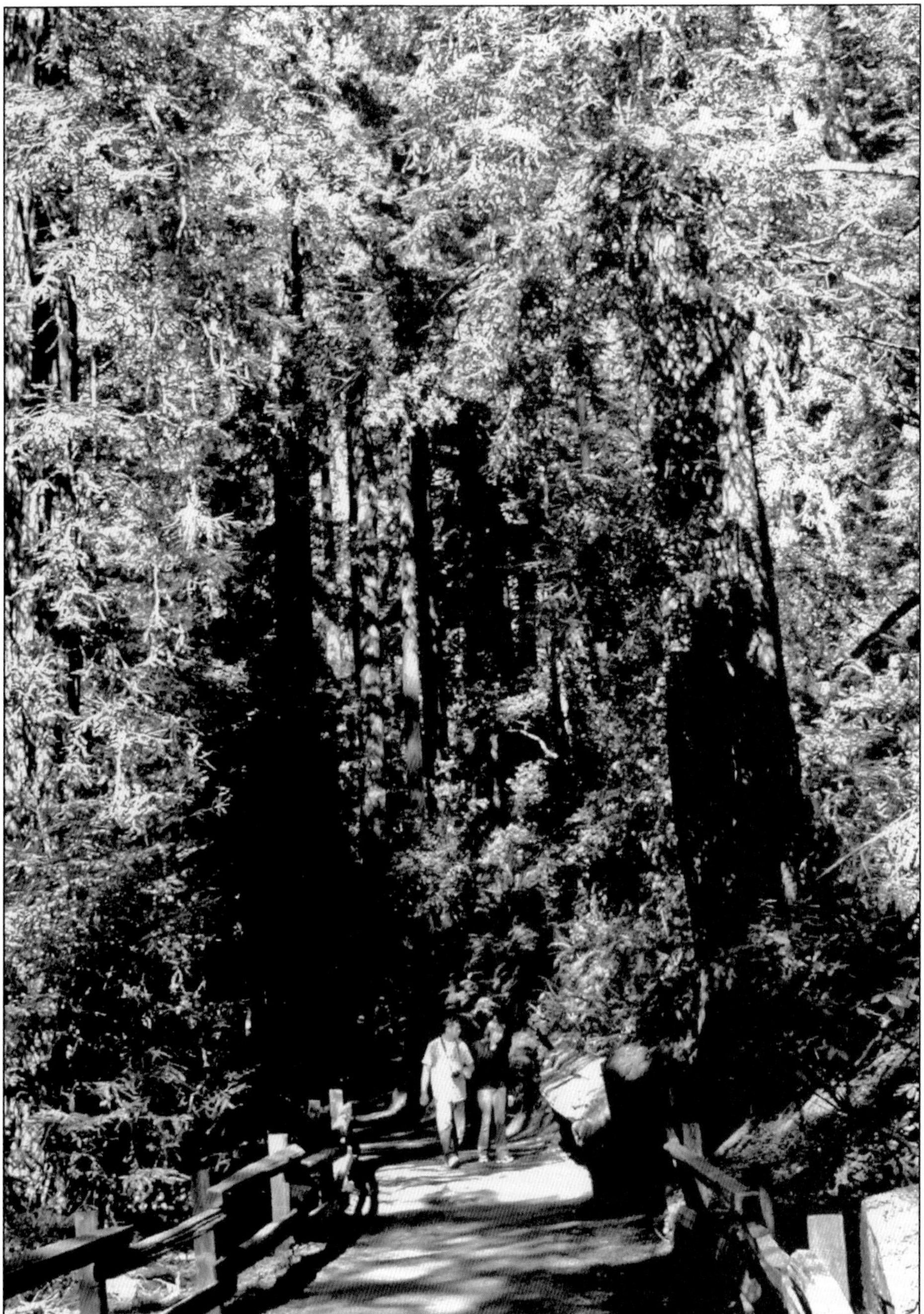

In 1905, a 611-acre grove of redwood trees owned by Congressman William Kent was threatened by a proposal from the Tamalpais Land and Water Company to dam Redwood Creek. In 1907, Kent donated 295 acres to the U.S. government to create the Muir Woods National Monument. It became the inspiration for Pres. Theodore Roosevelt to create the system of national parks. More than one million visitors come annually to the woods, which now spans the full 611 acres. During the meetings in San Francisco to organize the United Nations, a special ceremony was held in Muir Woods in memory of Franklin Roosevelt, who had recently passed away.

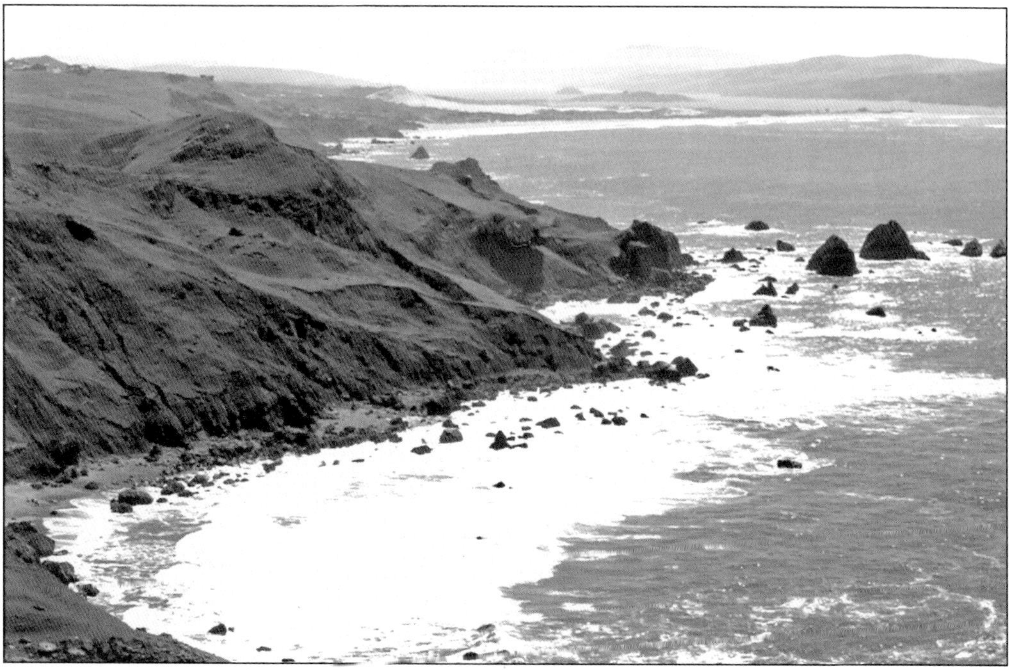

Dillon Beach, seen in the distance in this image, is not as popular as other Marin locations. It is at the mouth of Tomales Bay, the breeding ground of the great white shark. Operators of small boats are also warned of a "following surf," or a big wave coming over the stern, which can swamp or capsize the unwary.

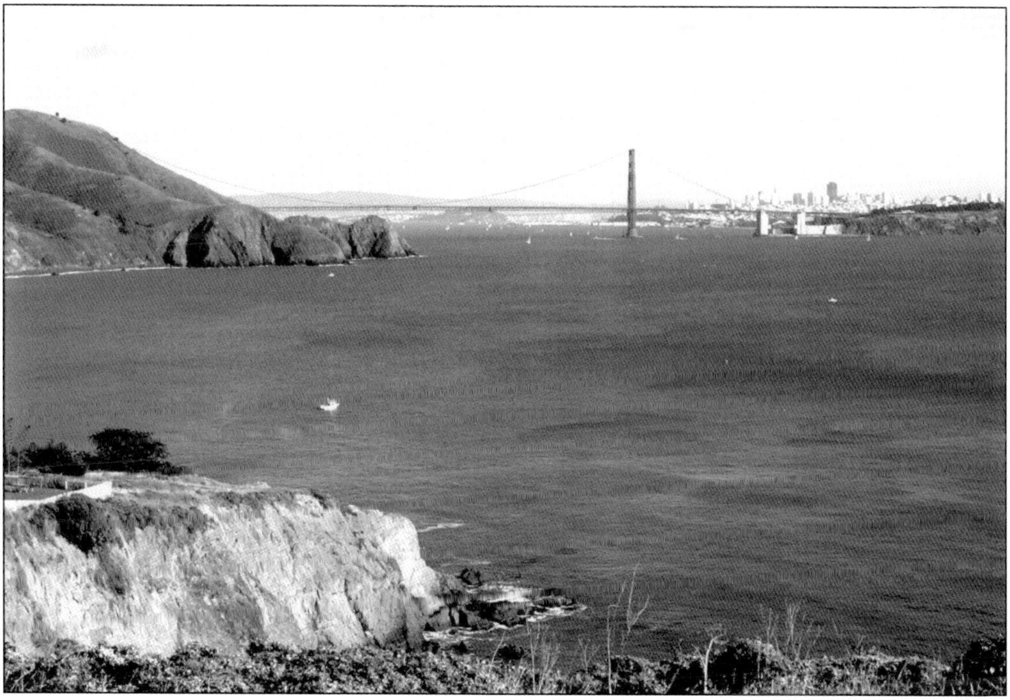

When traveling about the headlands—the Marin side of the Golden Gate—a view of the great bridge is always present, usually with San Francisco shining through.

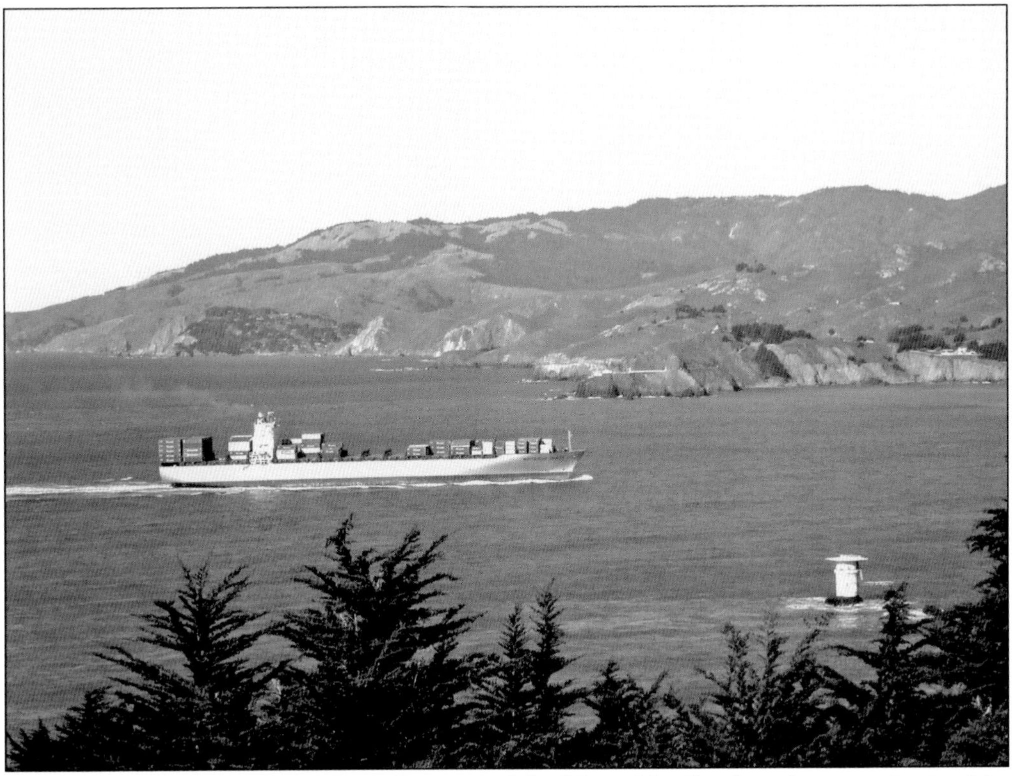

Ten thousand ships a year pass Point Bonita and the Marin Headlands with cargos destined for ports throughout the bay and as far inland as Sacramento and Stockton. Serving as the main defense for the Port of San Francisco since the Civil War, the Marin Headlands is honeycombed by abandoned coastal defense installations. Nike missiles were housed in the headlands during the cold war. A few are still there but without warheads. Once each week, visitors can see how the system worked.

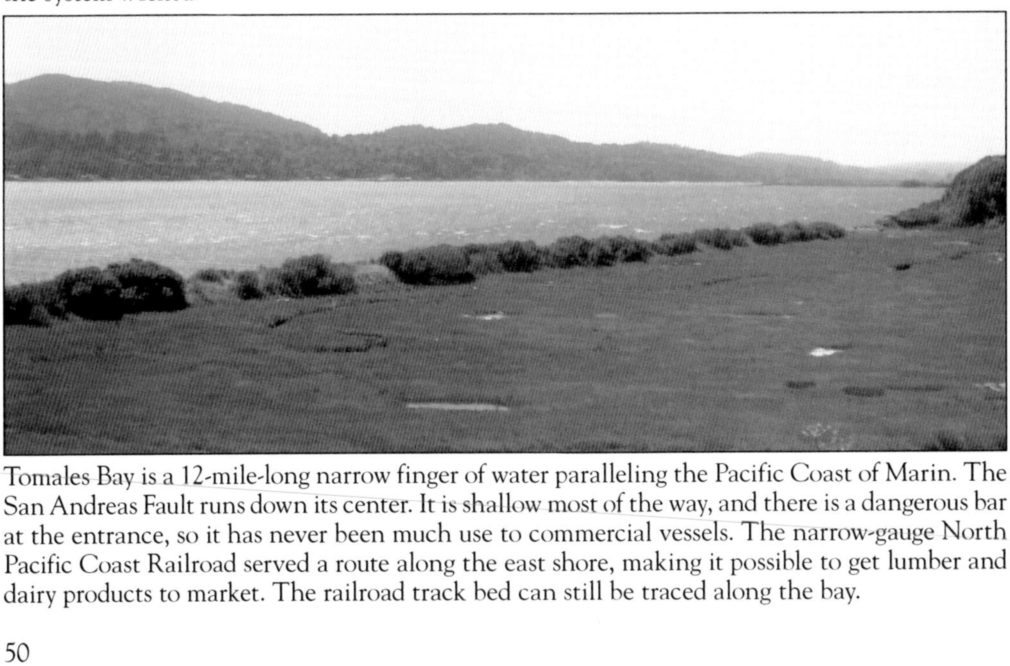

Tomales Bay is a 12-mile-long narrow finger of water paralleling the Pacific Coast of Marin. The San Andreas Fault runs down its center. It is shallow most of the way, and there is a dangerous bar at the entrance, so it has never been much use to commercial vessels. The narrow-gauge North Pacific Coast Railroad served a route along the east shore, making it possible to get lumber and dairy products to market. The railroad track bed can still be traced along the bay.

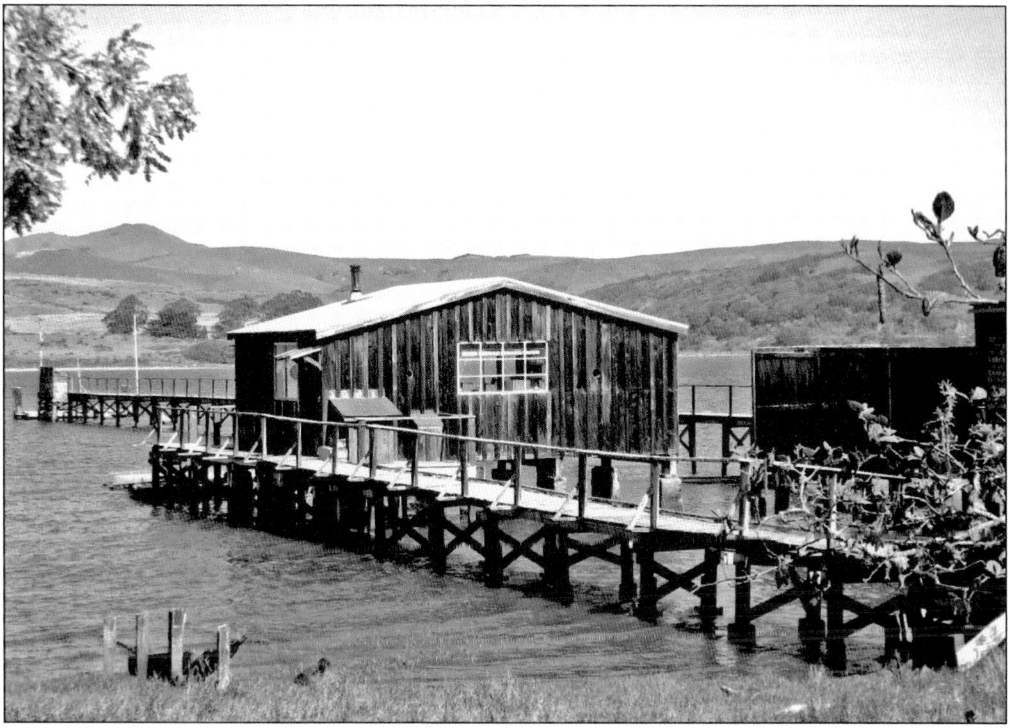

Inverness, on the west side of Tomales Bay, was a popular tourist spot and was one of the few places which opened up lots for sale. It is a long commute from Inverness to San Francisco, but those who do it maintain that it is worth it.

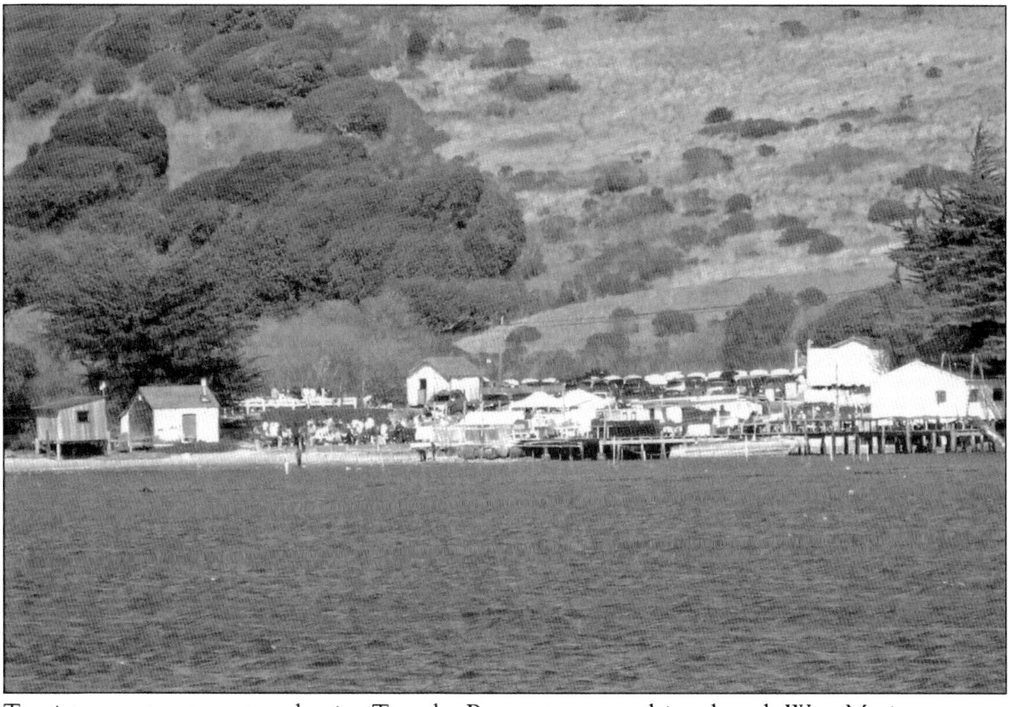

Tourists can stop to rest and enjoy Tomales Bay oysters on a drive though West Marin.

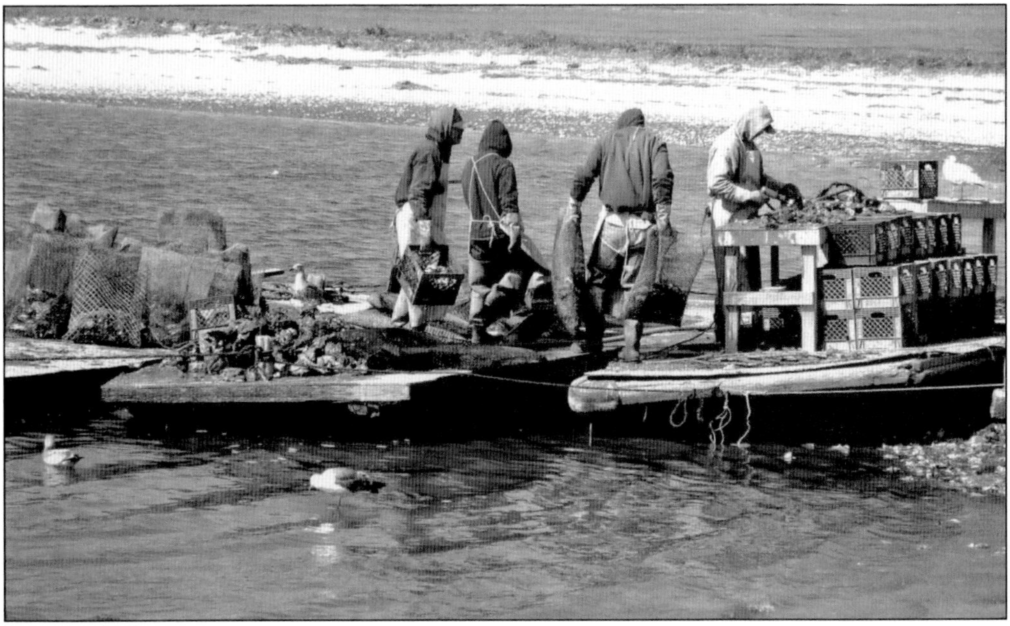

The Drakes Bay Family Farm produces 80 percent of the county's $3.3 million in farmed oysters each year. Oystermen bring crates of oysters to land at the farm on the Point Reyes peninsula, as they have for several generations.

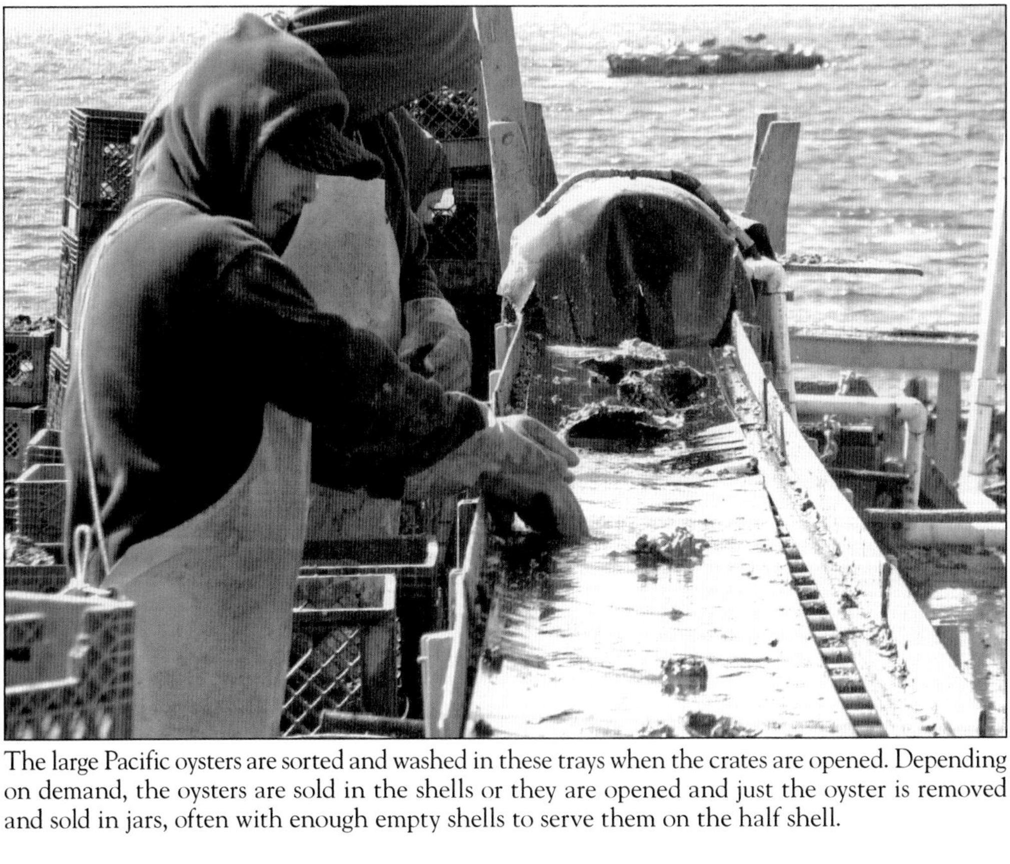

The large Pacific oysters are sorted and washed in these trays when the crates are opened. Depending on demand, the oysters are sold in the shells or they are opened and just the oyster is removed and sold in jars, often with enough empty shells to serve them on the half shell.

Four

Inside the Golden Gate

The first several exploration parties came overland from Monterey. The Golden Gate and the Carquinez Strait were barriers preventing them from proceeding further north. Finally, a courageous ship captain braved the unknown dangers of the Golden Gate and found a vast inland sea, which began at the delta created by the Sacramento and San Joaquin Rivers. Marin's long shoreline fronts on San Pablo Bay and central San Francisco Bay. The bay then was teaming with fish and other aquatic life. Sea otters and fur seals were everywhere. The hills were covered with timber for building and firewood. Freshwater was plentiful. Deer, elk, and bear provided food. First the Catholic missions and then American and Mexican settlers acquired vast ranches, raised cattle and horses, and lived an idyllic existence. But all was not well in this paradise. Lumberjacks soon began to clear-cut the redwood forests, allowing the topsoil to fill the creeks and rivers. Gold seekers using hydraulic mining in the Sierras flushed millions of tons of toxic minerals into the bay. Villages began to grow along the shore. Railroads were built. Cattle ranches became subdivisions. And that was just the beginning. Marshlands that were breeding mosquitoes that brought malaria and other diseases for which there were no cures were filled. Hundreds of acres were diked to create Hamilton Field. Hundreds more were filled to make the railroad yards in Southern Marin and the shipyards in Sausalito. Only 20 percent of the wetlands once surrounding San Francisco Bay are still subject to tidal action. Nevertheless, Marin blossomed into a place of incredible beauty. Connecting to a world-famous city by an engineering marvel only accelerated its attraction. Farsighted citizens stepped in and created many state, county, and federal parks. An agricultural land trust preserved thousand of acres. Wildlife sanctuaries were created to protect the marine environment. Today almost 80 percent of the county is open space. Combining one of the best educational systems in the nation with a shortage of building sites sent the prices of homes to levels matched by few other locations. Small-scale marine-oriented industries have generally flourished in Marin—marinas, boatyards, and environmental research centers, for example. Tourism has become the leading job-producing industry, and the film industry is close behind.

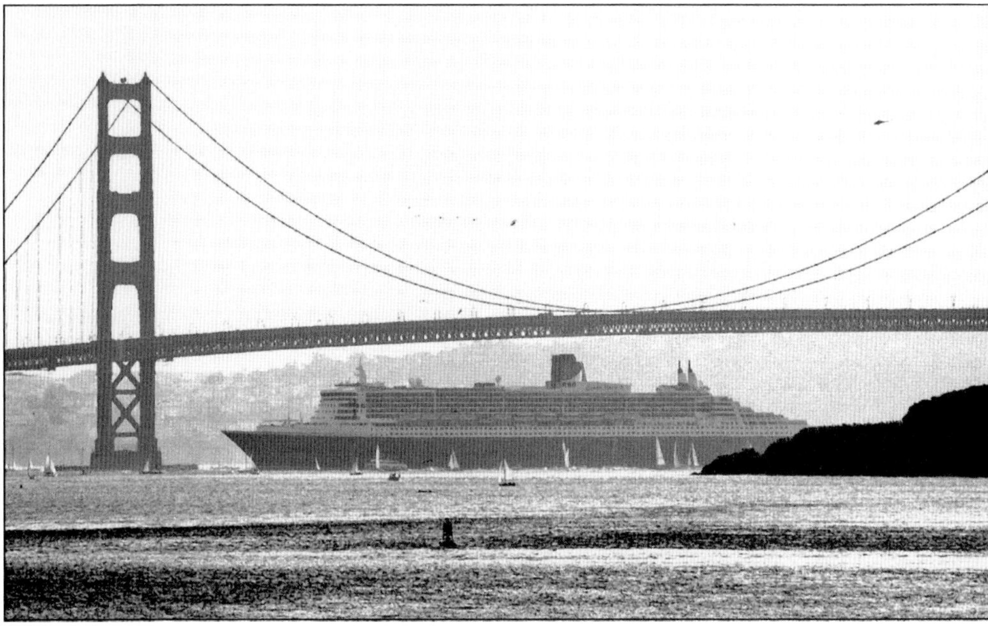

On a spring evening in 2007, the *Queen Mary 2*, then the largest passenger ship in the world, pushed aside centuries of battling the winds and tides, and majestically entered the Golden Gate. Ayala's little *San Carlos* could have rested comfortably on the afterdeck of this behemoth. Instead of the silence that greeted Ayala, a flotilla of yachts led the *Queen* into the bay, while thousands of spectators watched from every vantage point.

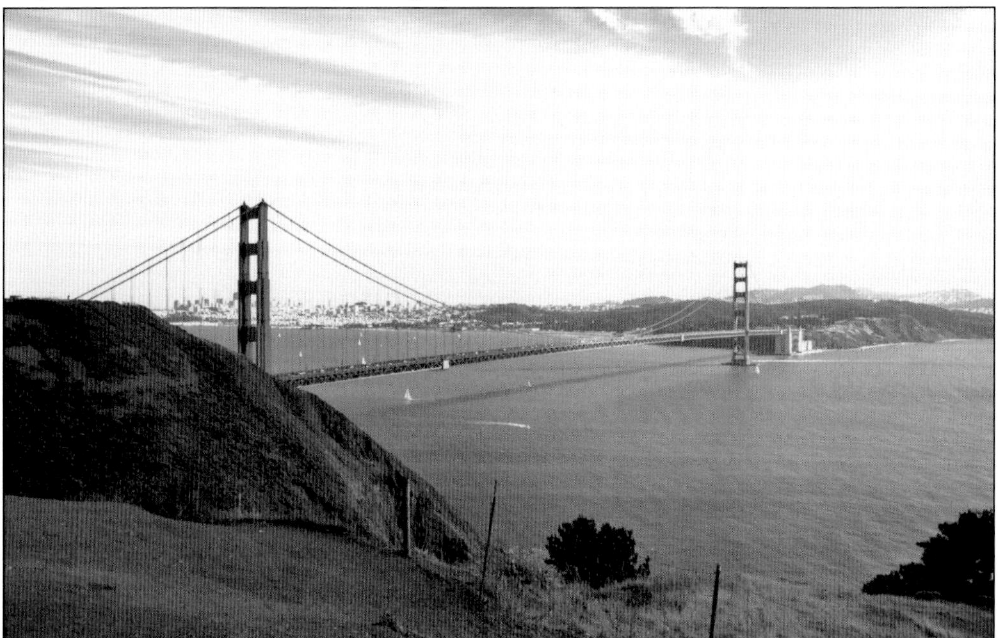

Marin's southern end is dominated by the Golden Gate Bridge, one of the most recognized landmarks in the world. It connects Marin to San Francisco, one of the most exciting cities in the world. The bridge put the ferries to San Francisco out of business, but the ferry from San Rafael to the East Bay continued to run for almost two more decades.

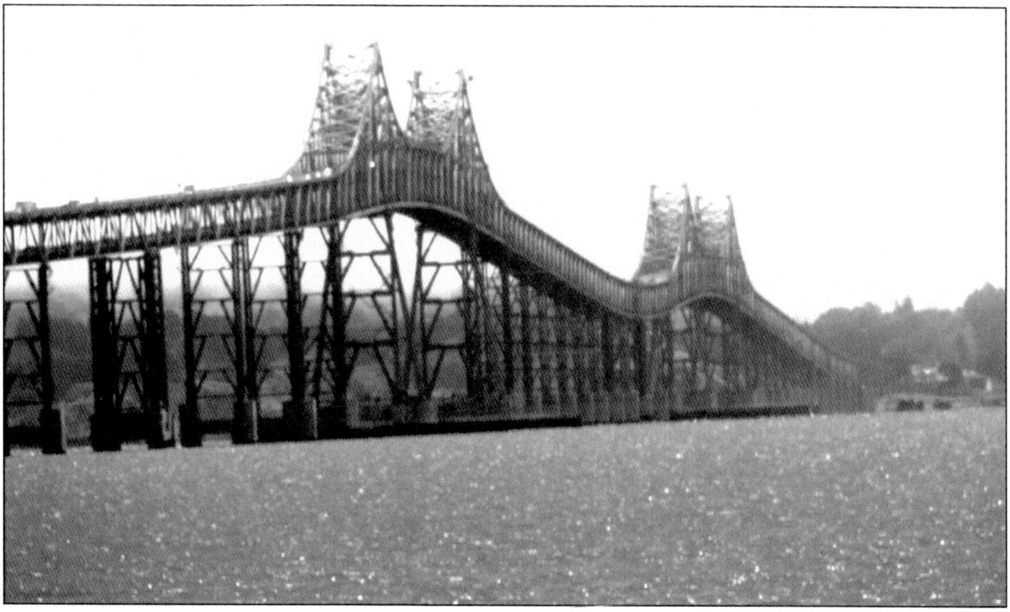

Finally, the San Rafael–Richmond bridge was built. Called an "ugly duckling," the bridge had a roller-coaster design that suffered when compared to its sister bridge, the Golden Gate. It connected Marin to the East Bay cities and educational centers at the University of California, Berkeley. The era of the large automobile-carrying ferryboats was over.

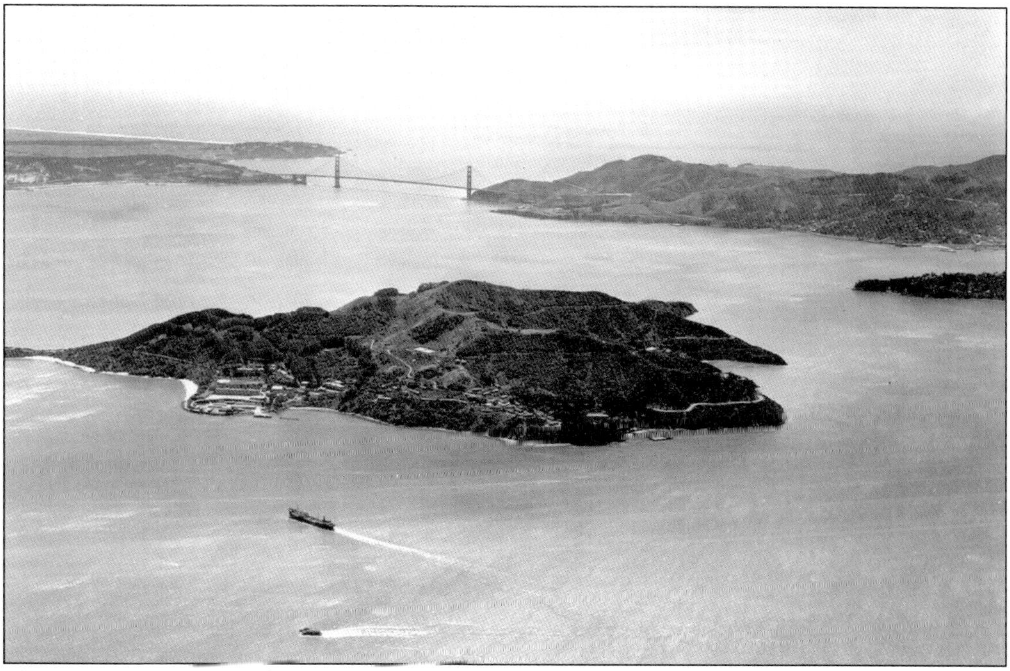

The largest island in the bay is Angel Island. It was the landing spot for the first explorers, then became an early cattle ranch. By the Civil War, its strategic location made it ideal for an army post with coast defense guns and the troops to man them. For almost a century, enlarged facilities housed thousand of trainees, until the end of World War II and even through the cold war. It is now a state park.

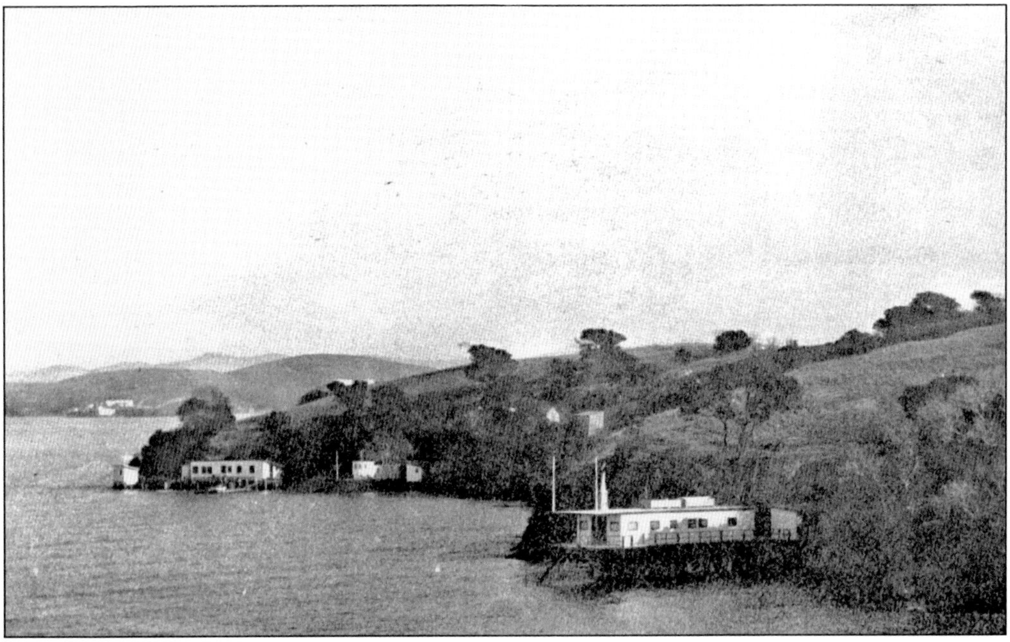

For several generations, an island near Point San Pedro in San Rafael was in private hands. Several small cabins provided a place for the owner's family to gather on weekends and holidays. Now this and its sister island are wildlife refuges.

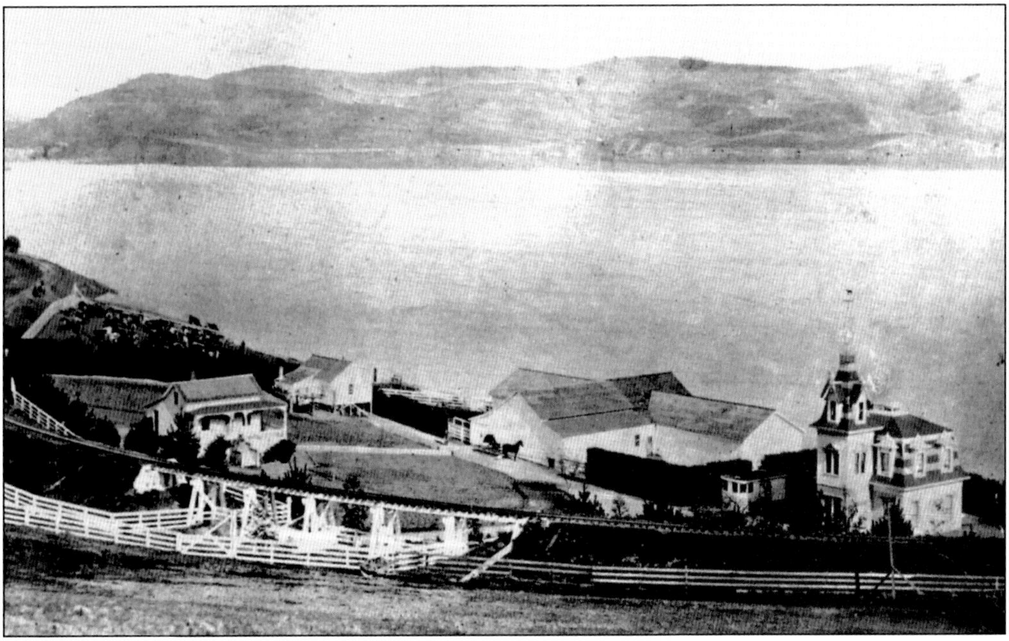

Among the first industries in Marin dependent upon its marine location was cattle ranching. Hides and tallow were the main products and were exported to Mexico and the Far East. When dairy cows were imported from Britain, milk, butter, and cheese proved profitable. The Eagle Dairy on Strawberry Point was one of the best. Everything at the Eagle Dairy was painted white, even the narrow-gauge railroad rails, in an early attempt at sanitation. (Courtesy the Landmarks Society.)

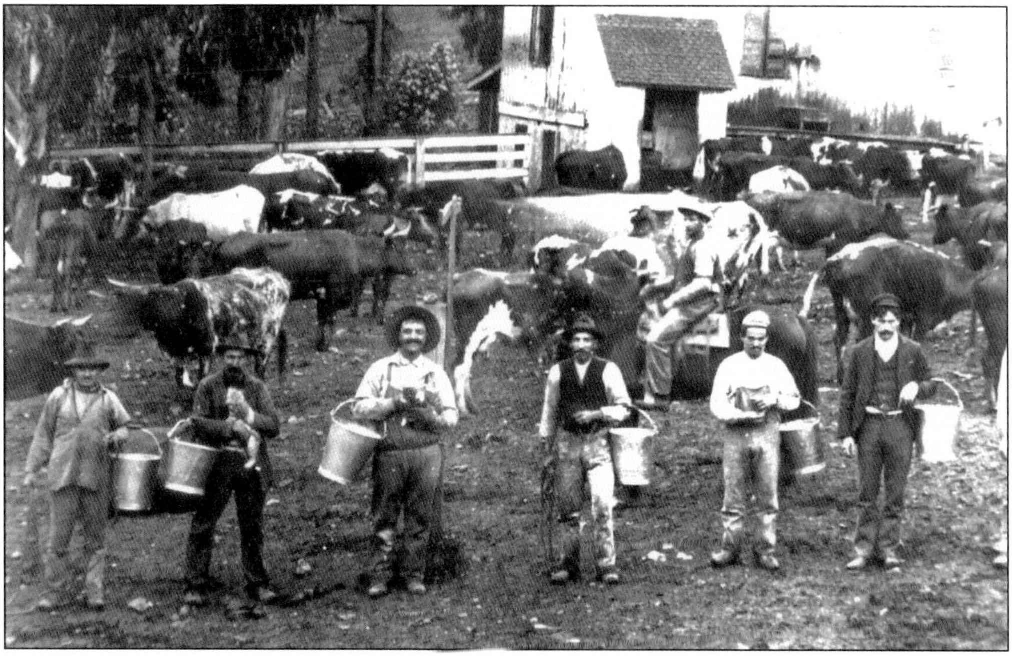

Portuguese dairymen were brought from the Azores to do the milking. Milk, butter, and cheese from Marin were considered the best and found a willing market in San Francisco. Native Americans managed the huge herds of cattle and horses on the ranches. The coming of the railroads in the 1870s and 1880s made it possible to get dairy products to market quickly. (Courtesy the Landmarks Society.)

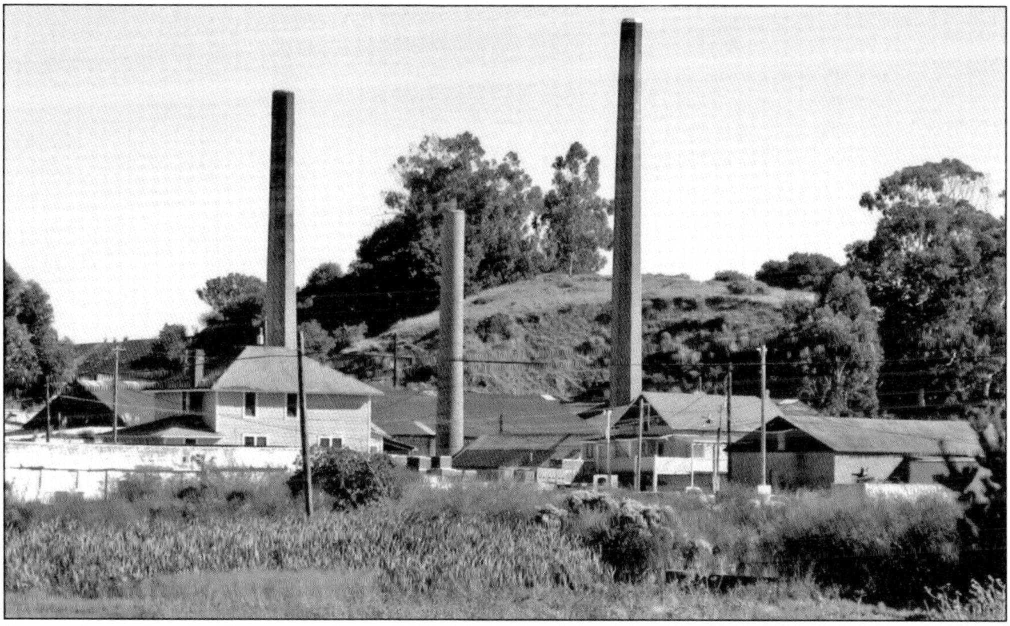

Barges loaded with Marin bricks traveled throughout the Bay Area to deliver the material to building sites. A million bricks a year were produced in local kilns. They were needed both before and after the 1906 earthquake to build and rebuild San Francisco. The tall smokestacks of many of the brick kilns are still visible on the Marin shoreline.

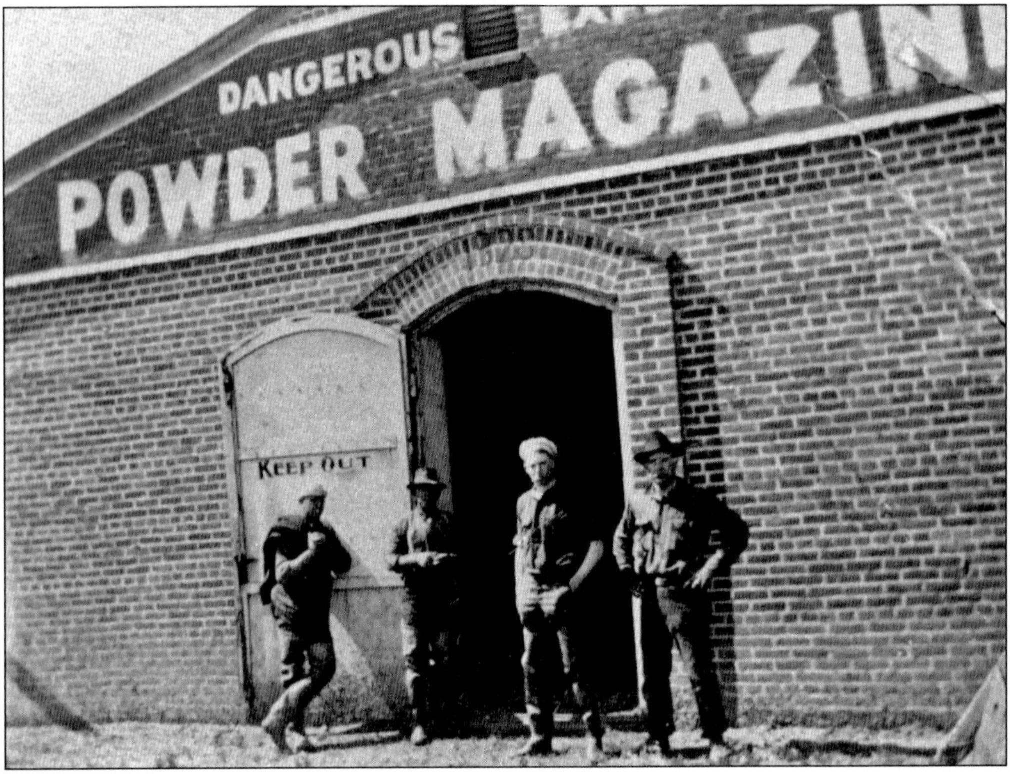

Building bridges and tunnels for the railroads and clearing land for the ranchers required lots of blasting powder. Marin's open space and water access made it ideal for explosive manufacturing. After an explosion of two ammunition ships at Port Chicago during World War II killed more than 300 people, the military decided to turn much of Southern Marin into an ammunition storage and loading center. However, within five months, the war ended and the plan along with it. (Courtesy the Landmarks Society.)

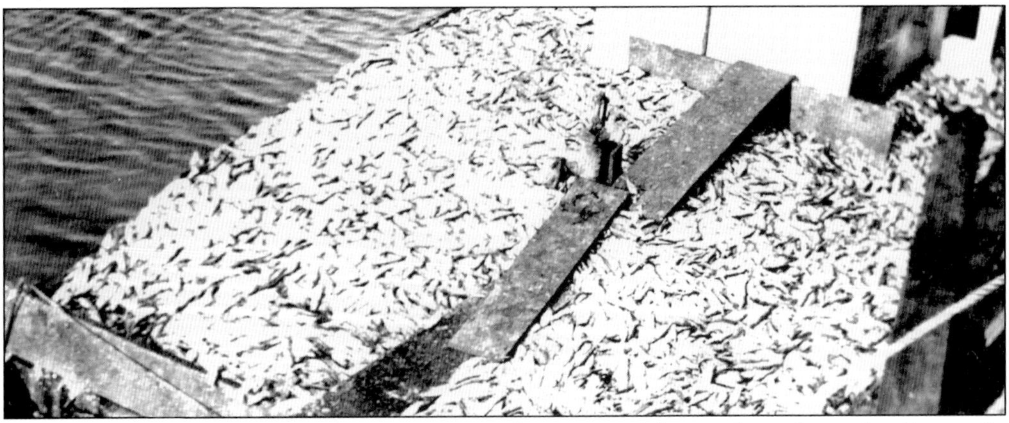

Once each year the bay is filled with herring. The roe is a delicacy throughout the Orient. In 1973–1974, Japanese demand for roe exploded. Fishing fleets from far and wide came to Marin to get as many as possible before thousands of birds and hundreds of seals and sea lions filled their stomachs. In 1976, the Fisheries Conservation Act was passed to protect the maximum sustainable yield. It was too late to save the sardines. They were gone after the 1950s. (Courtesy the Morrison Family Collection.)

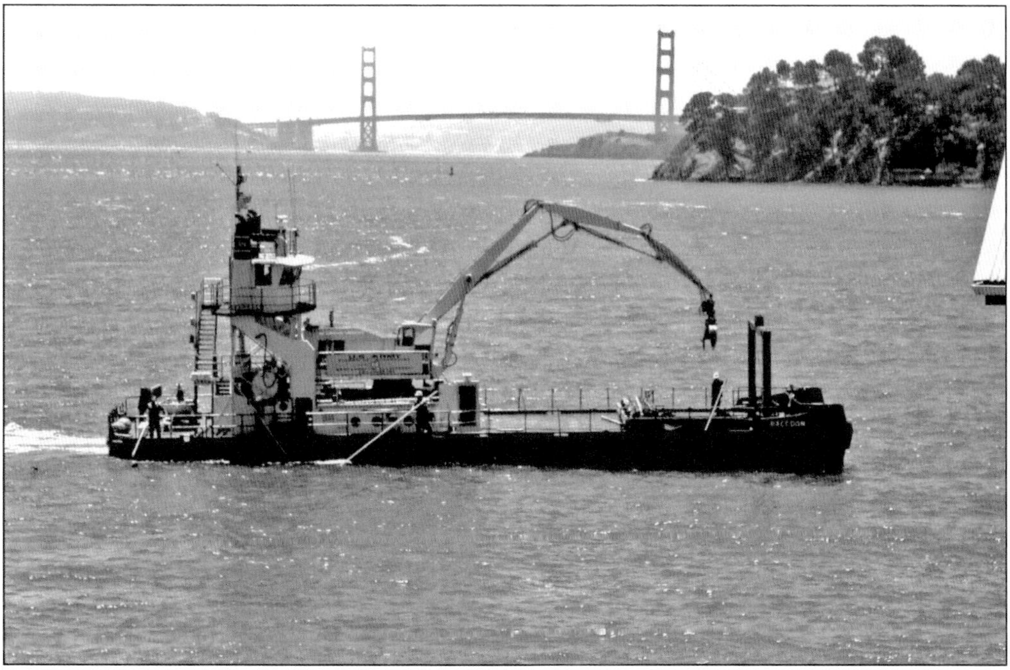

For all its beauty, San Francisco Bay is still a working port. Dredges are needed to keep the harbor and shipping channels open. For a long time, dredges were busy filling in the bay, but that is no longer possible. Care must also be taken during any dredging operation that soils still holding toxins from the Gold Rush era are not disturbed.

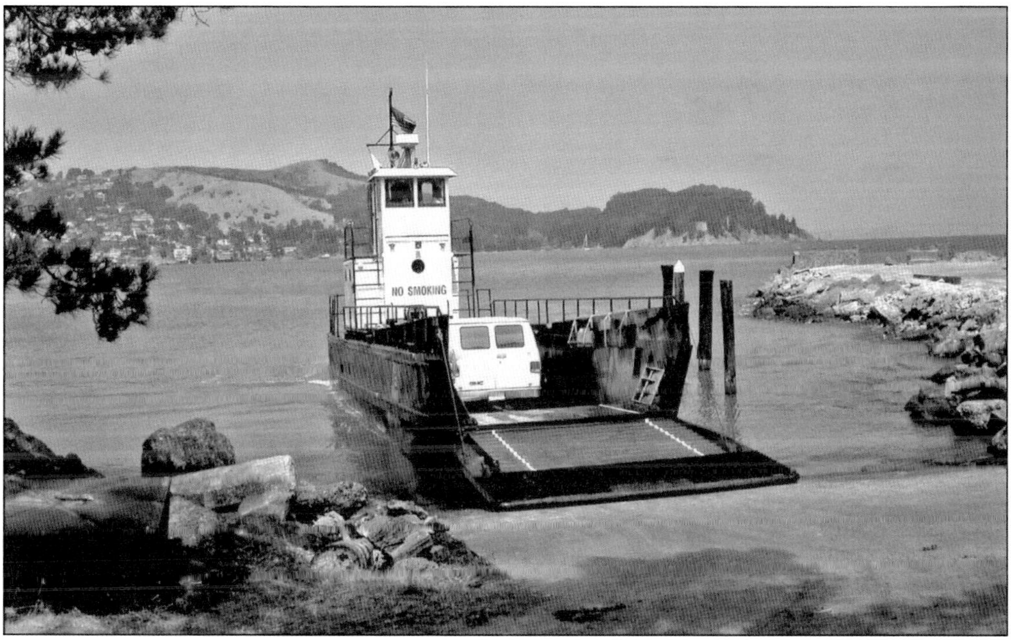

San Francisco Bay is a large body of water with a great deal going on besides the international shipping industry. Ferryboats and sightseeing vessels move people, and barges and tugs are busy with cargo. When a vehicle on Angel Island requires service, the State Park Department landing craft is ready to move it to shore.

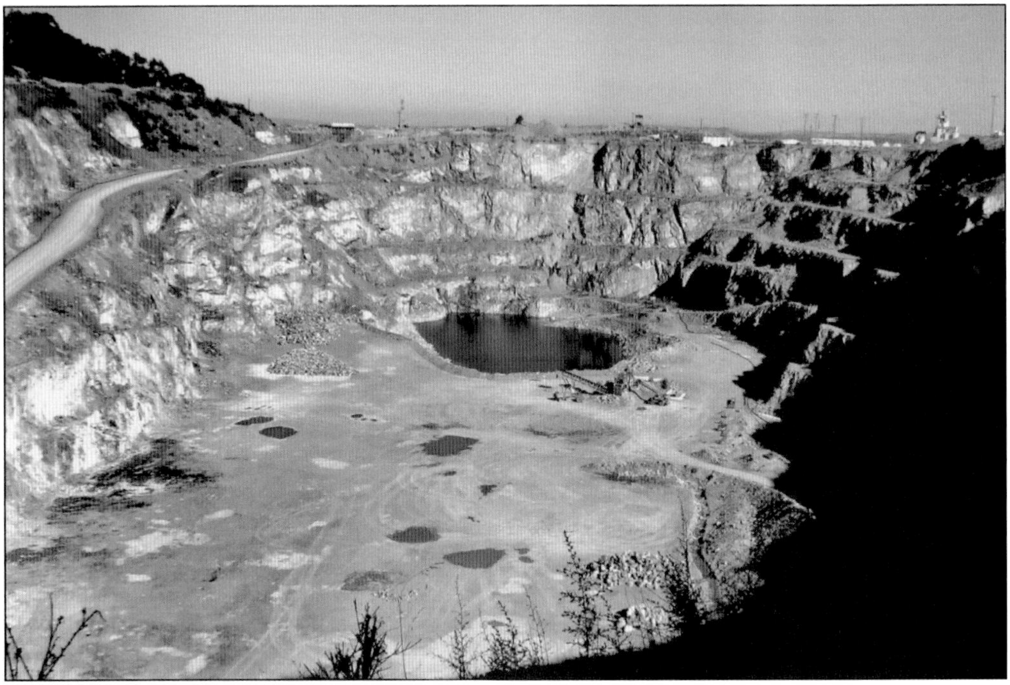

A huge block of limestone was discovered on the east end of the San Pedro peninsula. Each day, huge trucks carry crushed rock to building sites in Marin and other North Bay locations. But it is the bay-side location that is most important. This enables barges to take on loads at the quarry's deepwater dock. Tugs then move the rock directly to the delta, where it becomes riprap, protecting the levies flanking thousand of acres of some of California's best farm land.

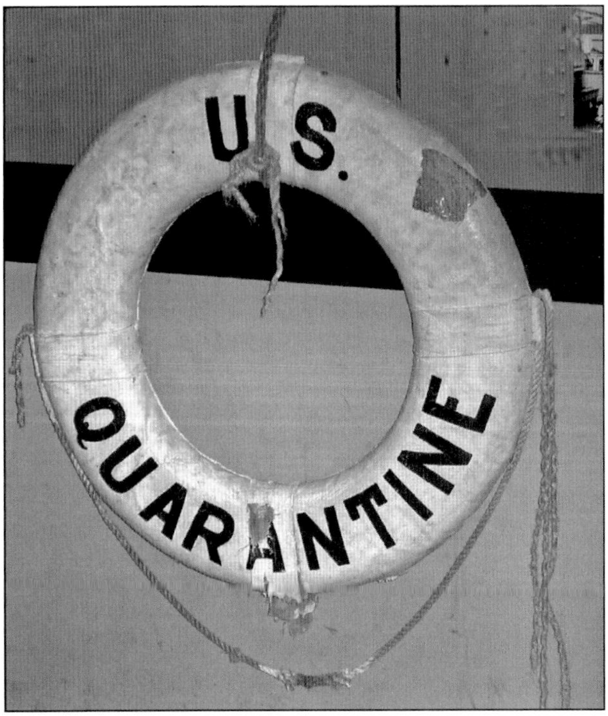

Because of the large number of travelers, particularly immigrants, arriving at the Port of San Francisco, the fear of a contagious disease for which there was no cure spreading through the population was great. In 1890, a quarantine station was established on Angel Island. All arrivals were detained through the incubation period of any fatal disease. (Courtesy Angel Island Association.)

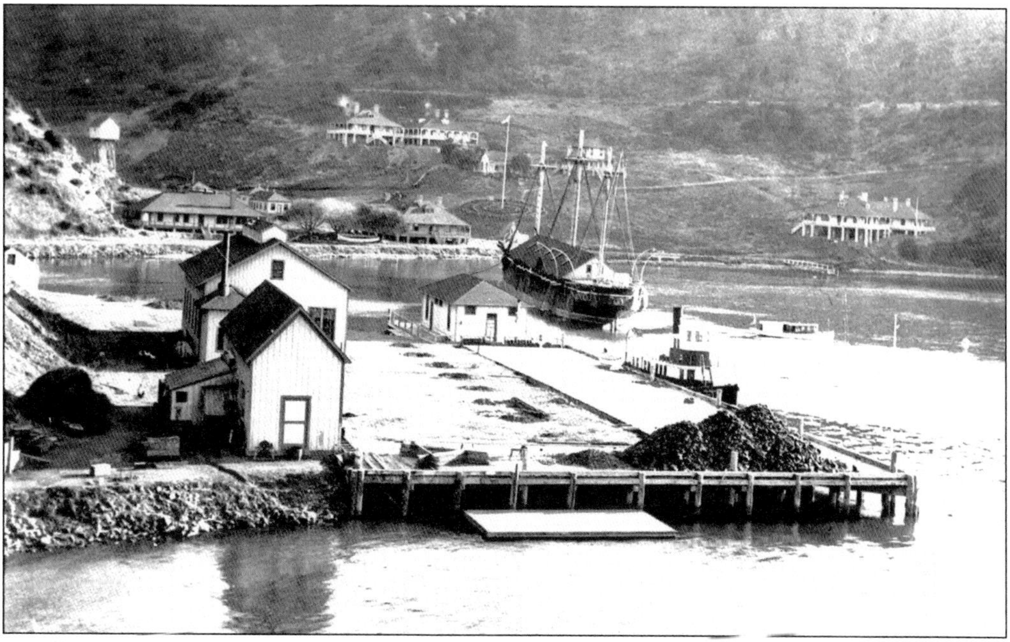

Smaller ships could dock right at the quarantine station. Passengers from larger ships were transported by ferry to the island. If small pox or other dangerous diseases were discovered, the passengers' stay was usually 21 days. Chinese and Japanese each had separate dormitories and kitchens. All baggage was unloaded and fumigated in large pressure tubes. Passengers were stripped and scrubbed with carbolic acid. The Angel Island Quarantine Station was phased out by 1940. (Courtesy Angel Island Association.)

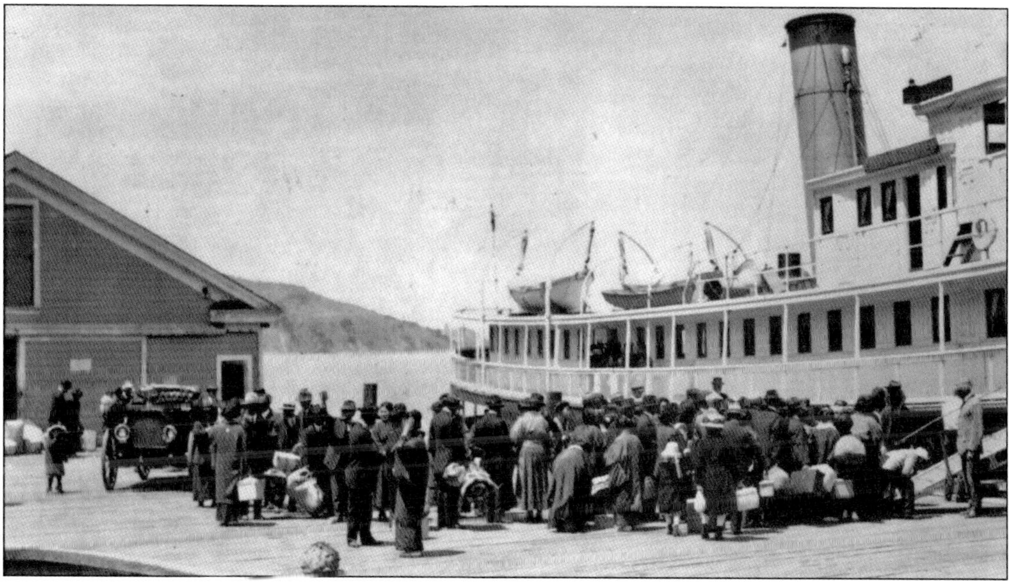

In 1882, Congress passed the Chinese Exclusion Act. From 1910 to 1940, the U.S. Immigration Service operated a station on Angel Island. All immigrants arriving in the Port of San Francisco were brought to the station. Most were cleared quickly, but for the Chinese, who had to prove they were not part of an excluded group, the wait could stretch for months or even, in a few cases, a year. (Courtesy Angel Island Association.)

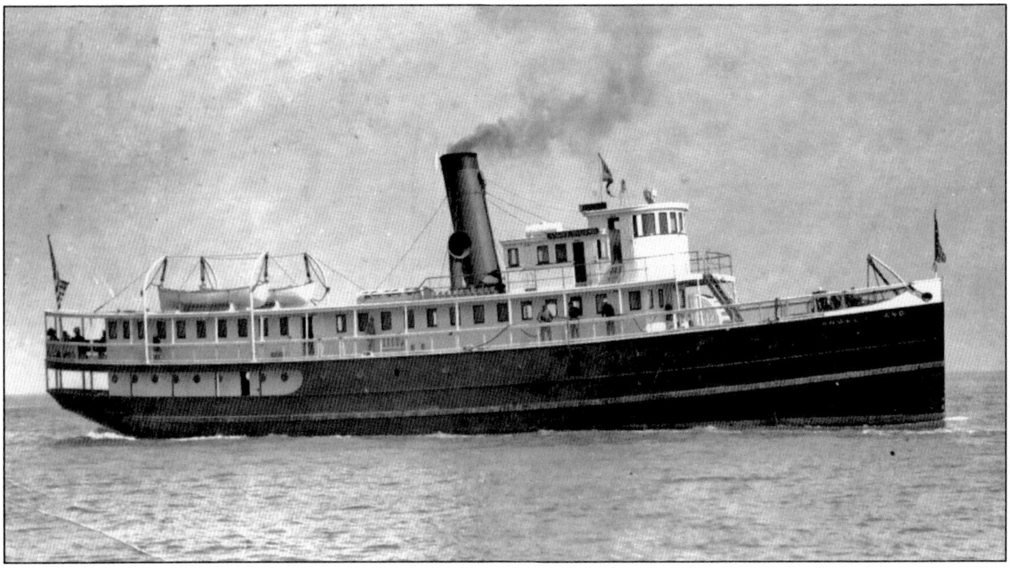

The SS *Angel Island* met the ships carrying immigrants at the dock in San Francisco and brought the new arrivals directly to the immigration station dock on Angel Island. A fire destroyed the administration building in 1940, and the immigration station was closed. The barracks were used as a POW camp until the end of World War II. The remaining buildings are being restored as a memorial to the Chinese immigrants. (Courtesy Angel Island Association.)

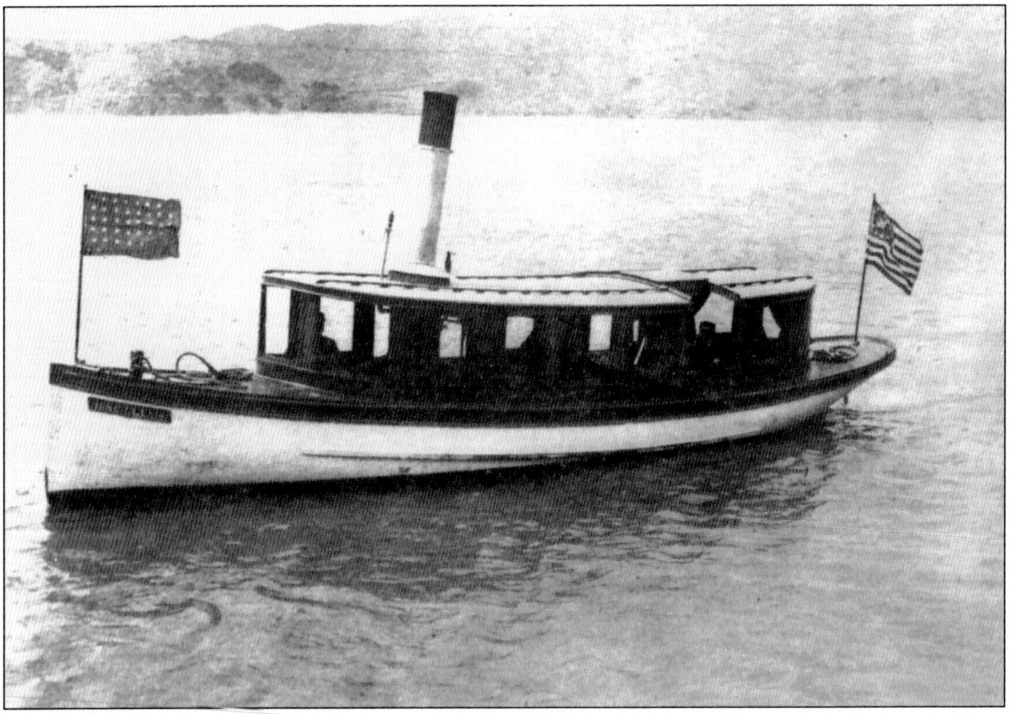

The steam launch *Bacilles* was typical of steam and power launches that served all the residents on Angel Island for almost a century. Everything had to be transported to the island. Older children had to be taken to Tiburon to get to high school in Mill Valley. (Courtesy California State Parks.)

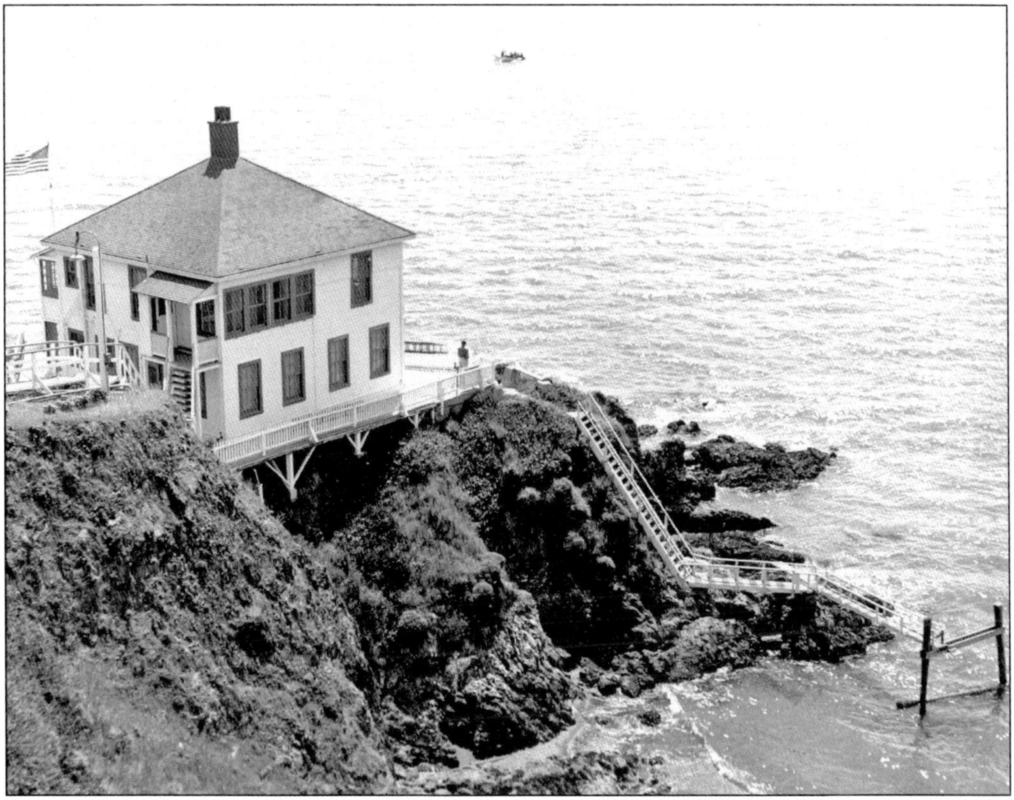

Lighthouses in Marin were not the picturesque tall cylinders seen throughout the world. Usually, the higher the tower and light, the farther out to sea it could be seen. This was not true with the fogs that were persistent in the bay. The lighthouses in Marin were built close to the water so the light could be seen underneath the weather. The lighthouse pictured above was one of three on Angel Island, making it the only island in the United States with three lighthouses. (Courtesy Angel Island Association.)

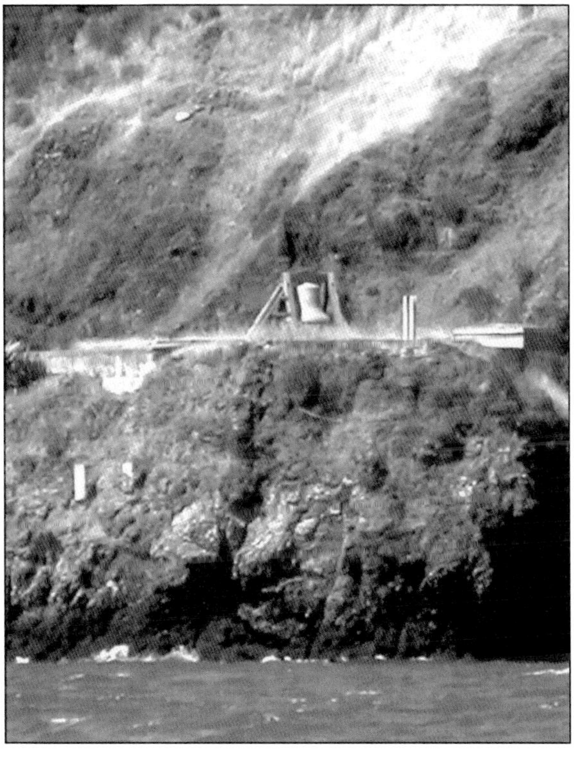

Even more valuable in a dense fog was a fog bell. In emergencies, the bells were struck every few minutes by hand. All of the fog-warning systems have been automated, and most of the light houses have been demolished. Although not in use, this bell has survived on Angel Island.

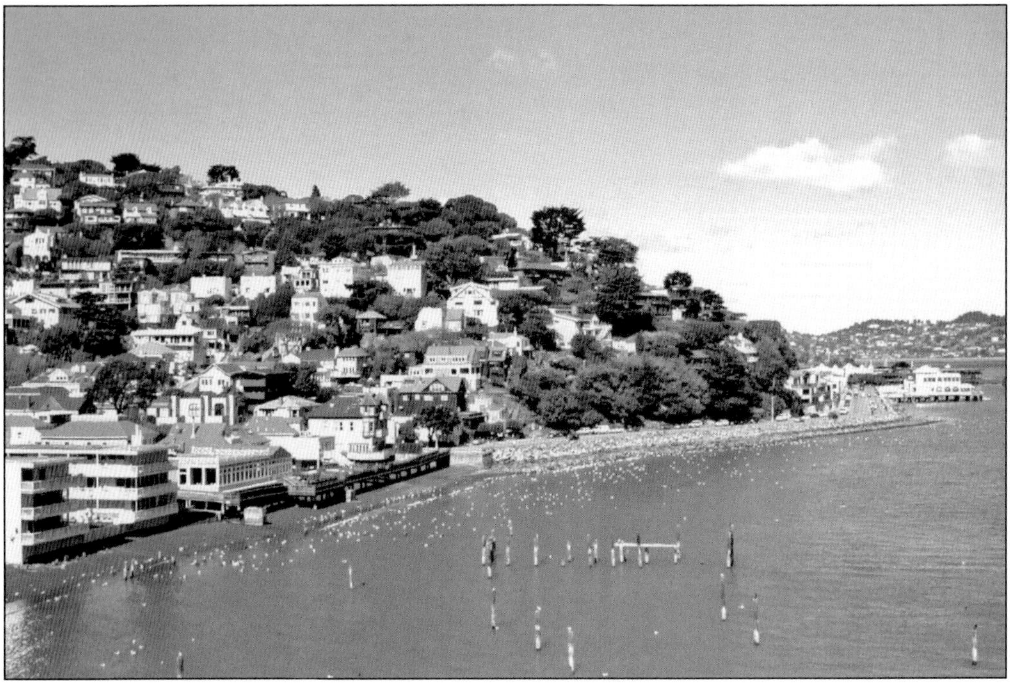

Marin is often compared to the French or Italian Riviera, with homes tumbling down picturesque hills to harbors filled with colorful yachts. That is an apt description of Sausalito today and has been since the first settlers came in the 1840s. San Francisco is just across the bay, and Sausalito has a better climate, so Sausalito has been a haven for those who do not mind a short commute.

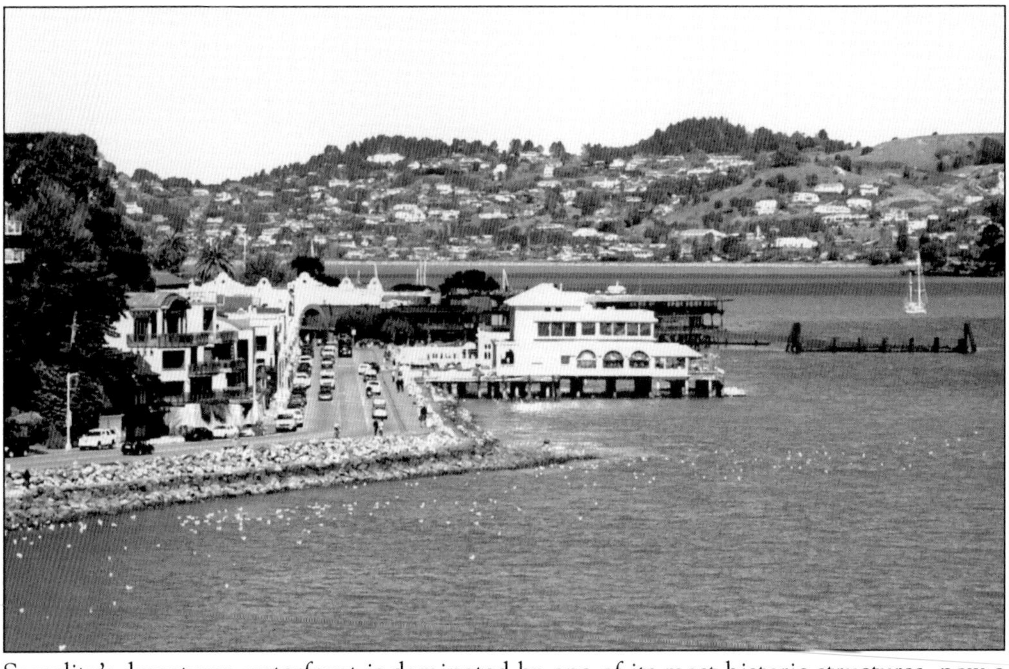

Sausalito's downtown waterfront is dominated by one of its most historic structures, now a restaurant. It was the home of the San Francisco Yacht Club until 1934, when the club moved to its present location on Belvedere Cove.

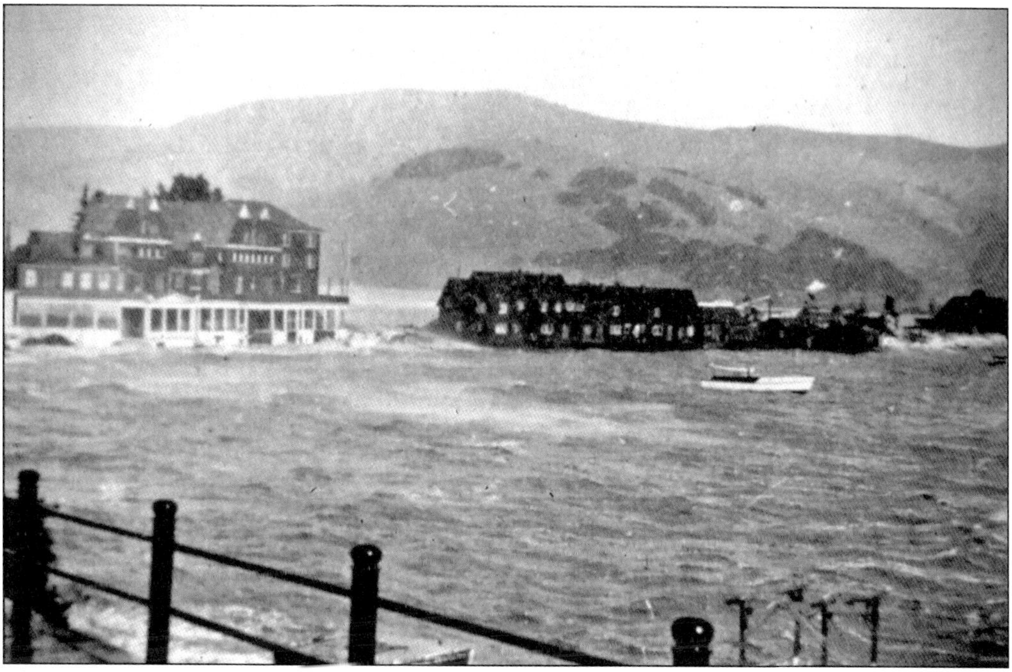

The Hotel Belvedere, pictured here during a violent storm, closed for financial reasons and was torn down. The site was acquired by the San Francisco Yacht Club, and in 1934, the club moved from Sausalito. (Courtesy the Landmarks Society.)

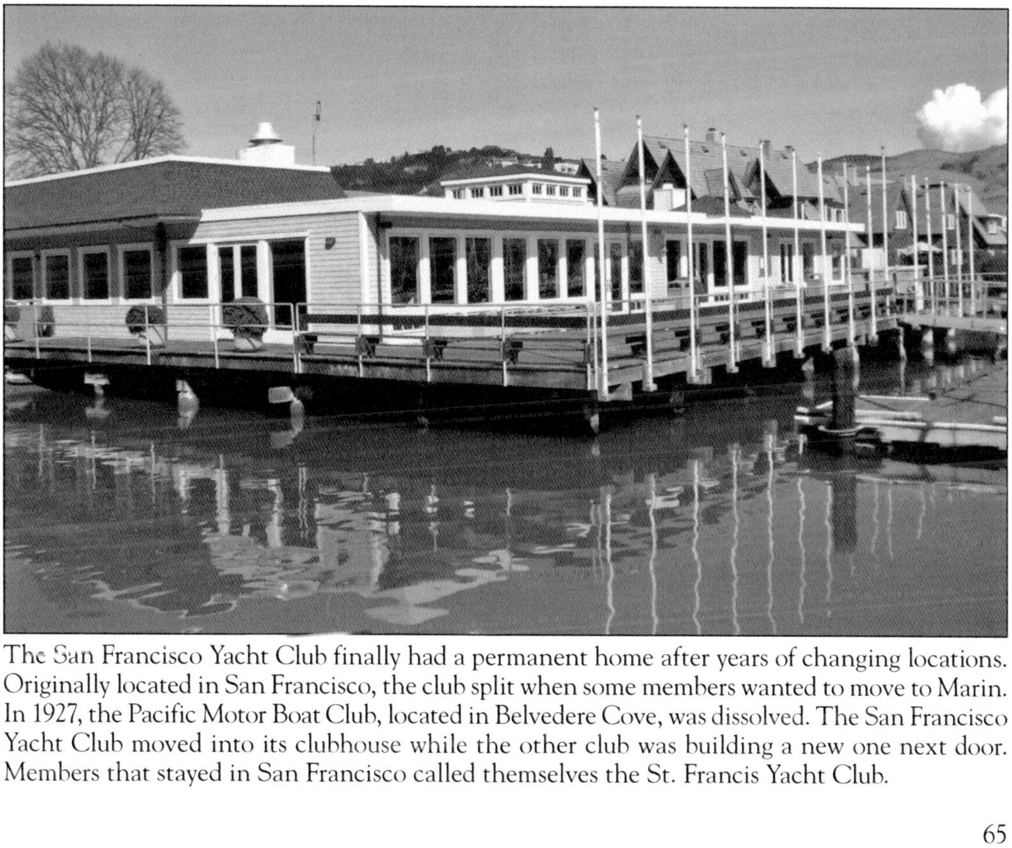

The San Francisco Yacht Club finally had a permanent home after years of changing locations. Originally located in San Francisco, the club split when some members wanted to move to Marin. In 1927, the Pacific Motor Boat Club, located in Belvedere Cove, was dissolved. The San Francisco Yacht Club moved into its clubhouse while the other club was building a new one next door. Members that stayed in San Francisco called themselves the St. Francis Yacht Club.

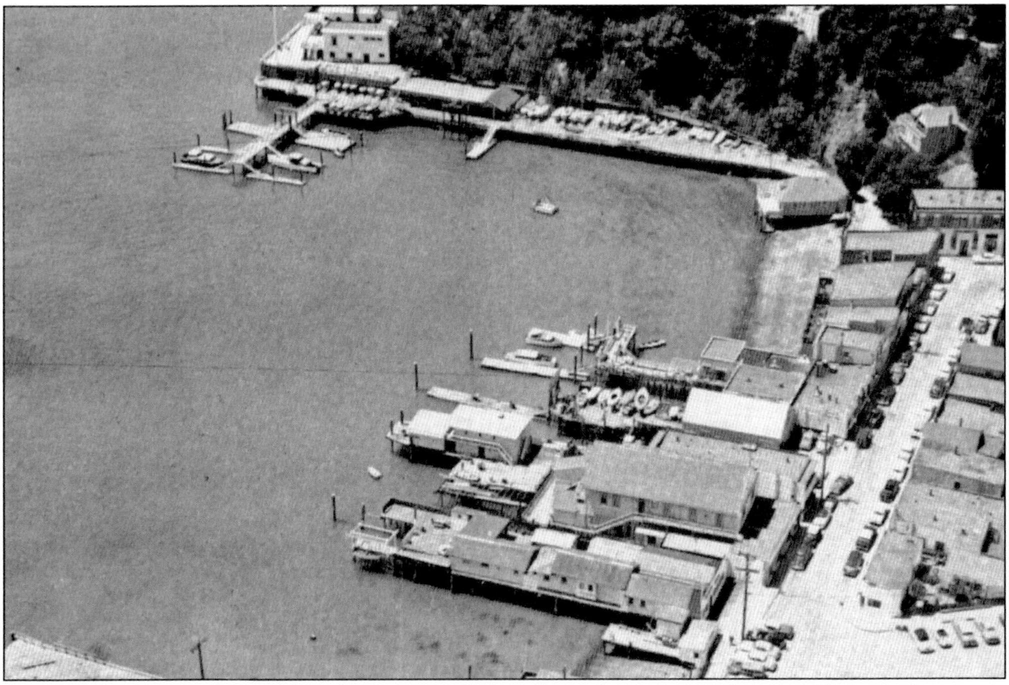

Tiburon's Main Street was a popular hangout for ranchers, dairymen, railroad workers, and cannery packers from the 1880s until the 1980s. By that time, all those industries had gone away, leaving Main Street for tourists and the new suburbanites. (Courtesy the Morrison Family Collection.)

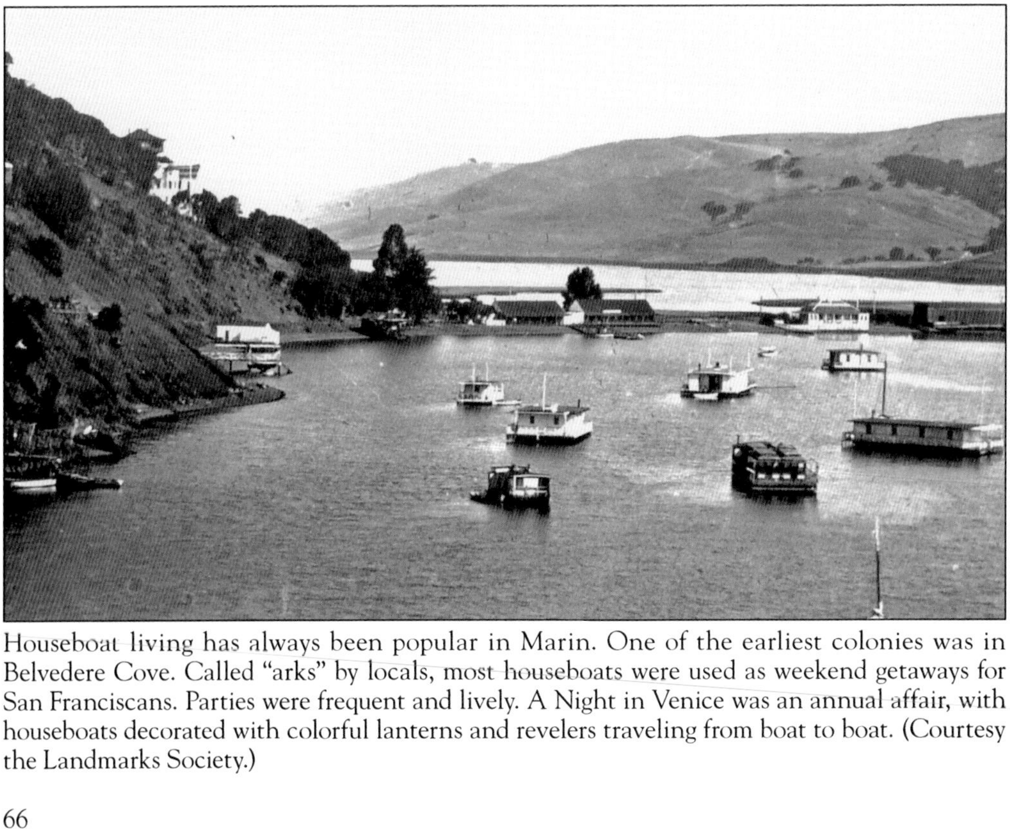

Houseboat living has always been popular in Marin. One of the earliest colonies was in Belvedere Cove. Called "arks" by locals, most houseboats were used as weekend getaways for San Franciscans. Parties were frequent and lively. A Night in Venice was an annual affair, with houseboats decorated with colorful lanterns and revelers traveling from boat to boat. (Courtesy the Landmarks Society.)

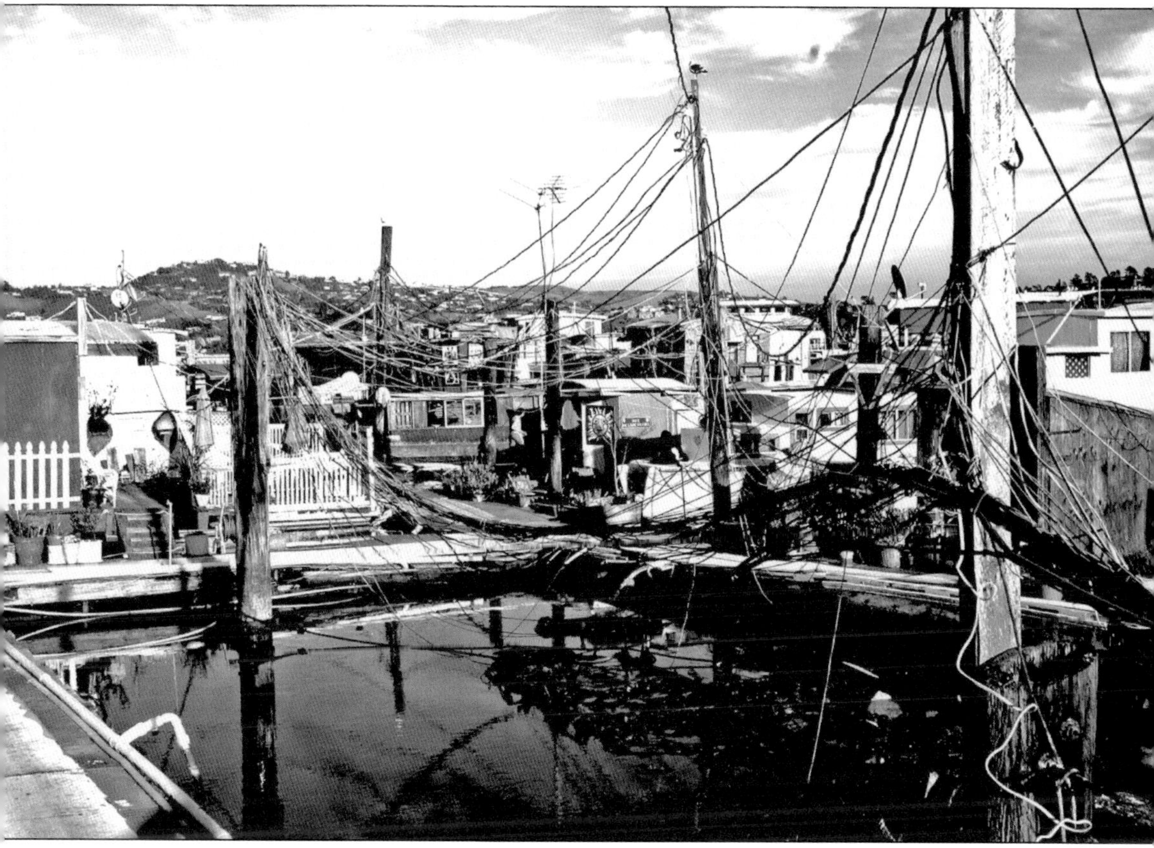

Sausalito became a haven for houseboats during the politically active 1960s and 1970s. Defying all rules and attempts to regulate them, houseboat colonies grew to unmanageable proportions. Lacking any connections to sanitary facilities or other public services, it was an inexpensive place to live. Timothy Leary, Alan Watts, and other exponents of LSD and marijuana were the community leaders.

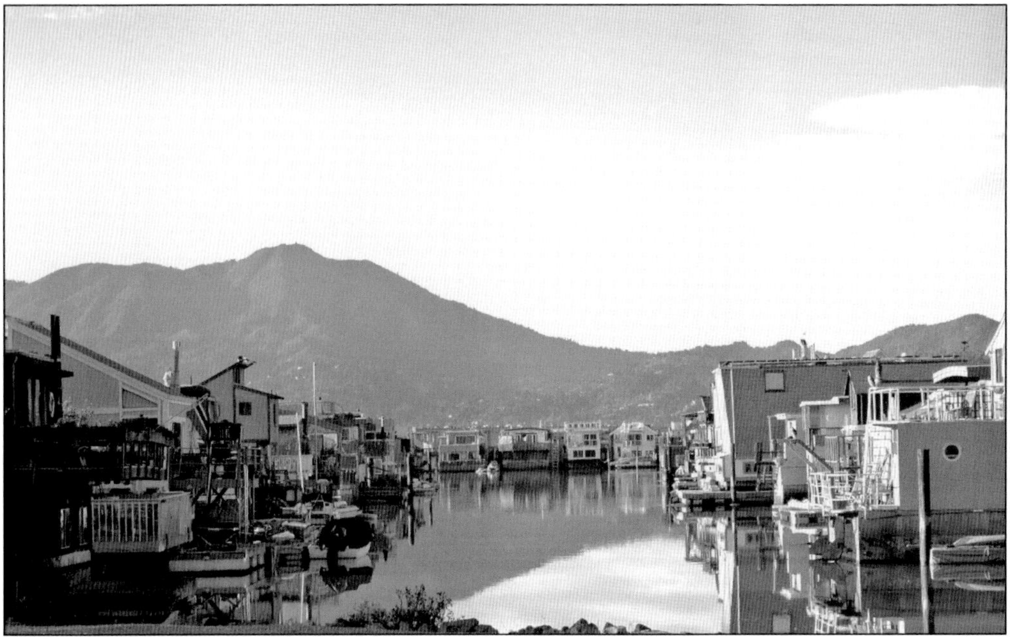

Sausalito authorities finally got control of the situation, and while some old houseboat colonies still look like floating junkyards, most now consist of expensive floating homes hooked up to public utilities.

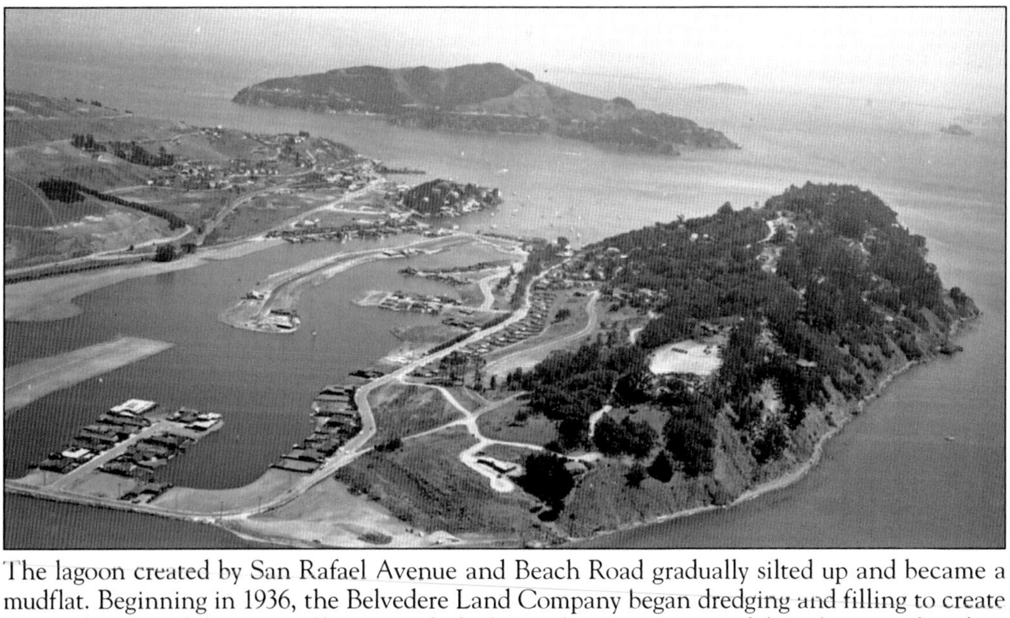

The lagoon created by San Rafael Avenue and Beach Road gradually silted up and became a mudflat. Beginning in 1936, the Belvedere Land Company began dredging and filling to create one of the first subdivisions of homes with docks on the water. Many of the arks were placed on pilings and became Tiburon's picturesque Ark Row of shops and restaurants, or were moved to Bolinas as private homes.

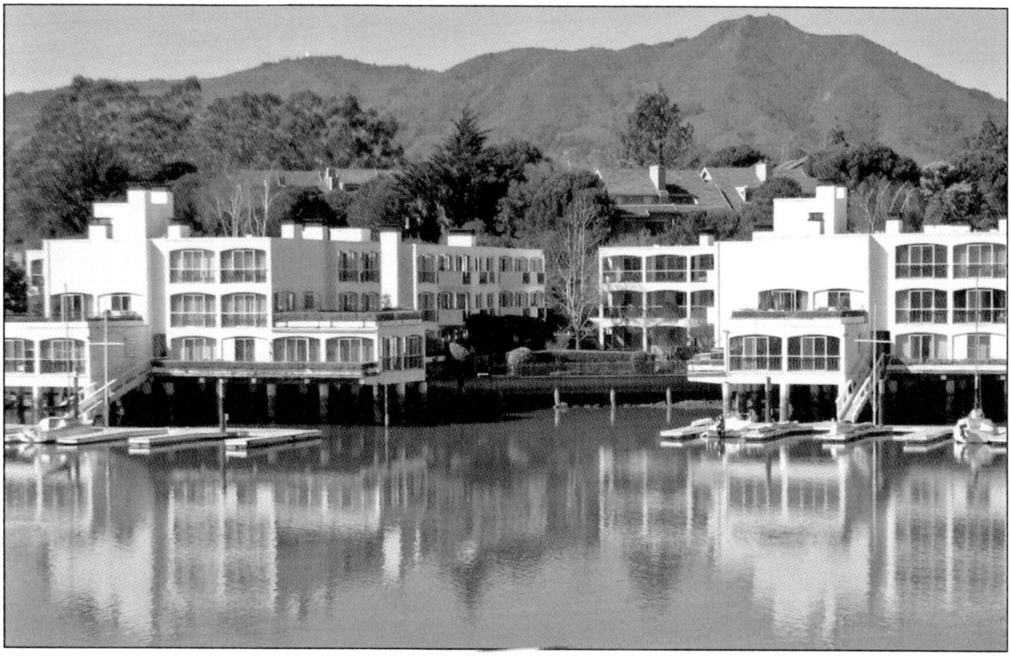

Shelter Bay, on Mill Valley's short window on Richardson Bay, is designed like one big yacht club. A Highway 101 bridge over Richardson Bay kept large yachts out, so it was a haven for the small boater who could have his boat at his door. The bay has gradually silted up, so most docks remain empty.

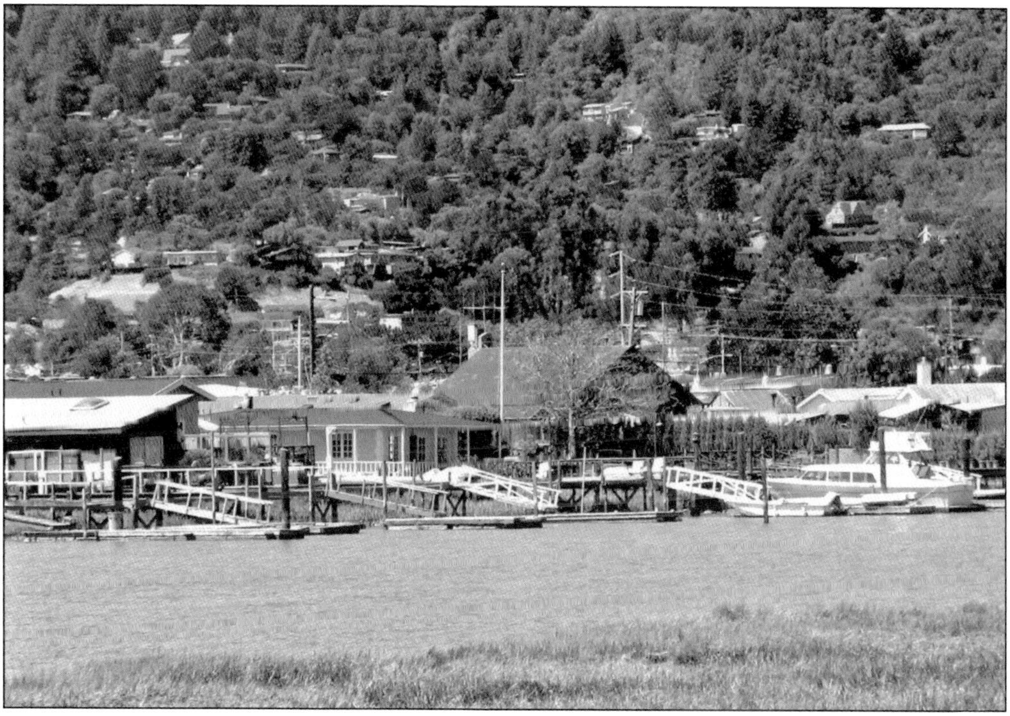

Elsewhere in Marin, waterfront lots with private boat docks still command a premium. These Larkspur homes are on Corte Madera Creek, which gives them an outlet to the bay.

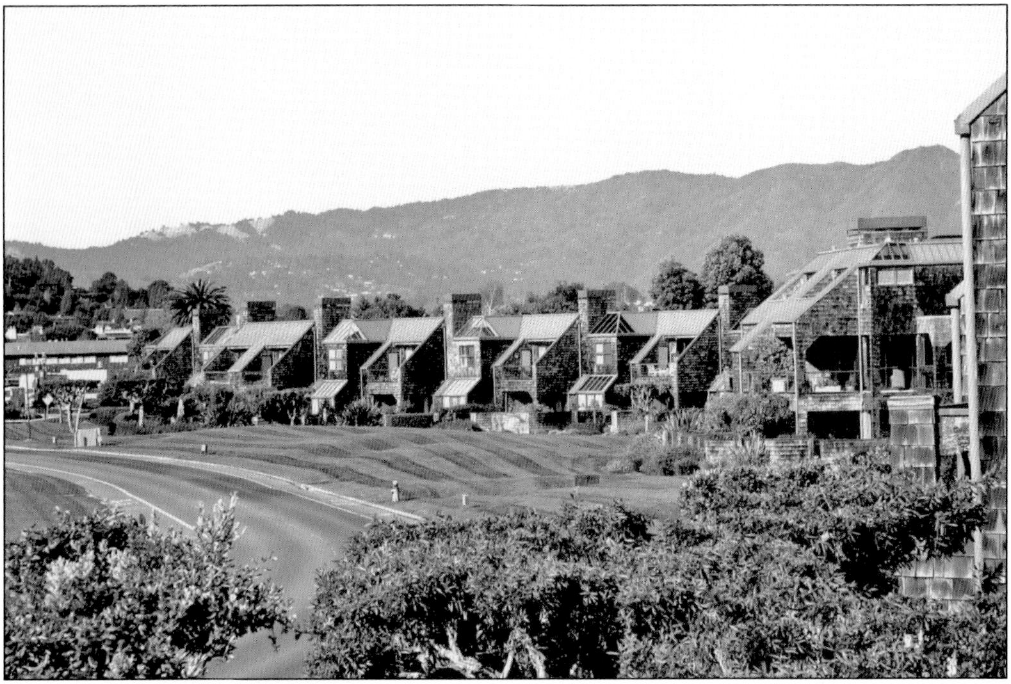

Even without private docks, having a view of the bay, bridges, or San Francisco brings a premium. These multimillion-dollar condominiums were built in the former railroad yards at Point Tiburon.

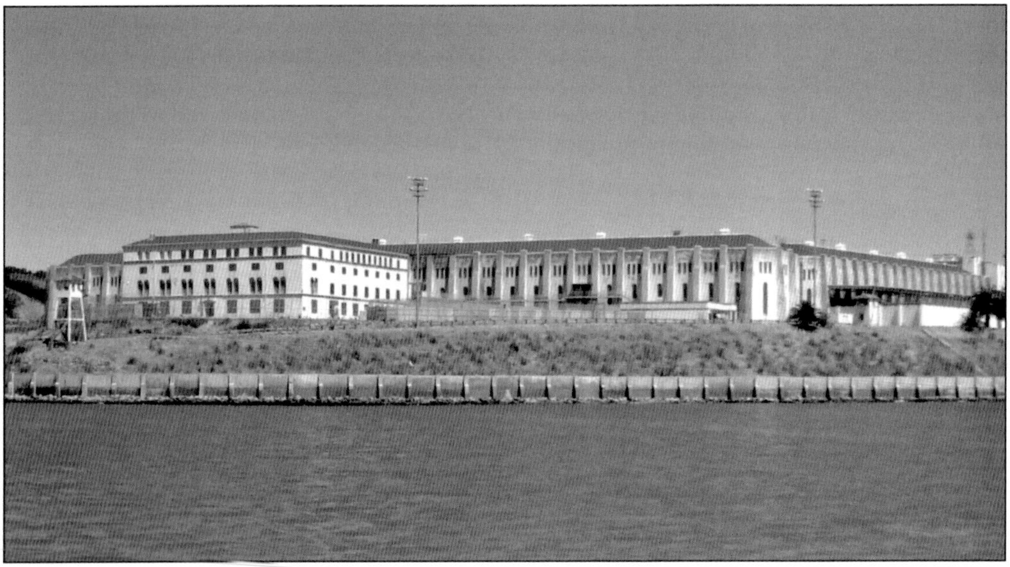

One of the most prominent buildings on Marin's shore is San Quentin Prison. A huge installation and California's first prison, it houses several thousand more than its design capacity plus 600 men on death row. Proposals for reuse of this desirable site are constantly being offered but are just as routinely lost in the system.

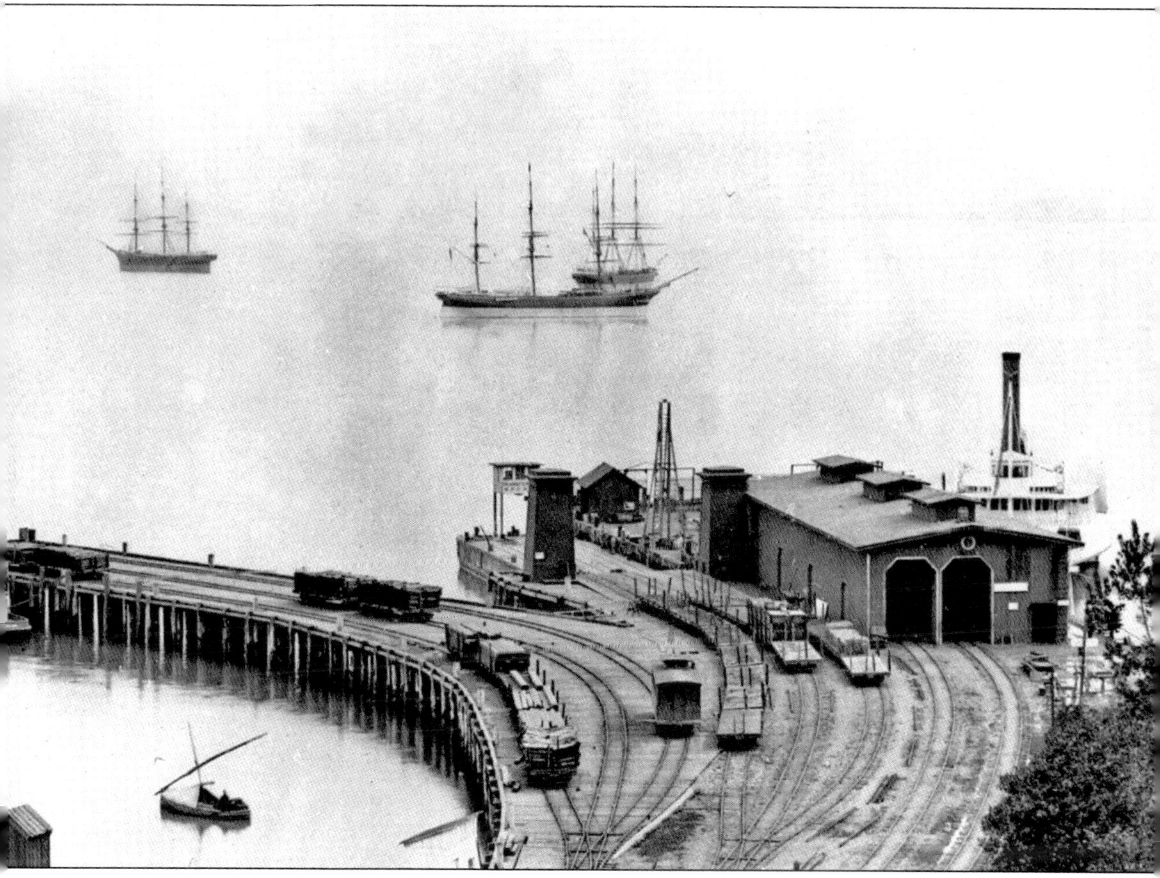

In 1871, the narrow-gauge North Pacific Coast Railroad (NPC) was incorporated. It had its terminal in Sausalito and ran north along the Pacific Coast to the Russian River. It had a big advantage over its rivals by being closest to San Francisco. In 1907, five lines were merged into the Northwestern Pacific Railroad, including the NPC. Freight traffic was moved to Tiburon, and passengers were concentrated in Sausalito. (Courtesy San Francisco Maritime National Historical Park.)

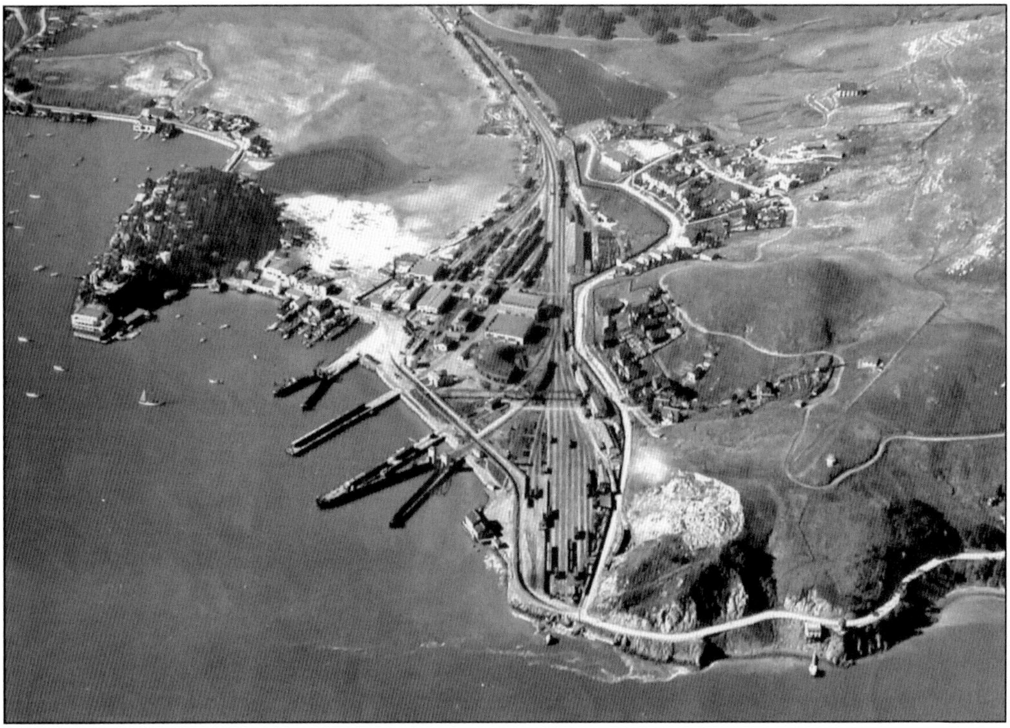

Named Punta Del Tiburon, or Shark Point, by the first explorers of San Francisco Bay, the town of Tiburon was part of the huge Rancho Corte Madera Del Presidio, which covered 8,000 acres of southern Marin. Because of its proximity by water to San Francisco, it became the junction between the railroad and the ferry system. Its industrial shops could build locomotives and ferries. When the railroad era ended, it became a popular tourist destination and an exclusive residential area.

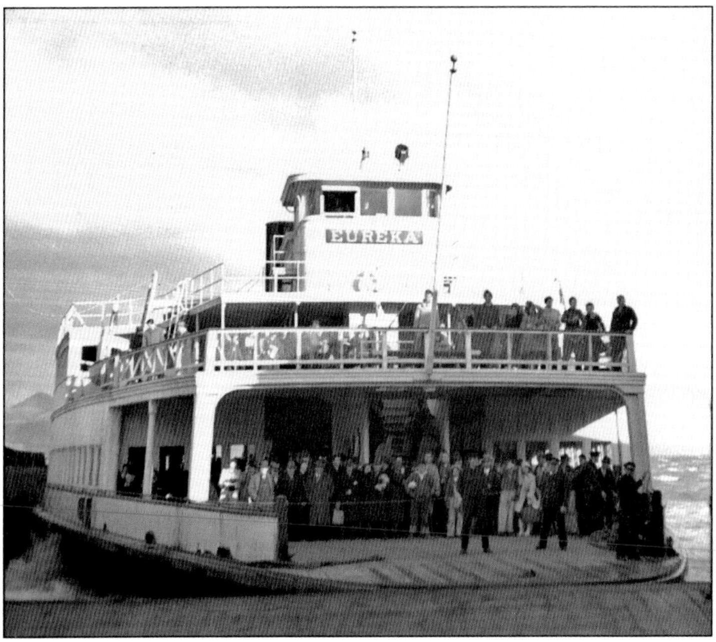

One of the ferries built in the Tiburon yards was the *Ukiah*, launched in 1890. It could carry 16 railroad cars and 3,000 passengers on the Tiburon–San Francisco run. Rebuilt in 1920, it then became the *Eureka*, carrying 100 automobiles instead of railcars. This picture was taken on its last run to Sausalito on February 28, 1941. The Golden Gate Bridge made the ferries obsolete. The *Eureka* is still afloat at the historic ship collection in San Francisco.

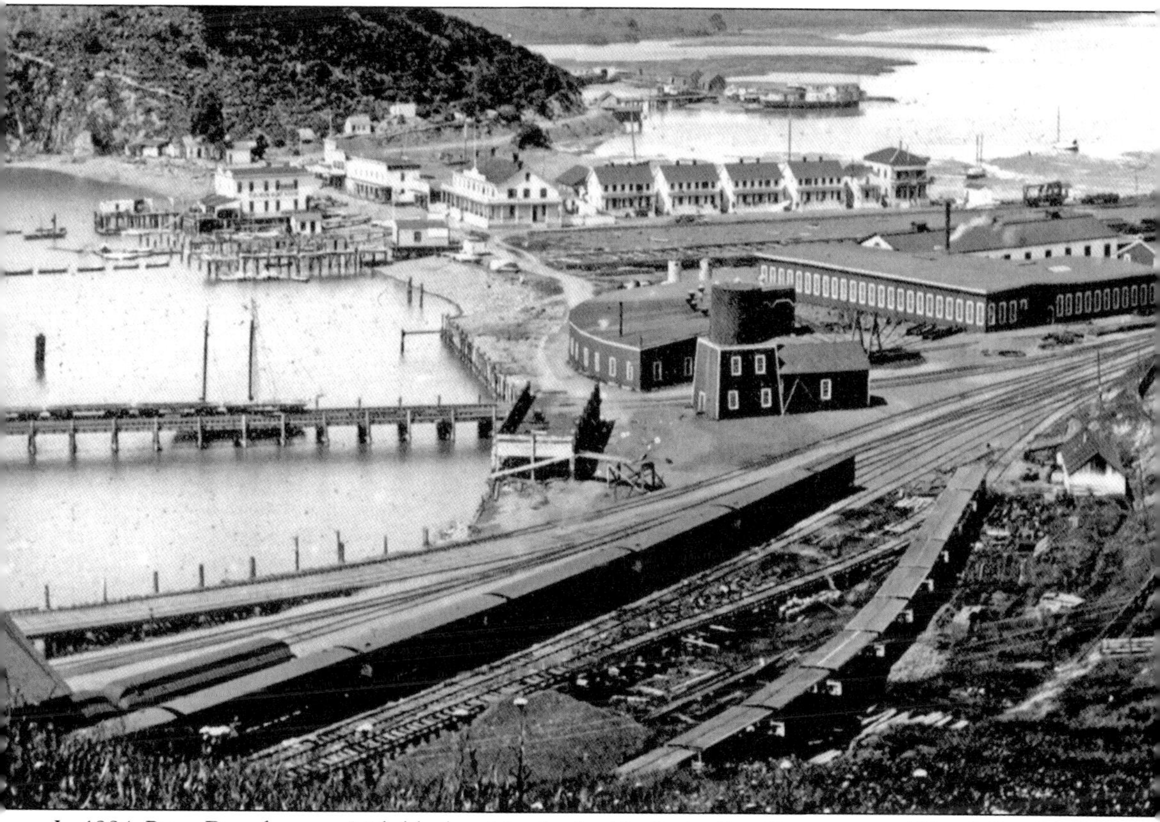

In 1884, Peter Donahue, an Irish blacksmith who had built the San Francisco and North Pacific Railway (SF&NP), brought the line all the way to Tiburon, where it was in a position to compete with the North Pacific Coast Railroad in Sausalito. The ferry piers later added adjustable ramps to allow loaded cars to be pushed onto barges, avoiding the double handling of cargo. The SF&NP railroad was standard gauge and originally ended on the Petaluma Creek, where cargo was transferred to Donahue's fleet of riverboats. Many of the buildings in this scene, including the residence buildings on Tiburon Boulevard and the 40-room hotel, were barged down from Petaluma. Several large fires destroyed all but a few of the original buildings. Replacements have become popular restaurants and shops.

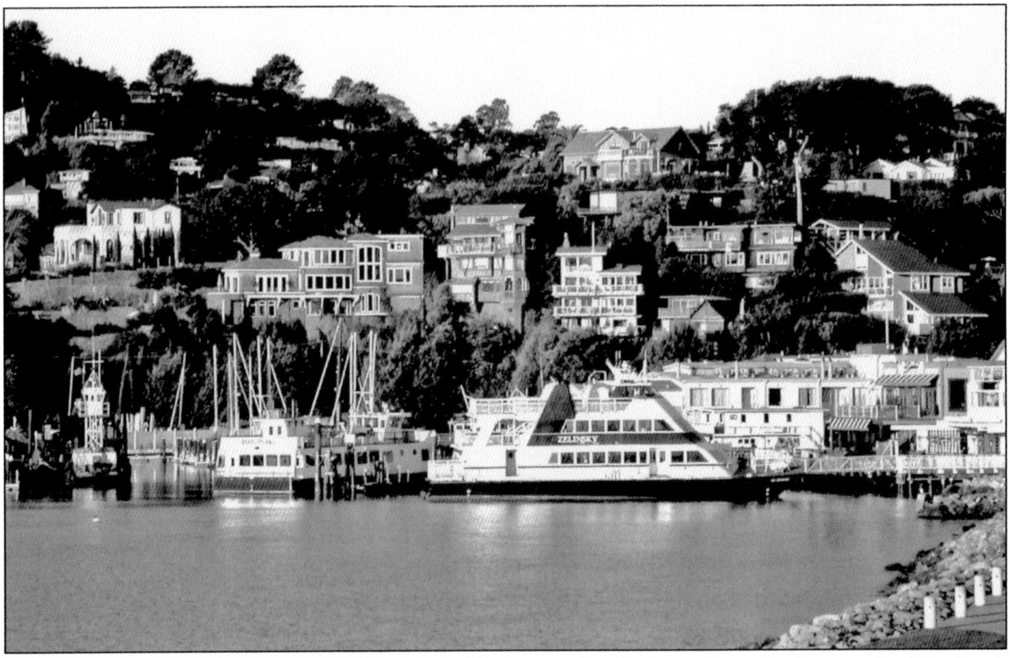

In spite of occasional tinkering with the traffic lanes, the Golden Gate Bridge reached its limit in only 20 years. As traffic backed up for miles, commuters from southern Marin chartered bay sightseeing vessels for an impromptu ferry service. The San Francisco commuters and the Angel Island ferry make the Tiburon waterfront a busy place.

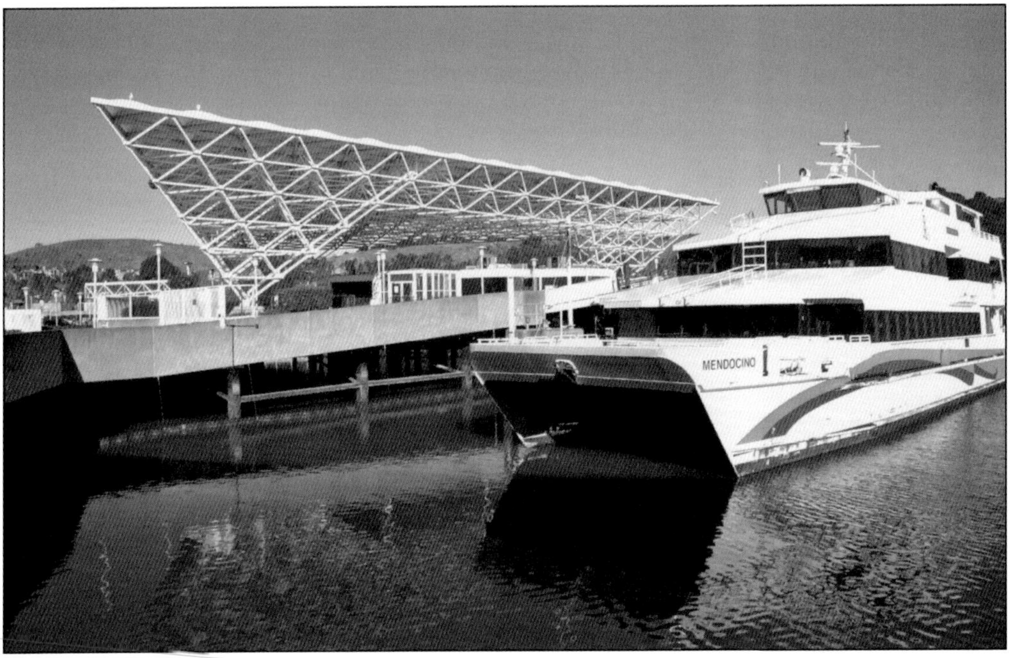

Operations from Sausalito and Larkspur using modern high-speed passenger ferries were instituted by the Golden Gate Bridge District to ease the traffic on the bridge. Large and fast, they provide a way for Marin commuters to get to the city. Playing bridge, reading a newspaper or report, or working on a laptop is far more enjoyable or productive than sitting in traffic.

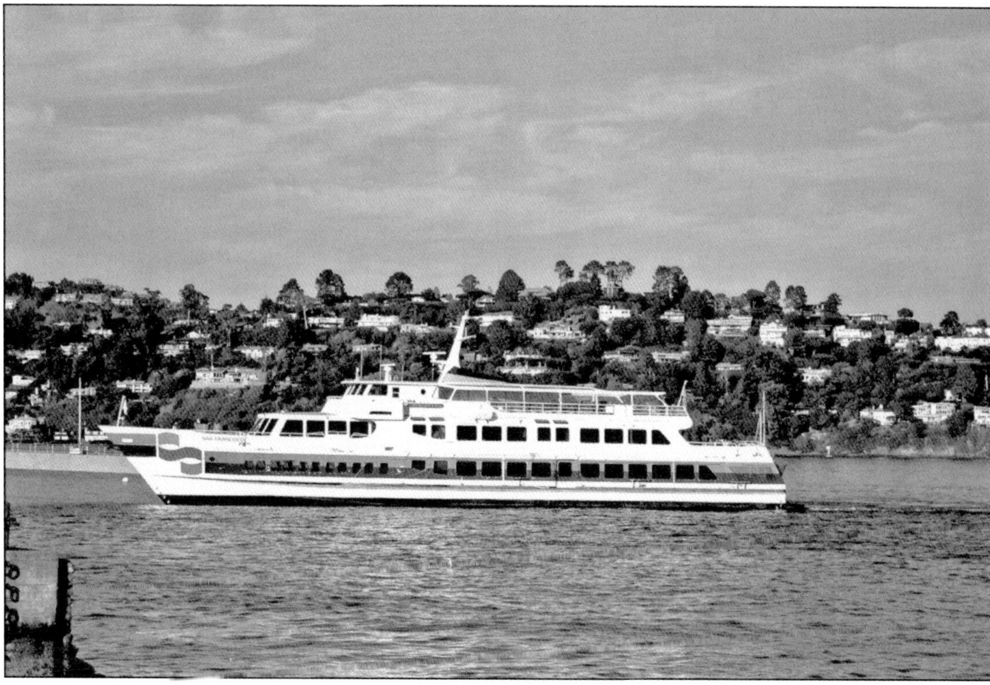

Looking like a fleet of miniature cruise liners, the ferry fleet crisscrosses between Marin and San Francisco all day long. In the evenings, another fleet of slightly larger cruise boats appears so diners can enjoy the sunsets.

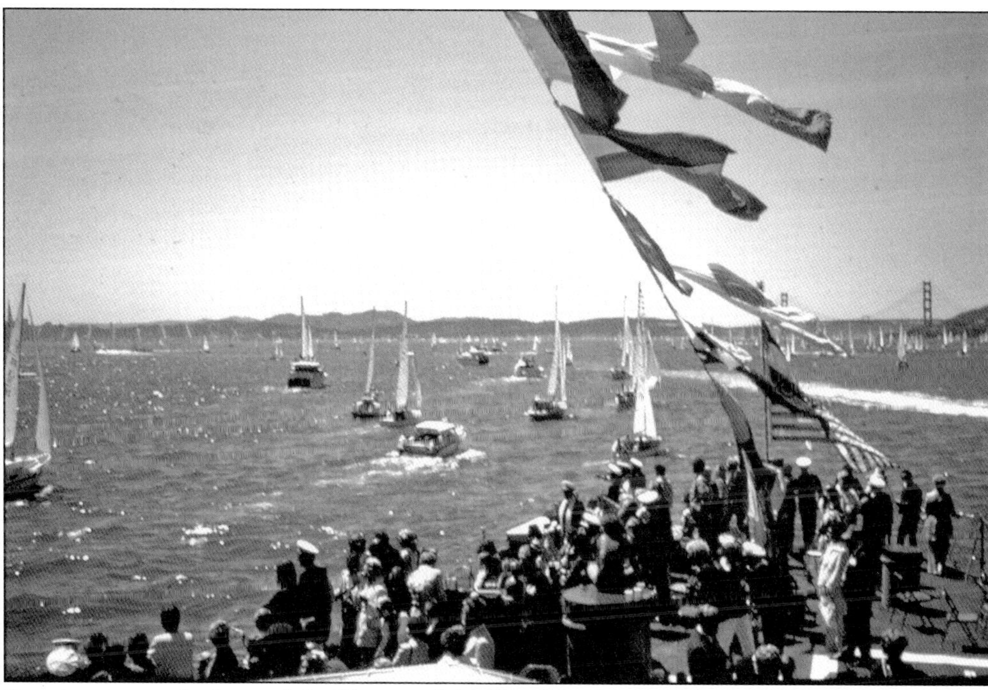

Opening day on the bay and the Blessing of the Fleet have been combined into one big celebration coordinated by the Corinthian Yacht Club. The pleasure boats line up and pass by a navy or coast guard vessel moored in Raccoon Strait.

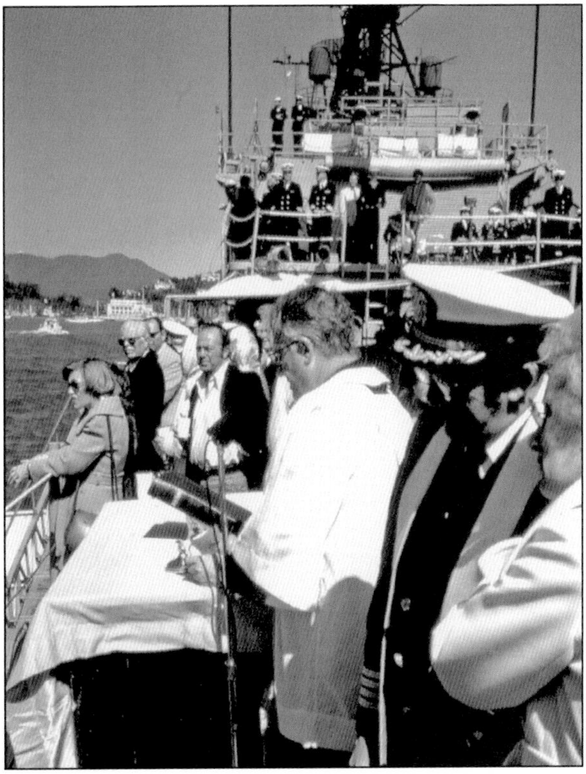

The tradition of the Blessing of the Fleet began with the fishing fleet out of San Francisco. In 1963, it was decided that the pleasure fleet should obtain divine protection as well, and the ceremony was held on the afterdeck of a navy destroyer in Raccoon Strait. Two thousand yachts pass by while a rabbi, priest, and minister bless the boats and their crews. With the U.S. Navy no longer operating in the world's finest harbor, the service has been transferred to a coast guard vessel, when available.

When the protective tree cover was destroyed, the creeks that had provided access to much of inland Marin were filled with the eroded top soil. Pictured here in 2008, Ross Landing, once the busiest port in California, was no longer able to provide service to ships of any size.

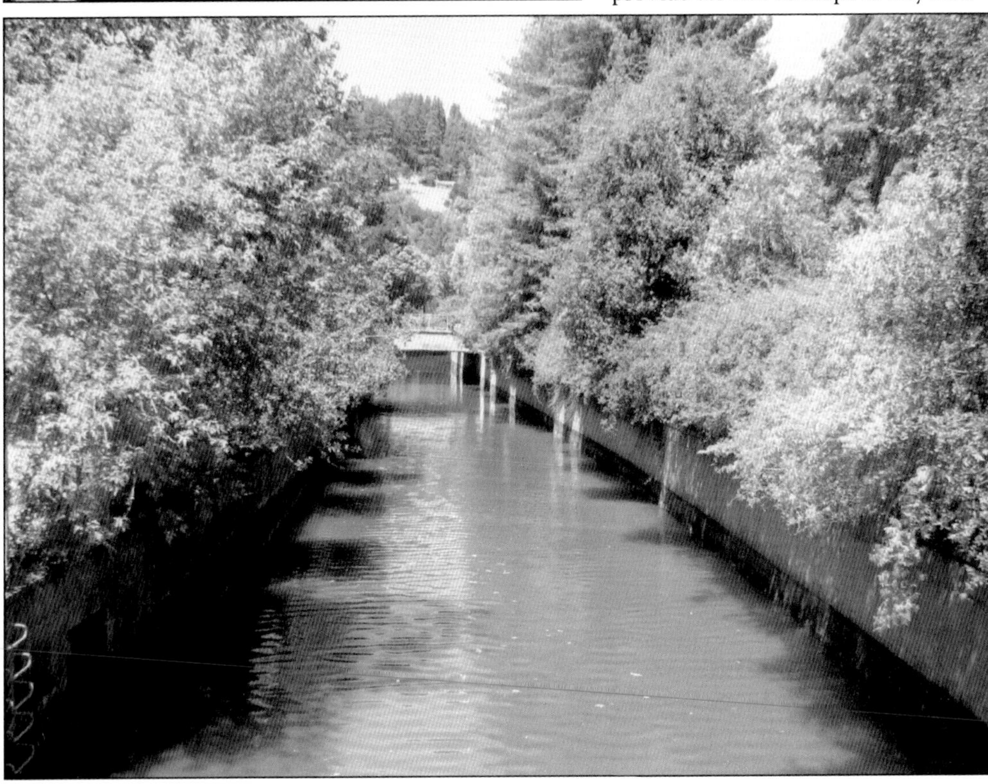

Five

Ships and Boatbuilding

Some could say that maritime construction in Marin actually began when the Miwok Indians, who bundled reeds together to serve as flotation devices. These crude vessels remained afloat long enough for short voyages around the bays and waterways. The early settlers brought boatbuilding skills with them and thus began Marin's long association with the construction of everything from workboats to pleasure yachts and even oceangoing merchant ships.

It is estimated that there were 3,500 square riggers still roaming the seas by 1905. Suddenly, iron ships and screw propellers made them obsolete. Many of the grand old clipper ships and trans-Pacific side-wheelers ended their days in ship breaking yards in Marin. Retired sailing ships that had escaped a watery grave on Marin's coast met their fate at the salvage yards in Marin. But Marin was noted for more than being a ship crematorium. As the main port on the West Coast, waterborne commerce was the lifeblood of the San Francisco Bay area. Large ships were built on the East Coast and delivered via Cape Horn, an arduous journey of many weeks. The hundreds of smaller ships serving the coastal communities and the agricultural industry were built here. Ferries, riverboats, and lumber schooners were built in Marin shipyards. Serious shipbuilding was a wartime interlude that ended in 1945 when the last of 93 Liberty ships and tankers slid down the ways in Sausalito. With the end of the war, Marin boatyards returned to building and repairing the thousands of pleasure craft dotting the bay on any reasonably good day with a fair wind.

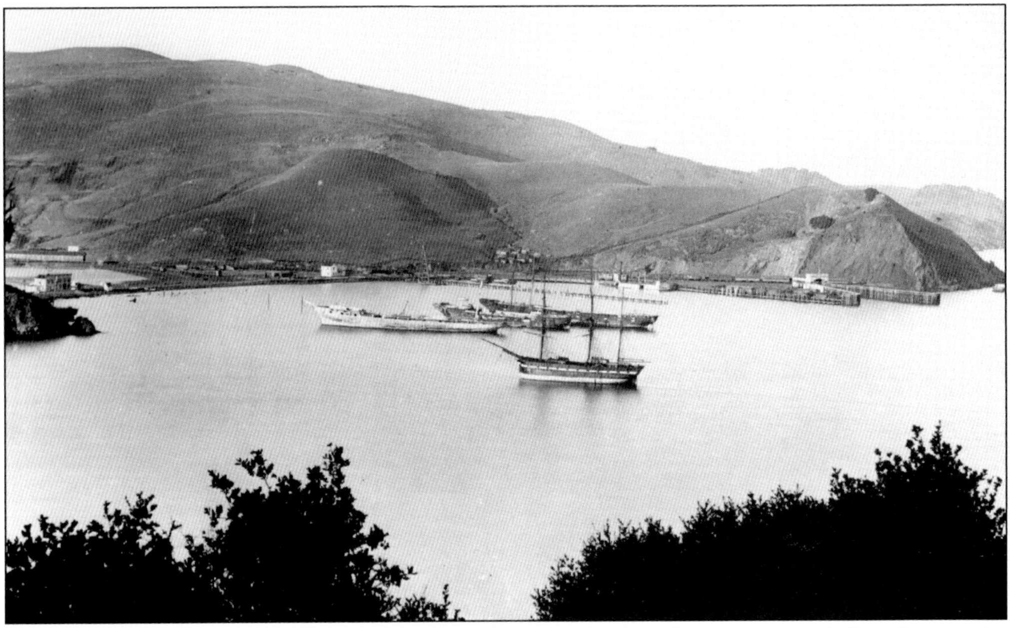

Retired sailing ships that had escaped a watery grave on Marin's coast awaited their fate at the ship breaking and salvage yard in Tiburon Cove. Belvedere and Paradise Coves were also used to dispose of ships that had lost out to the new technology of steam and iron. After everything that could be reused was removed, ships would be burned to the waterline. Metal was then salvaged, and the remaining hulk would be sunk at sea. (Courtesy the Landmarks Society.)

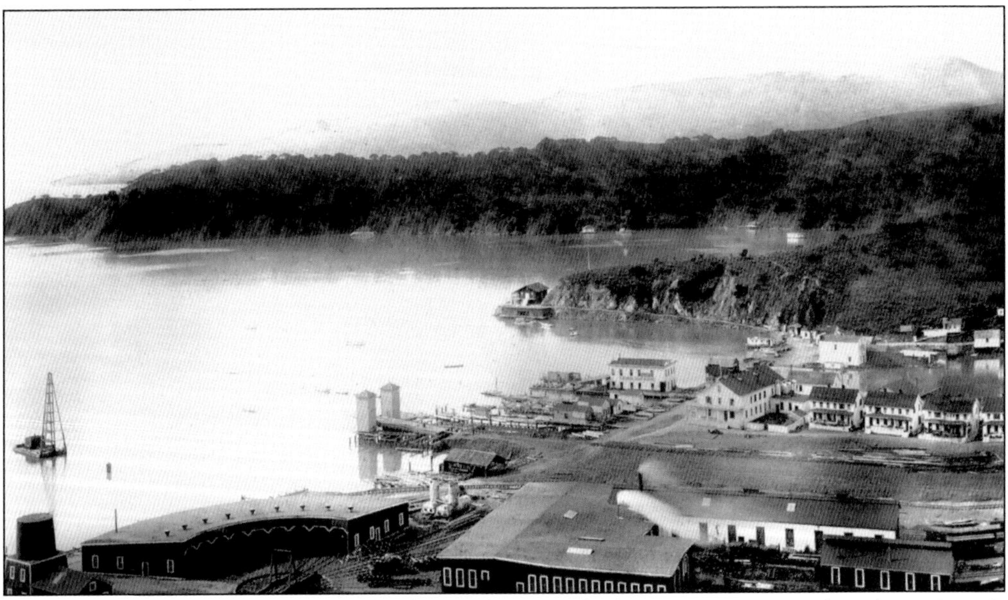

The *Ukiah*, one of the largest ships built anywhere on the bay, was constructed in the rail yards of Tiburon in 1891. The San Francisco and North Pacific Coast Railroad (SFNPC) had moved its southern terminal from Donahue Landing on the Petaluma Creek to the end of the Tiburon peninsula. The SFNPC had shops that could build locomotives and railcars, and could begin building their own ferries. The first Corinthian Yacht Club can be seen on the point overlooking downtown. (Courtesy San Francisco Maritime National Historical Park.)

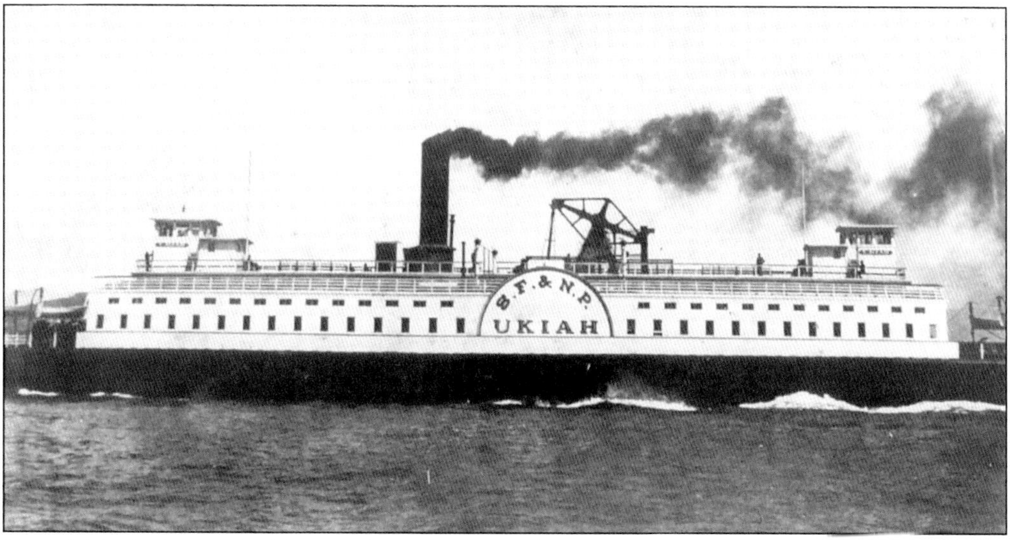

The *Ukiah*, the largest double-ended ferry in the world at 271 feet long, could carry 2,300 passengers and 16 railroad cars. After World War I, it was rebuilt to carry 3,000 passengers and 100 automobiles, was renamed the *Eureka*, and was moved to Sausalito. It made its last San Francisco–to–Sausalito run on February 28, 1941. After several more decades on the Oakland run, it joined the historic ship collection of the National Park Service on the San Francisco waterfront.

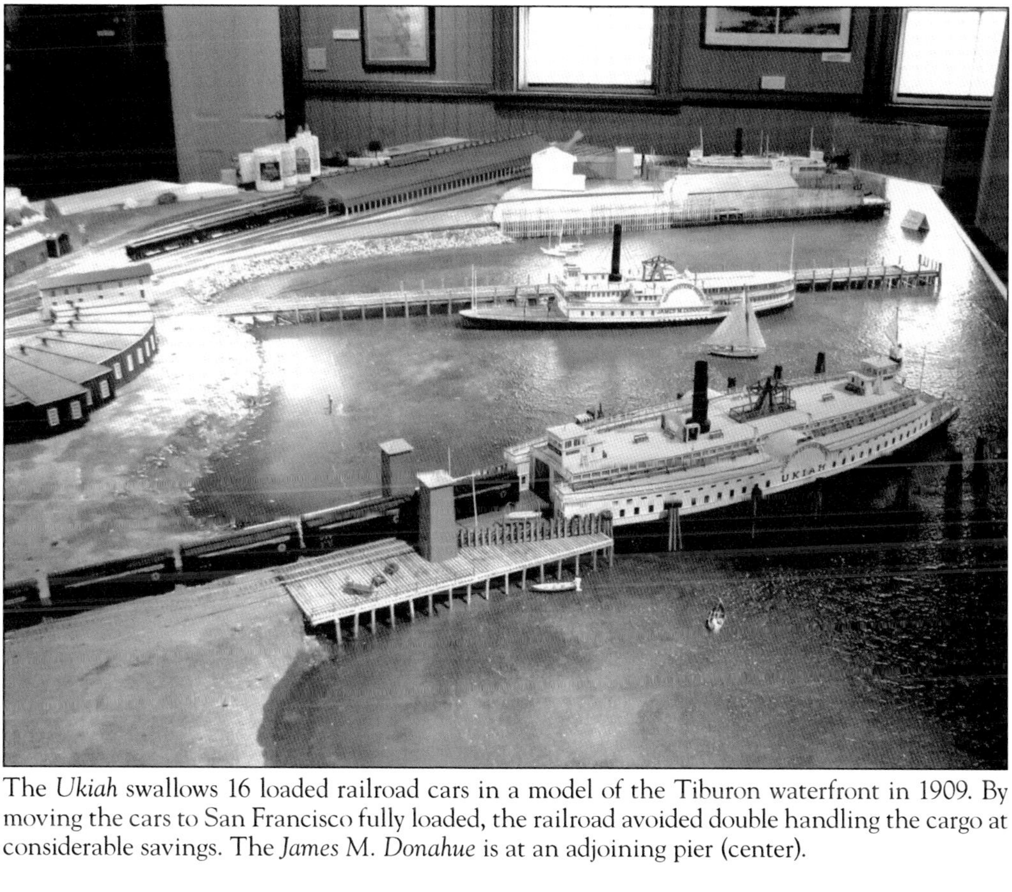

The *Ukiah* swallows 16 loaded railroad cars in a model of the Tiburon waterfront in 1909. By moving the cars to San Francisco fully loaded, the railroad avoided double handling the cargo at considerable savings. The *James M. Donahue* is at an adjoining pier (center).

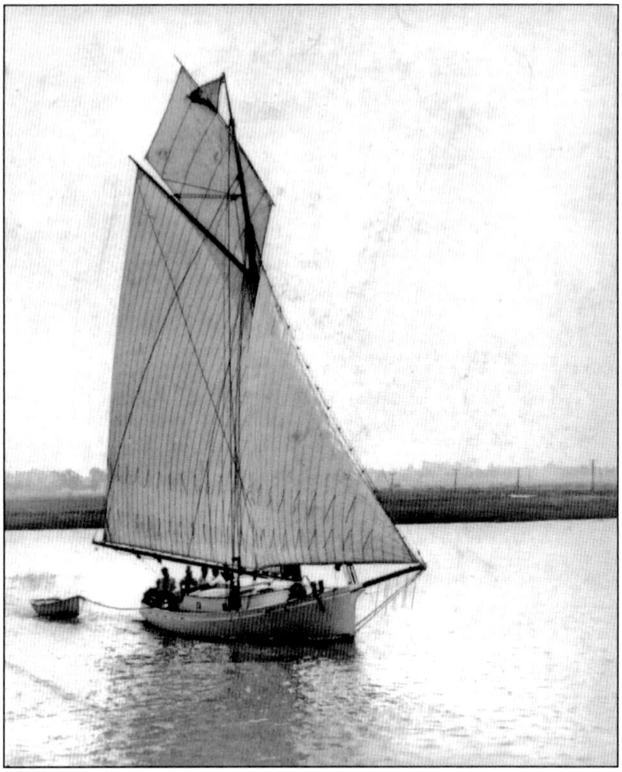

In 1885, people were still breaking up old sailing ships in Belvedere and Tiburon Coves when the *Freda*, the oldest yacht on San Francisco Bay, was built on the sand spit that became Beach Road in Belvedere by Harry F. Cookson, a Tiburon saloon keeper. It is not known whether Cookson had any shipbuilding plans to follow or if he just used his own talent as a woodworker. The style is that of an American sloop, popular in those days. (Courtesy Spaulding Wooden Boat Center.)

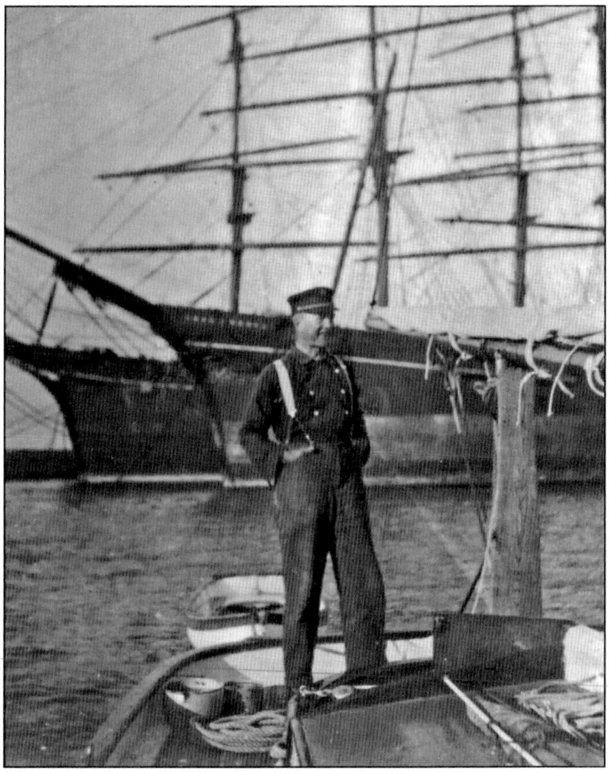

The owner of the *Freda* from 1895 to 1916 was Theodore Tracy. Like many sailors of the times, he had grown up in the clipper-ship era. (Courtesy Spaulding Wooden Boat Center.)

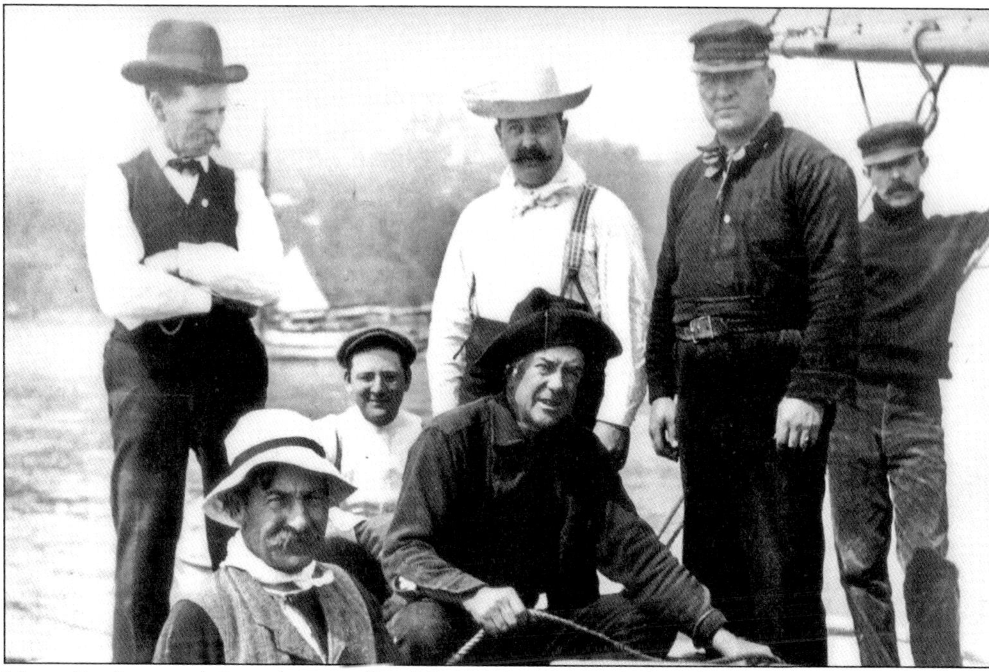

Harry Cookson, at left, and some of his fellow sailors get ready for a day's sail. The *Freda* measured 32 feet on the deck and 54 feet overall. With a gaff rig, she carried 1,250 square feet of sail. Cookson sold *Freda* to the Corinthian Yacht Club commodore, a fervent racer. (Courtesy Spaulding Wooden Boat Center.)

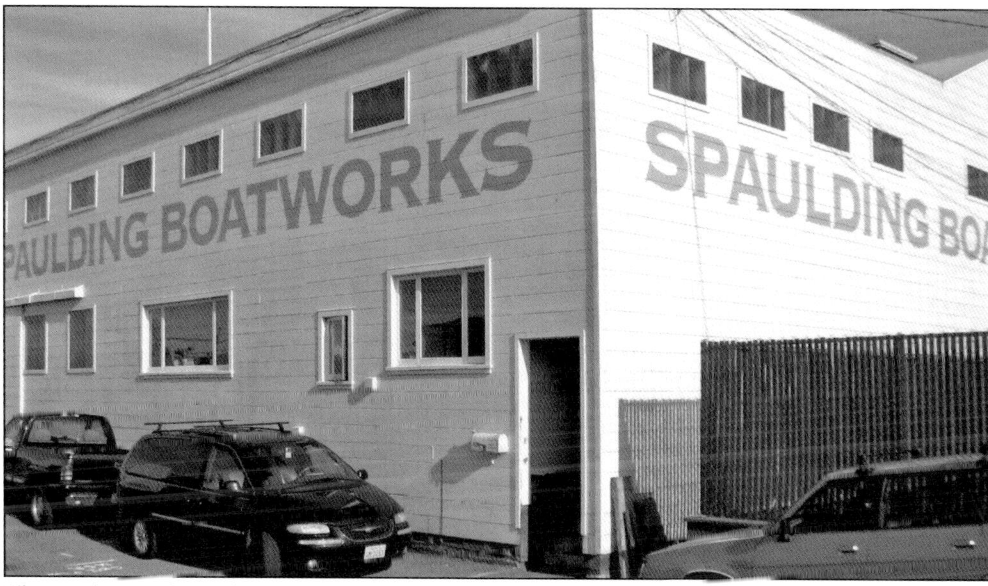

The tradition of wooden boats did not die with the scuttling of the clippers. At the Spaulding Boatworks in Sausalito, famed yacht designer Myron Spaulding designed and built some of the finest wooden racing yachts of his era. He died in 2000 at age 94. Spaulding was a champion sailboat racer and played first violin with the San Francisco Symphony. Spaulding left his business to a charitable trust, the Spaulding Wooden Boat Center, to restore historically significant wooden boats.

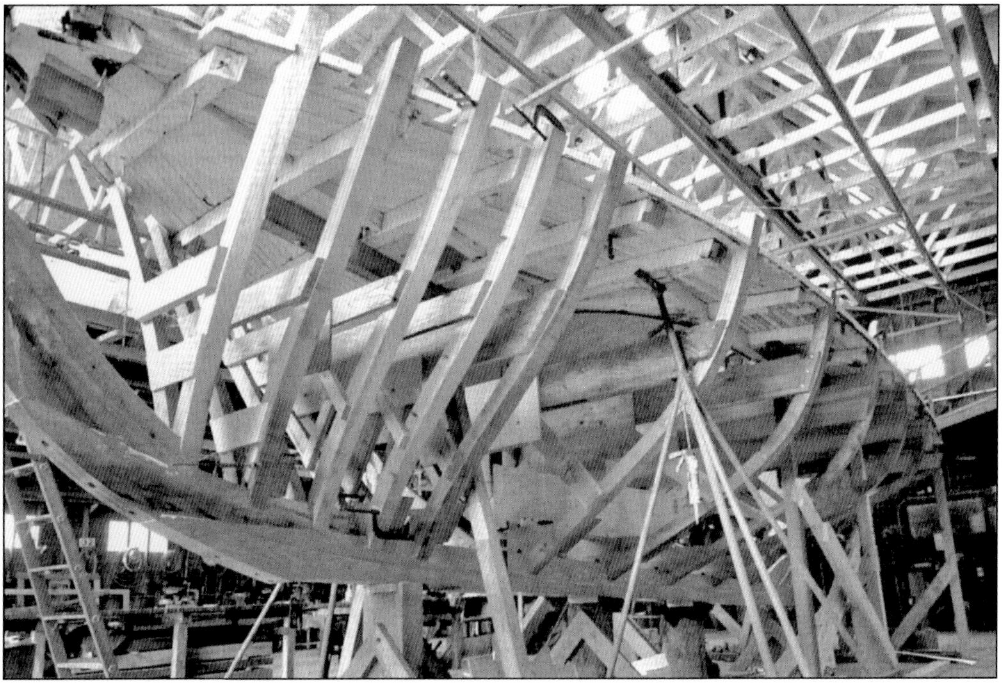

The fine art of restoring wooden boats is still practiced at the Spaulding Boatworks. In the reconstruction of the *Freda*, parts from the original are replaced or replicated to keep the final vessel true to the original. The *Freda* should be back in the water about 2009.

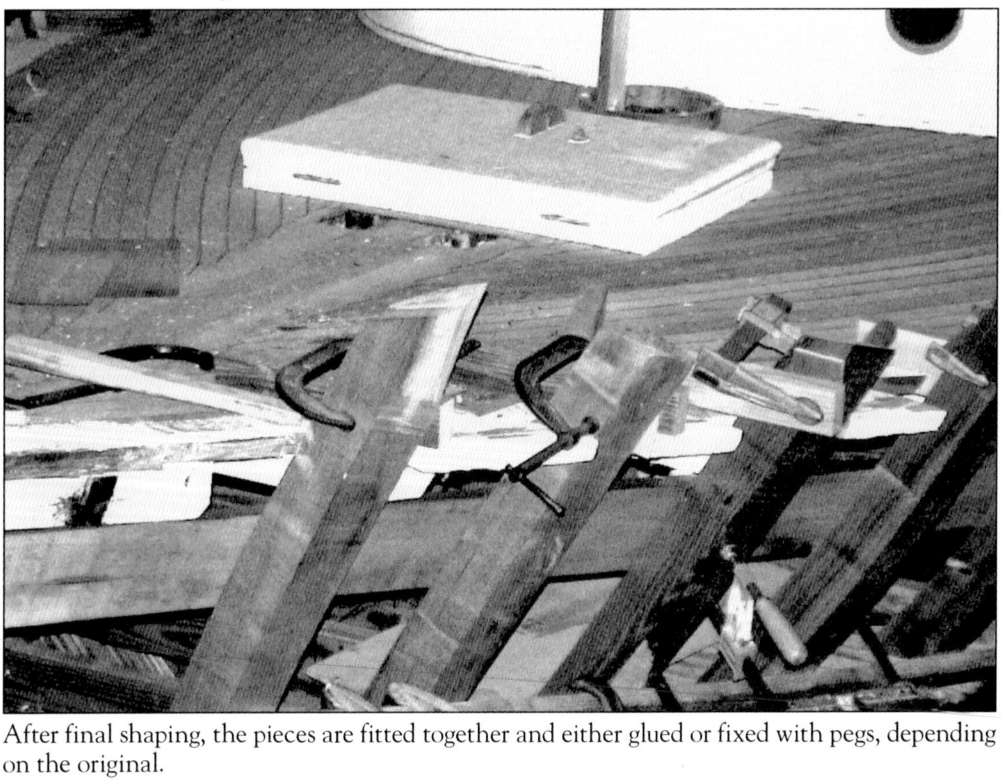

After final shaping, the pieces are fitted together and either glued or fixed with pegs, depending on the original.

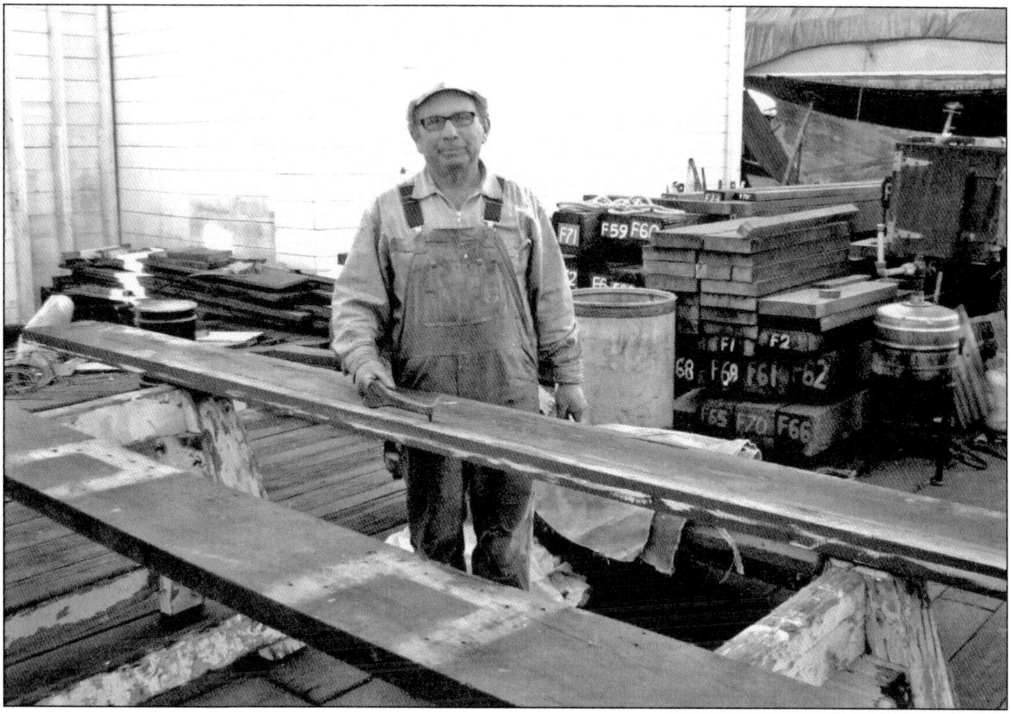

Mike Wiener, the manager at Spaulding Boatworks, is typical of the master craftsmen who carry on the tradition of wooden boats.

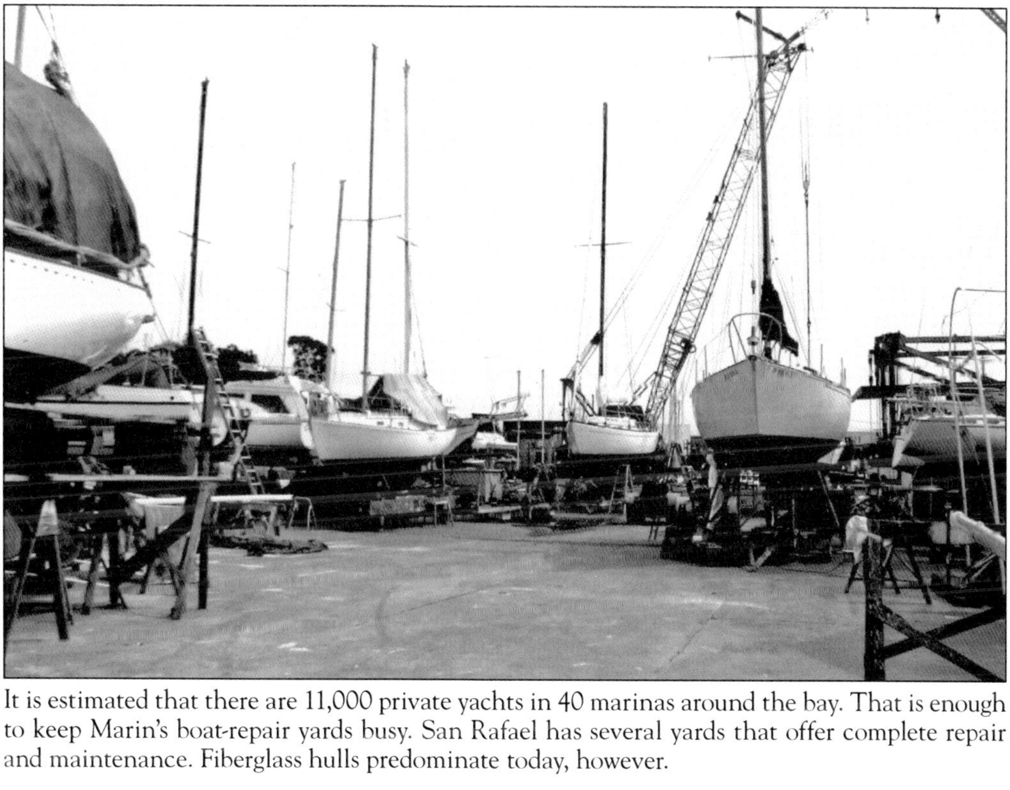

It is estimated that there are 11,000 private yachts in 40 marinas around the bay. That is enough to keep Marin's boat-repair yards busy. San Rafael has several yards that offer complete repair and maintenance. Fiberglass hulls predominate today, however.

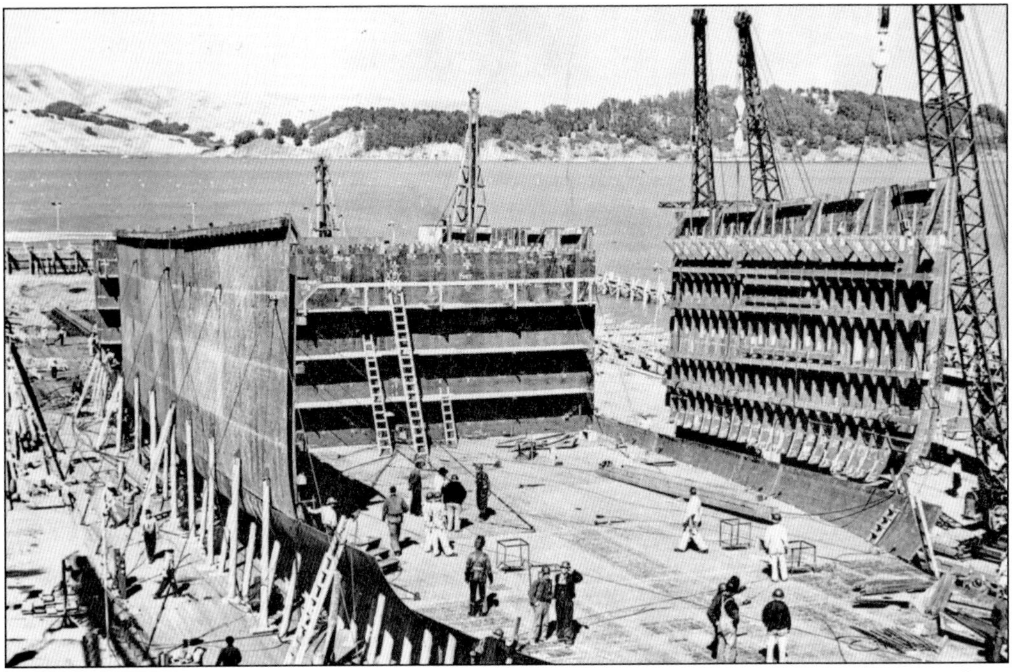

In December 1941, the call went out for 5,000 new vessels to rebuild the navy and merchant fleet, which had been ignored between wars. Not only did the United States have to supply ships for American military needs but also for half the world and in seas filled with hostile submarines. The W. A. Bechtel Company answered the call. In less than a year, a hill in Sausalito was leveled; 21 buildings, 6 shipways, and 2 docks were constructed, housing for more than 20,000 workers; and 5 Liberty ships were delivered. (Courtesy San Francisco Maritime National Historical Park.)

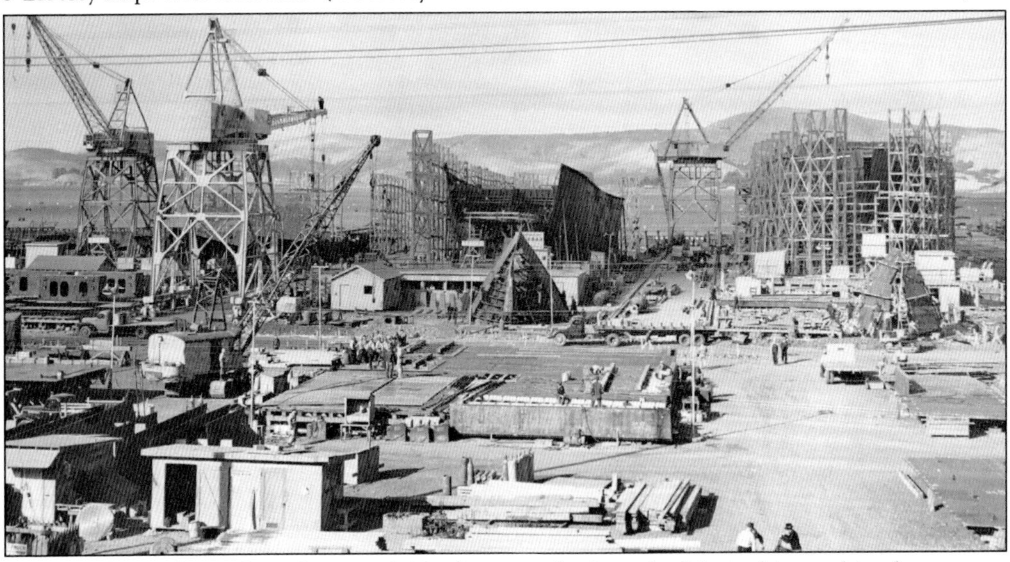

Fifteen Liberty ships, 62 tankers, and 16 oilers were built at the Marinship yard in three years. The shipyard worked around the clock using automobile assembly-line techniques. Steel plate came in at one end, where it was then cut and shaped before being welded into subassemblies, which were lifted by a giant crane into the hull. A finished ship left the yard by the other end. (Courtesy San Francisco Maritime National Historical Park.)

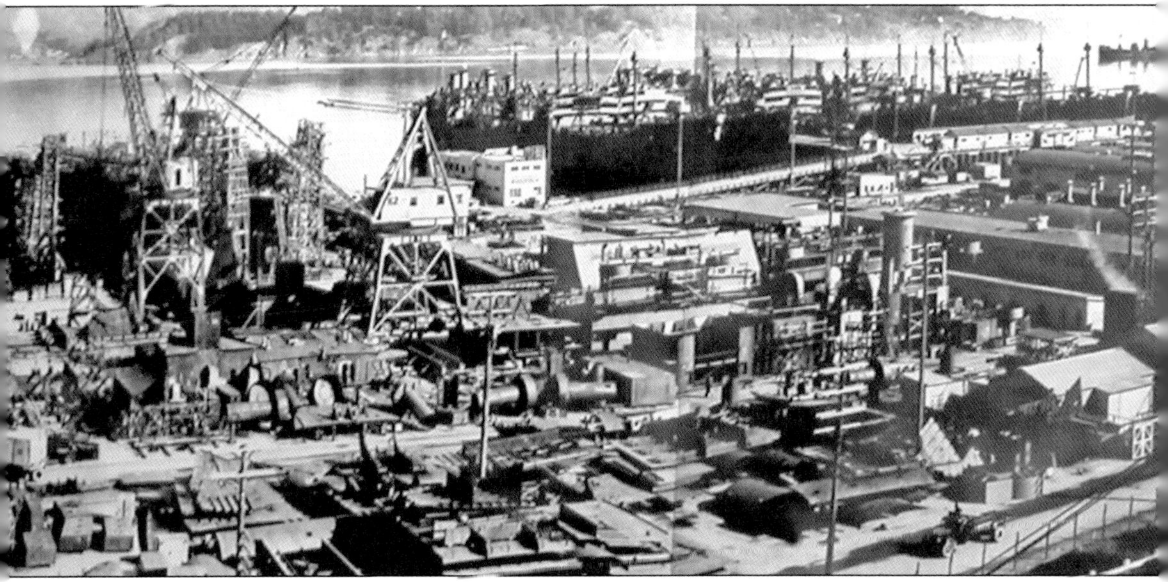

The keels were laid and subassemblies were fitted in the six shipways at left in this image. After launching, the hulls were towed to the fitting-out docks on the right. Marinship workers produced a ship every 13 days; one ship was even built from the keel up in 33 days. Many of these workers had never seen an ocean, let alone an oceangoing ship. The last of the 93 Liberty ships and tankers built in three and a half years in the mudflats of Sausalito was launched in September 1945, three weeks after the end of the war. (Courtesy San Francisco Maritime National Historical Park.)

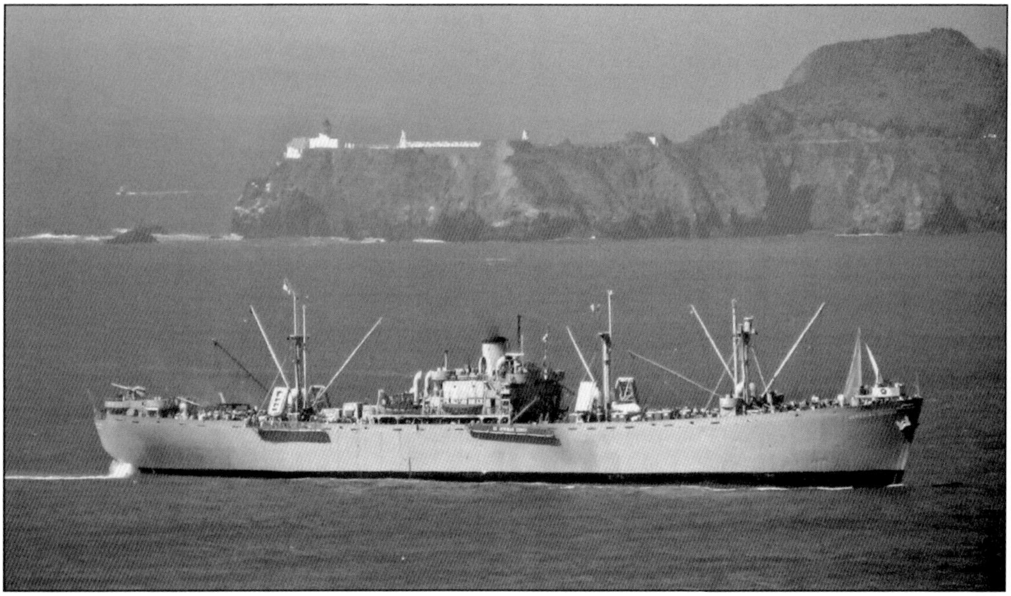

Typical of the Liberty ships built at Marinship is the *Jeremiah O'Brien*, the last surviving ship of this type from World War II. Permanently based in the Bay Area, it is lovingly cared for by old salts who served in Liberty ships with help from seamen who were not even born in time to dodge World War II torpedoes. A surplus of merchant shipping after the war doomed the slow Liberty ships, but some of the tankers were reported to be still in use somewhere in the world into the 1980s.

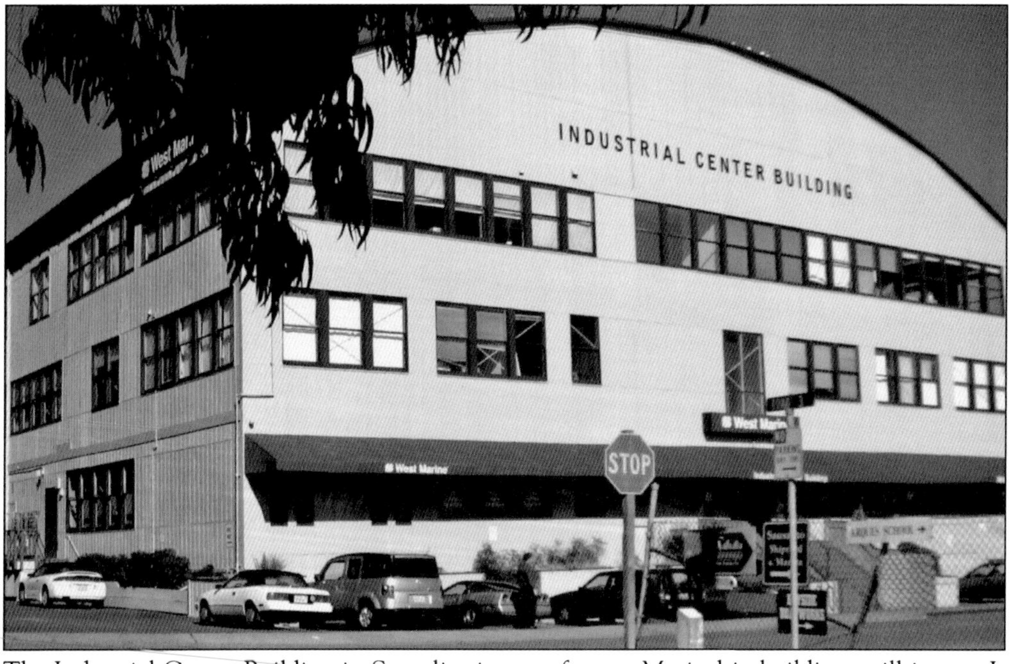

The Industrial Center Building in Sausalito is one of many Marinship buildings still in use. It was originally the Pattern Shop, where full-sized drawings of ship segments were laid out and cut. The largest surviving building houses a complete model of the San Francisco Bay made by the U.S. Army Corps of Engineers to test water flows and changes in the bay.

Six

MILITARY

At the end of World War II, the view from an airplane's window as it circled the bay was staggering, even if one had been living and working on the bay. Someone who had cruised throughout the bay on a daily basis would have been aware of a solid wall of ships but could not get the full impact unless seeing it from the air. Troop ships, aircraft carriers, battleships, and cruisers occupied every pier on all sides of the bay. Three hundred more were swinging at anchor. The victorious fleets that had defeated the empire of Japan returned through the Golden Gate. In addition, there were the ships from the Atlantic battle with Hitler's wolf packs, plus the hundreds that had massed for the no-longer-needed invasion of the home islands of Japan. Until seen from the air, it had been impossible to imagine the vastness of the sea power that this country had built from the ruins of Pearl Harbor in 1941.

Marin played a small but important part in this buildup. Except for a brief skirmish during the Bear Flag Revolt and several uprisings of the Miwok Indians, Marin has been spared any actual combat; however, the military has played an important part in its history long before 1941. Since the Civil War, army-manned gun batteries have been guarding the approaches to the bay from positions in the headlands and on Angel Island. Troops trained in Marin have served in every theater of every war. Hamilton Field was a key player in the West Coast defense. Ninety-three Liberty ships and tankers were built in the mudflats of Sausalito. Navy bases on Tiburon had supplied fuel for the coal-burning navy and later constructed massive nets to stop enemy submarines and trained crews on floating drydocks to repair ships in combat zones. The air force built huge radar domes on the top of Mount Tamalpais during the cold war to control the antiaircraft missiles launched from hidden sites in Marin. These were all tools of another era and another time, and by the 1970s, they were no longer needed. Attempts were made to develop these spectacular military sites, but most have been converted to parks, open space, and research institutions.

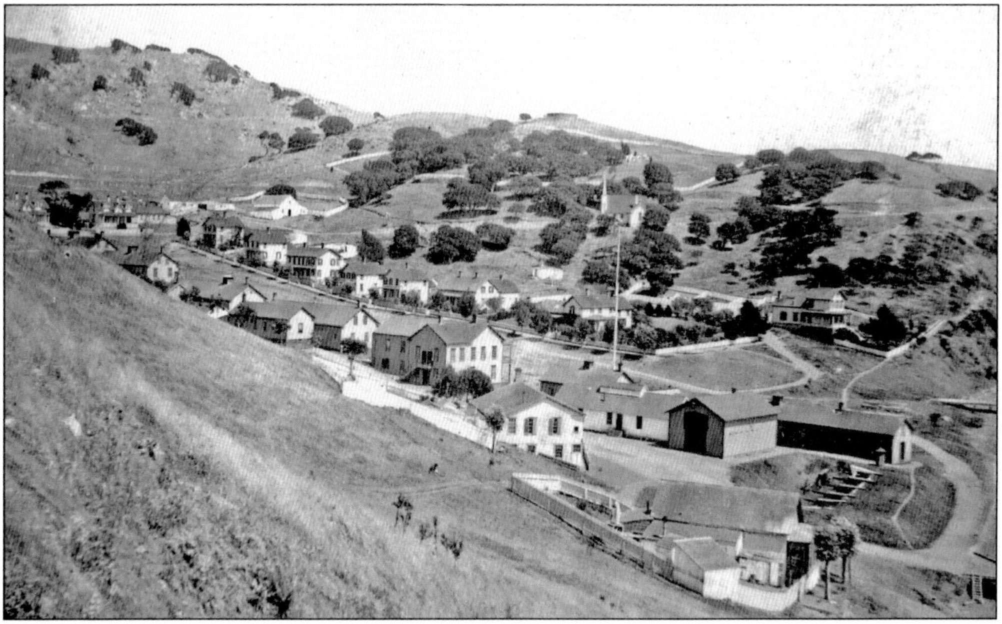

After the Civil War, the importance of the artillery installations faded quickly, so Camp Reynolds on Angel Island was expanded to house and train infantrymen from around the West. This 1870s photograph shows a long row of barracks in the foreground and a number of officers' homes opposite. The cannon in the lower right are more ceremonial than useful. (Courtesy Angel Island Association.)

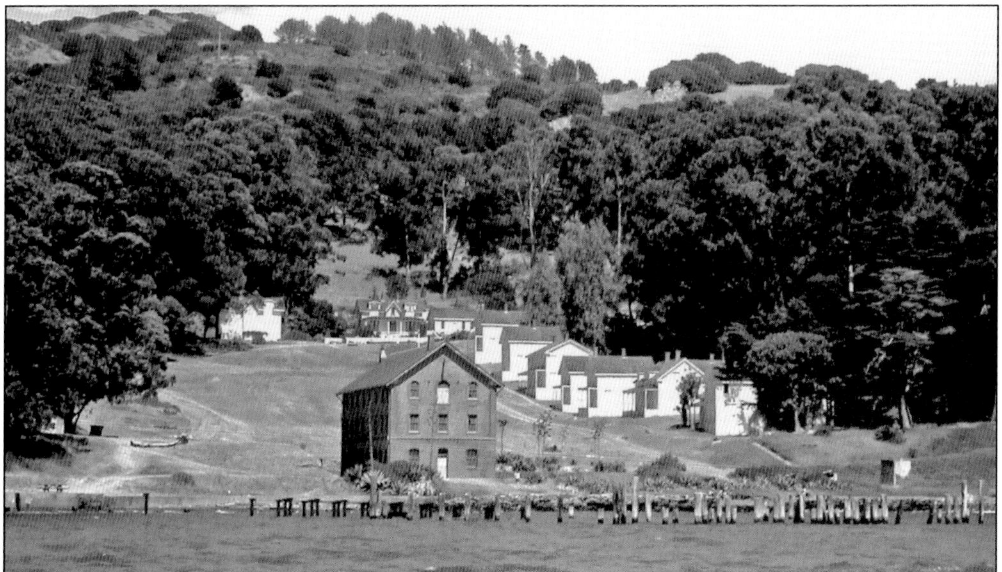

By 1876, Camp Reynolds had facilities for 200 soldiers, complete with barracks for the enlisted personnel, homes for officers and their families, a bakery, blacksmith, laundry, shoemaker, and barber. Roads were nonexistent on the island, so everything came in or out by a fleet of small ships. Even communications between the various island installations were by water. (Courtesy Angel Island Association.)

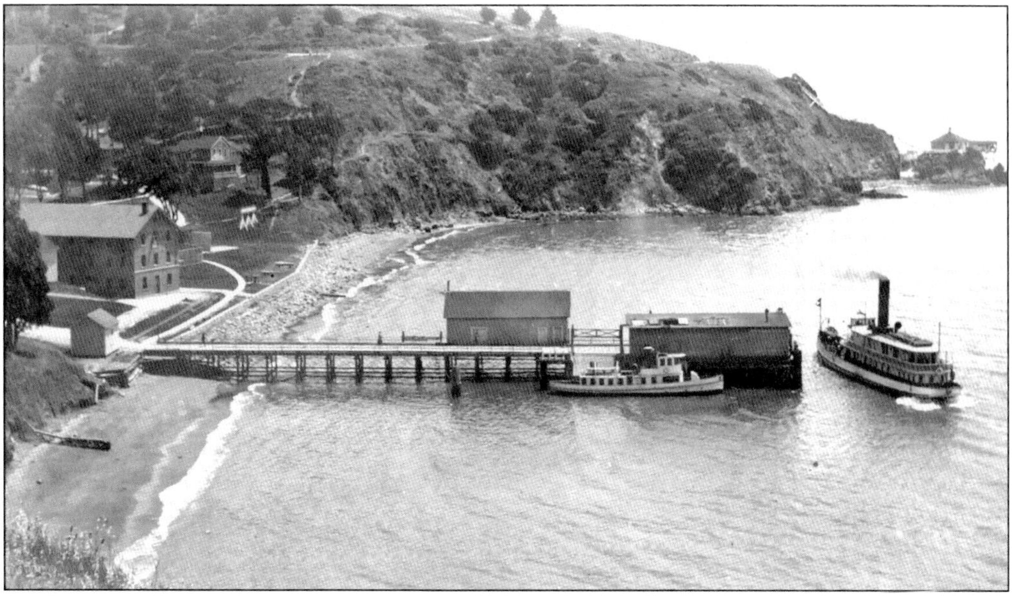

Most supplies for the island came across this wharf, built in 1864. Warehouses and camp administration buildings were close. Most of these buildings are gone except for the brick warehouse, built in 1909, which is now used by youth organizations for overnight visits. This was the main gateway for supplies, equipment, and men for the post. Regular service by a government steamer to San Francisco was available for all residents, military and civilian. (Courtesy Angel Island Association.)

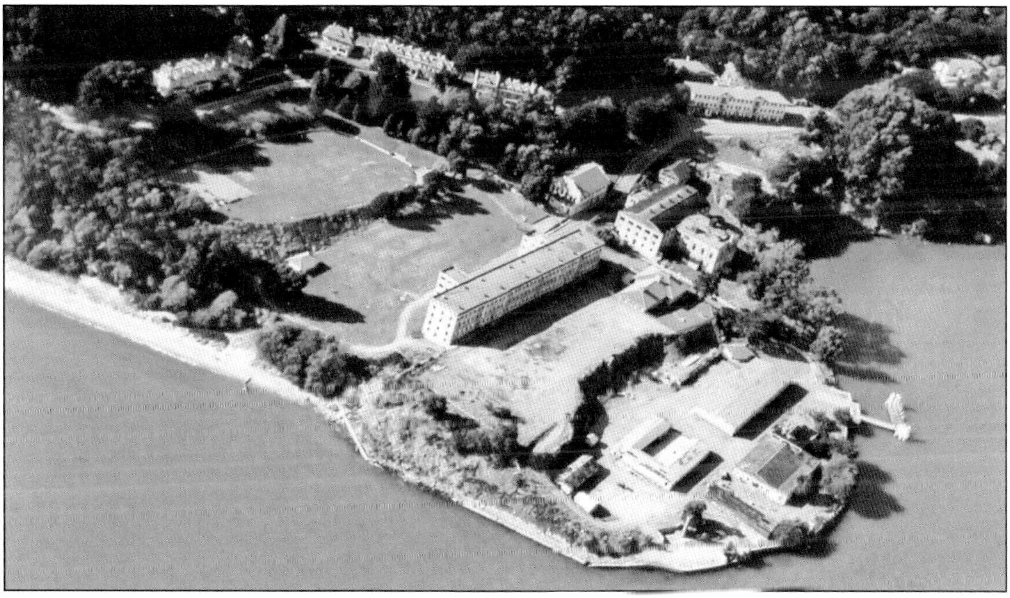

Fort McDowell became the headquarters for all army installations on Angel Island. The recruit barracks alone could house 1,000 men, giving it the unofficial name of the "Thousand Man Barracks." At the peak of World War II, temporary barracks were added as Angel Island became the main staging base for troops heading to the Pacific theater. More than 300,000 men passed through here during the war. Officers' housing is still in use for park personnel. (Courtesy Angel Island Association.)

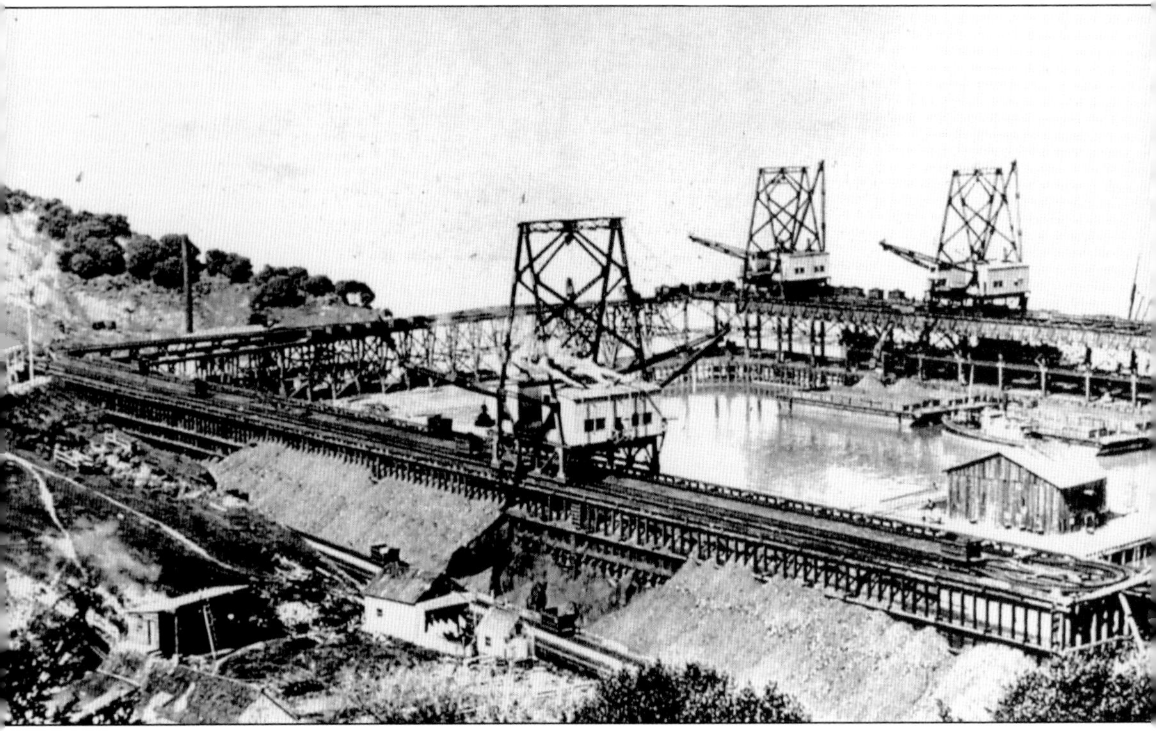

When steam power replaced sails, the U.S. Navy turned to coal, so a former codfish plant on Paradise Drive in Tiburon was transformed into a coaling station. The coal had to come around Cape Horn from the East Coast. Colliers, ships transporting coal, provided the same function as oil tankers would in later years. After the colliers unloaded their cargo of coal, the ships of the Pacific fleet would line up and refuel. (Courtesy Romberg Tiburon Center.)

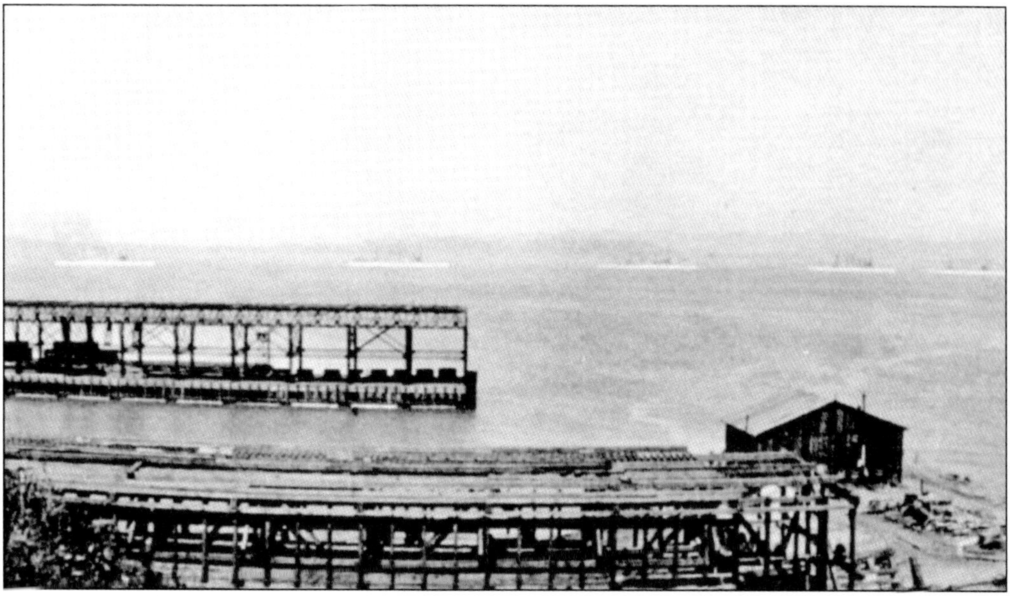

Sixteen battleships and support vessels, part of Pres. Theodore Roosevelt's Great White Fleet, had to stop at Tiburon to refuel before continuing on around the world in 1908. The completion of the Panama Canal made this long trip unnecessary, and the navy's switch to oil-burning ships eliminated the need for the Tiburon facility. (Courtesy Romberg Tiburon Center.)

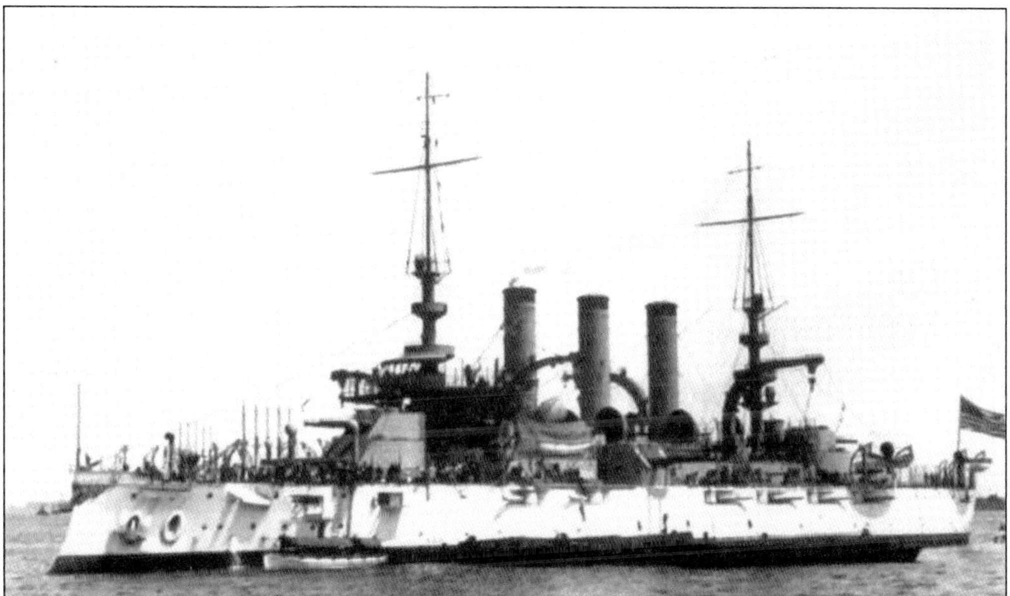

The USS *New Jersey* was typical of the navy ships in the Great White Fleet, which refueled in Marin. The fleet was on a goodwill trip around the world, but it also was out to impress potential foes of U.S. naval strength. (Courtesy Romberg Tiburon Center.)

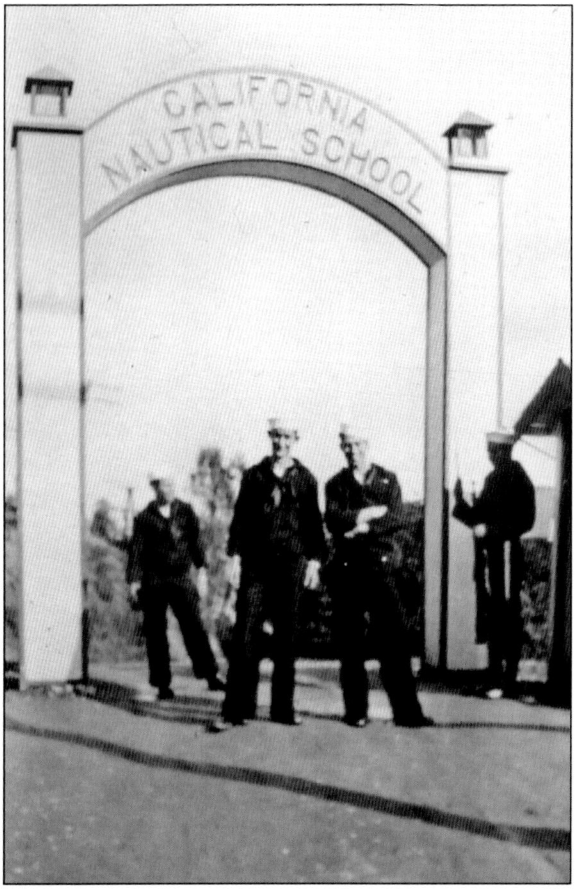

After its service as a coaling station was no longer needed, the navy transferred the base to the State of California for use as the California Nautical School to train merchant marine officers. This became the California Maritime Academy and moved to Vallejo before World War II. (Courtesy Romberg Tiburon Center.)

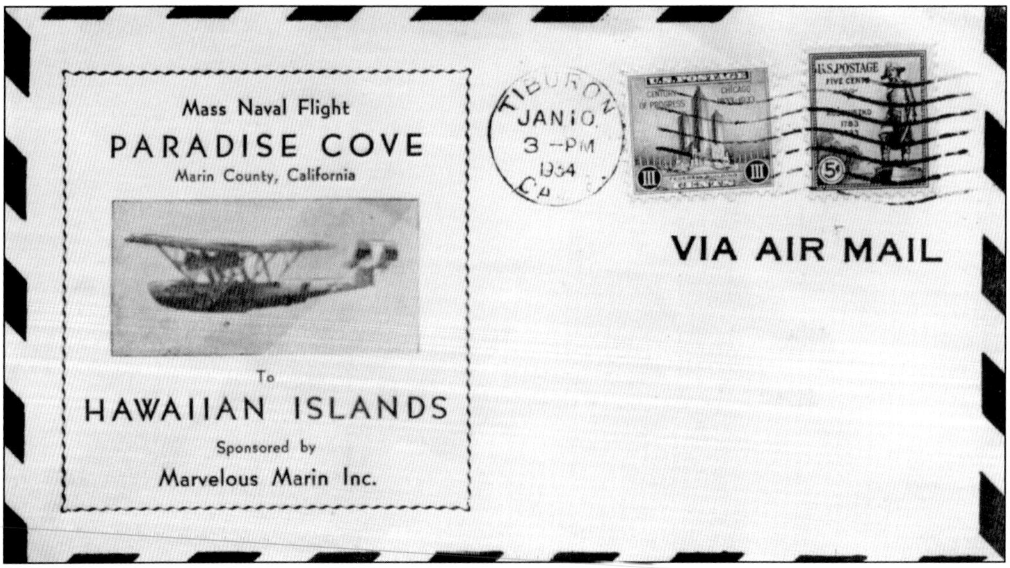

The calm waters of Paradise Cove made an ideal seaplane landing spot. In 1934, the navy made a demonstration flight to Hawaii from this cove between Corte Madera and the Tiburon Peninsula. (Courtesy the Morrison Family Collection.)

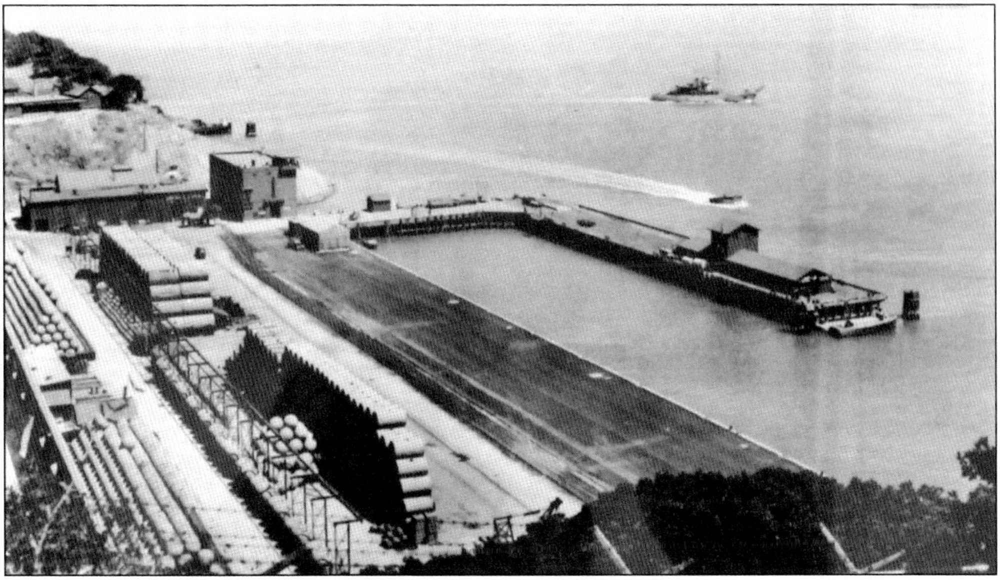

As World War II loomed, the navy reclaimed the old coaling station and started constructing antisubmarine nets and training the crews in the care and handling of these huge, ungainly but necessary devices that protected the harbors from Seattle, Washington, to Sydney, Australia. The net guarding the Golden Gate was seven miles long. More than 20 types of harbor nets and booms were constructed at the U.S. Navy Net Depot in Tiburon for use throughout the Pacific theater. (Courtesy Romberg Tiburon Center.)

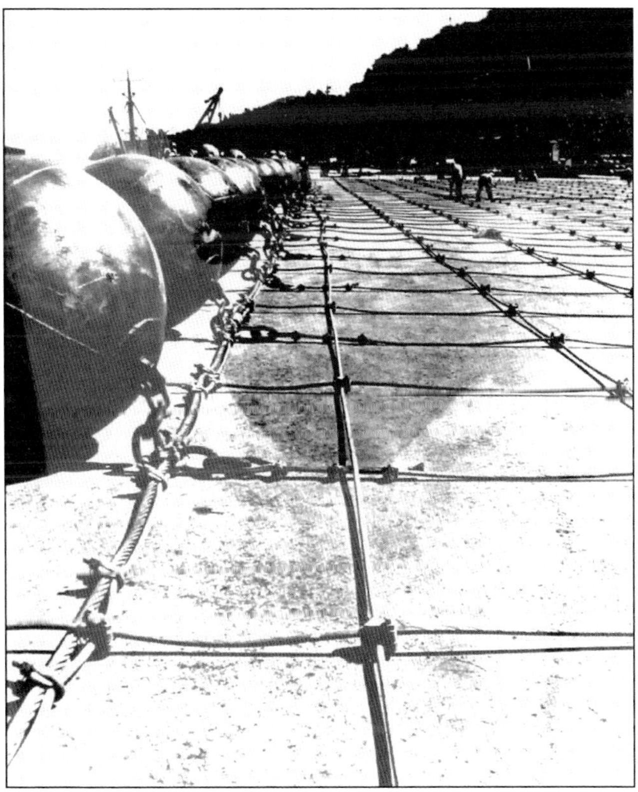

The former coaling station at Tiburon had served as the staging depot for the construction of the Golden Gate Bridge. Ships brought the steel sections from the East Coast steel mills, unloaded them here, and the parts were then barged to the construction site. The suspender cables were spun at the former coaling station from steel coils brought from the East Coast. It was not a big jump to making antisubmarine nets. (Courtesy Romberg Tiburon Center.)

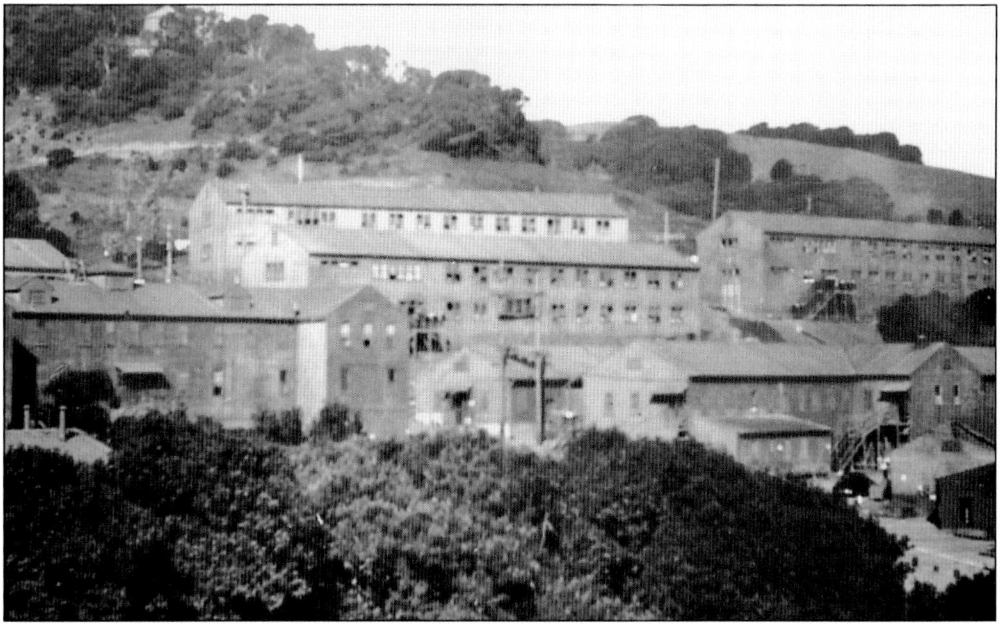

Early in World War II, the enemy captured all of the shipyards west of Pearl Harbor, and the navy was about to send a thousand ships in harm's way. The solution: build floating drydocks and bring them to Tiburon. Here men were trained in the operation of three sizes, which when paired with navy repair ships could fix anything from a PT boat to an aircraft carrier in the most remote part of the Pacific. The buildings pictured here housed up to 3,000 instructors and trainees.

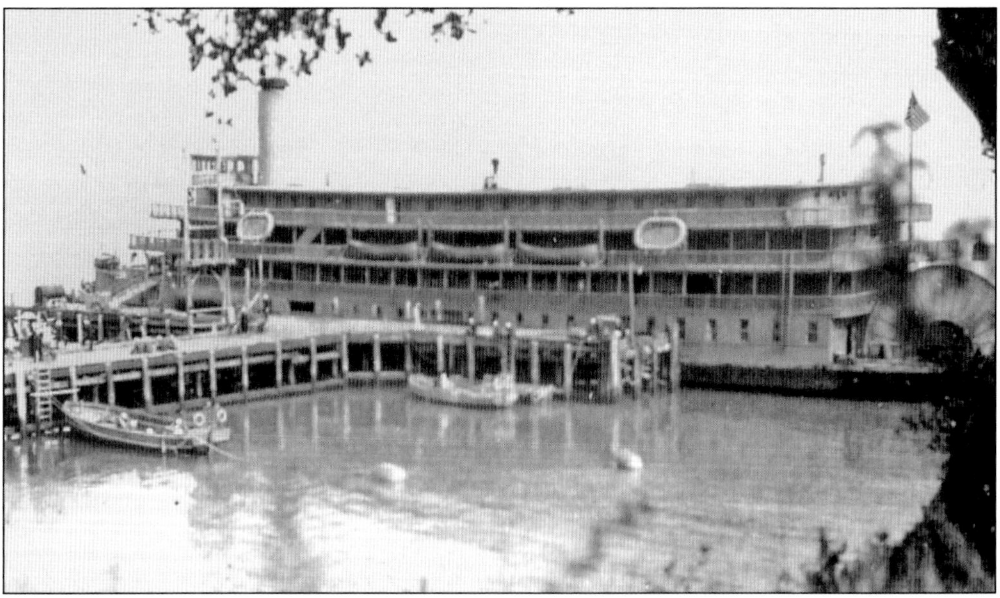

This cove near the net depot is now the lovely Paradise County Park. However, when this photograph was taken, it was the main port of supply and activity for the navy's Floating Drydock Training Center in World War II. It was difficult for liberty parties to get into Tiburon or San Francisco from here, so the old Sacramento riverboat, the *Delta Queen*, YFB-56 (pictured here), was pressed into service as a water taxi. As the war wound down, many of the fleet submarines were laid up here until being moved to the mothball fleet.

Even the Floating Drydock Training Center had it own logo.

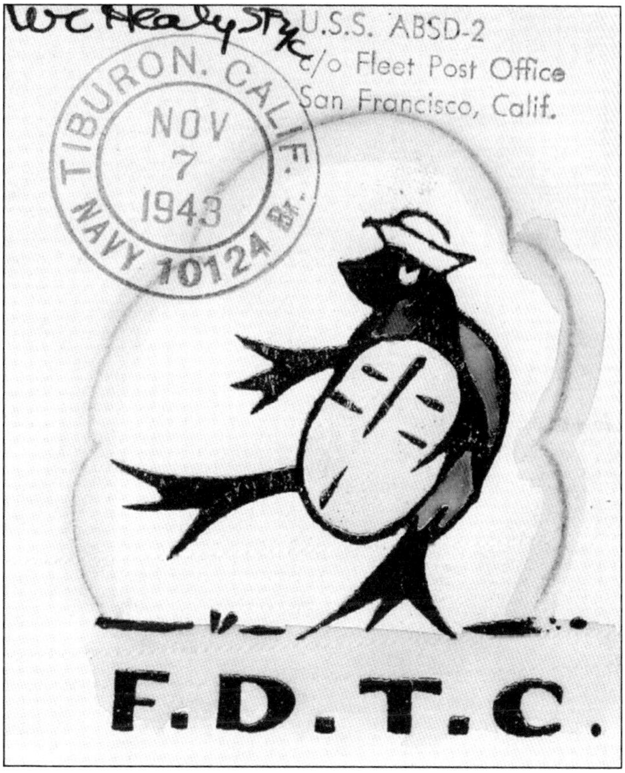

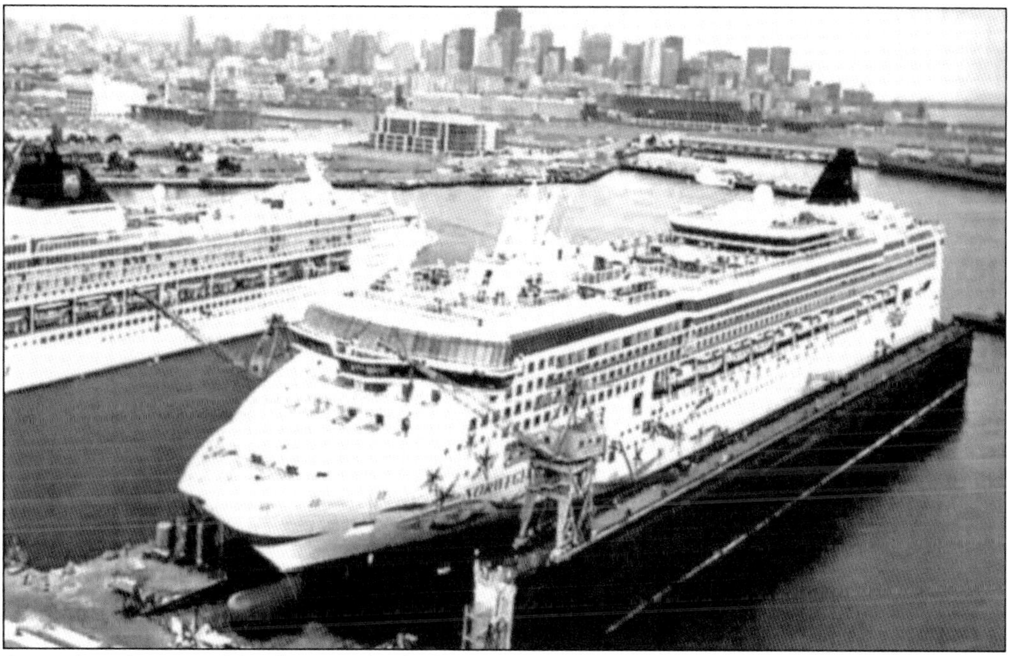

At war's end, some of the floating drydocks returned to the bay, and a few are still in use at local shipyards. Some proved almost indestructible, like two that bedeviled the Sausalito waterfront for years. Drydocks of the type that had to be towed to sea in sections and then joined together could hold an aircraft carrier. They were huge!

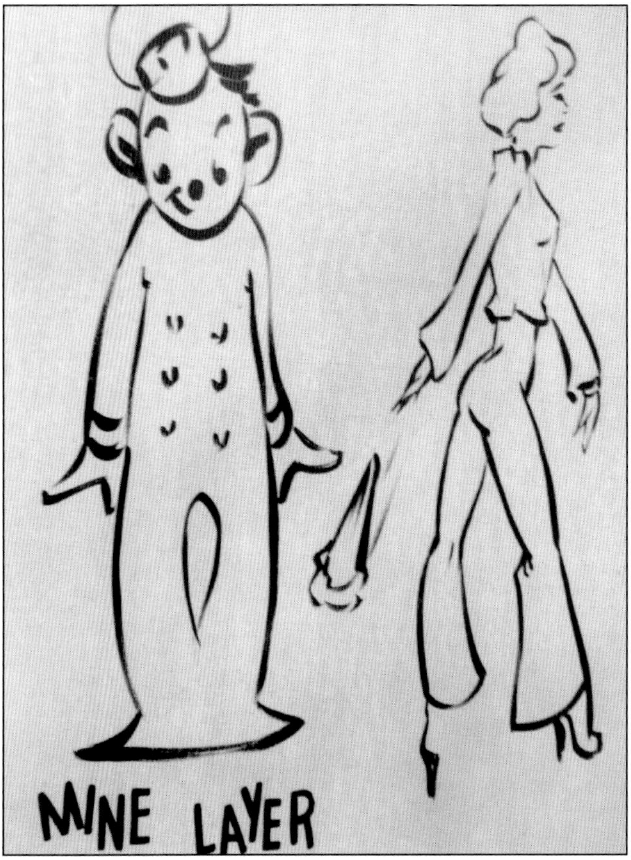

It was definitely never "all work and no play" at the Marin navy bases. Deep in the underground passages of the Tiburon Naval Net Depot was an officers' club. On the walls were what has been described as "graffiti" by some and by others as irreplaceable works of art. Not only were the drawings not particularly flattering to U.S. enemies, but they also poked fun at U.S. naval sailors. They will be preserved in any reconstruction.

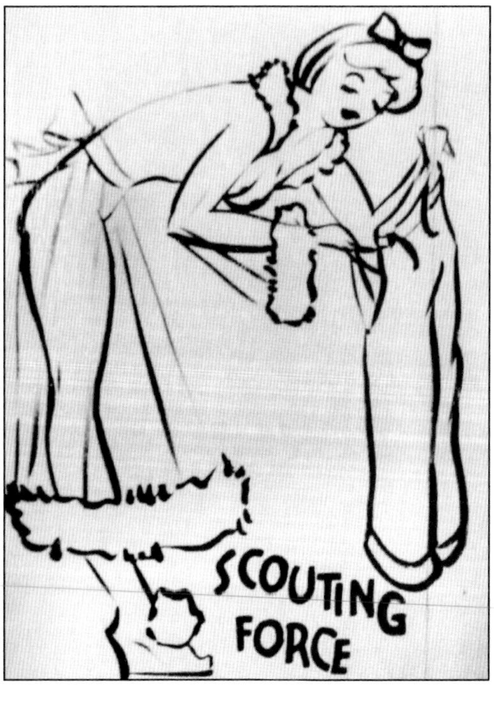

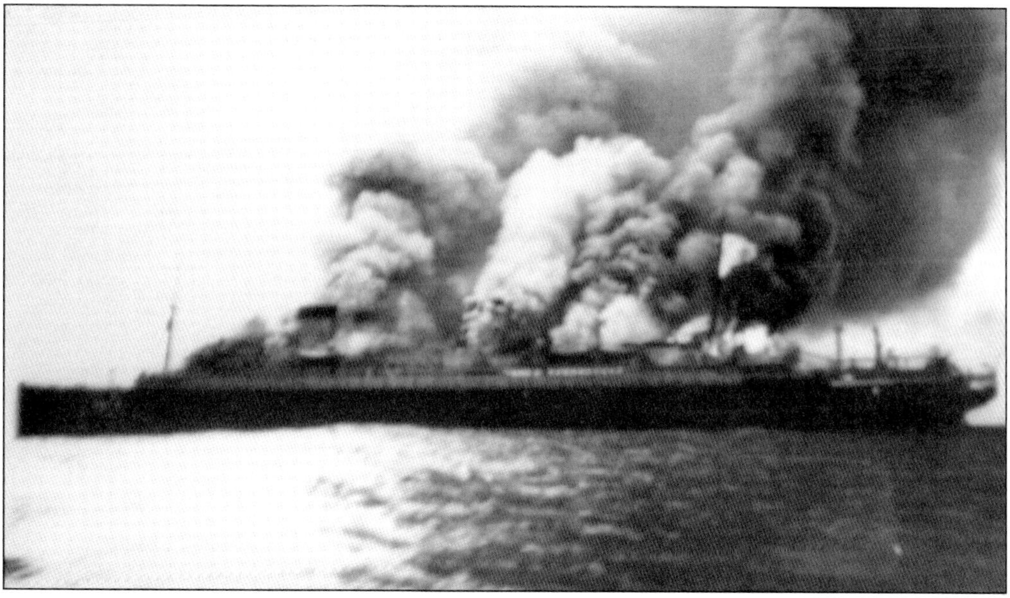

During World War II, the former immigration station on Angel Island became a POW camp. Before the United States formally entered the war, 700 members of the civilian crew of the German luxury liner *Columbus*, which had been set on fire in the Atlantic to avoid capture by the British, were held for 14 months on Angel Island. Eventually, these crewmen returned home after Germany's surrender. (Courtesy the Angel Island Association.)

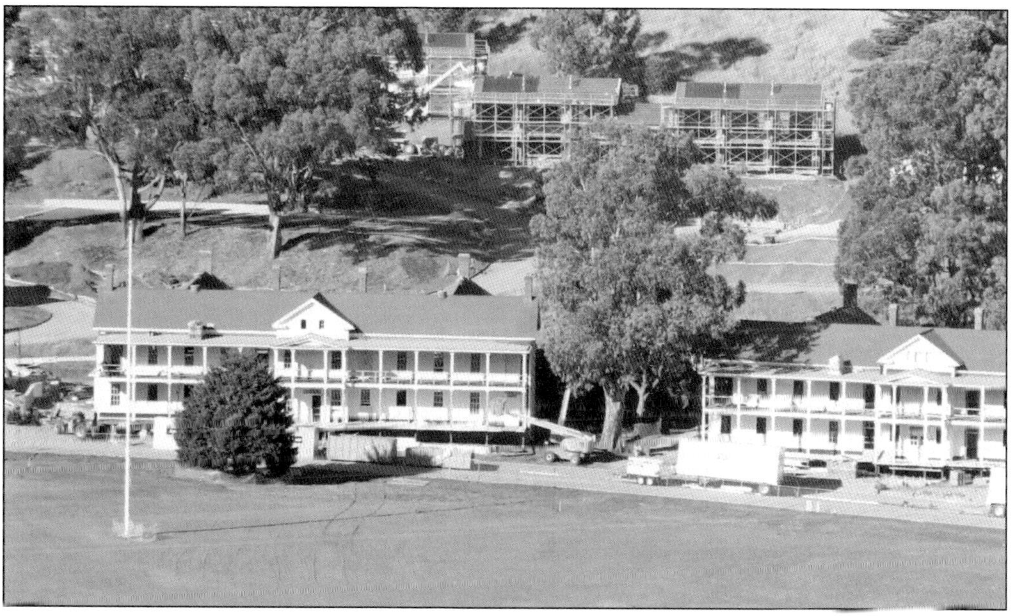

To support coast artillery units on the north side of the Golden Gate, Fort Baker was built in 1897 on an early Miwok village site. It expanded through the years to become the home of the army's Coast Artillery Corps until after World War II. The 91st Division, the Bay Area's army reserve unit, used the fort as its headquarters until 2002. The surviving 28 historic buildings were turned over to the GGNRA and the Institute at the Golden Gate for future focus on environmental issues.

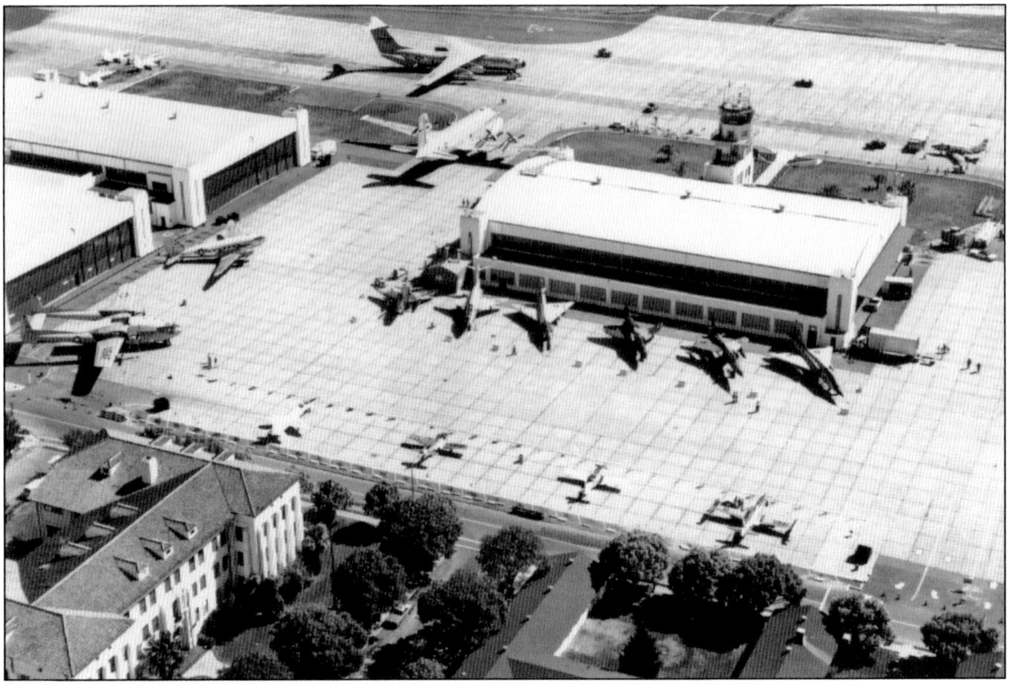

Hamilton Field, built on land diked from San Pablo Bay, was ready when World War II began. The people of Marin had purchased the land and donated it to the army during the Depression in order to create jobs. During the attack on Pearl Harbor, B-17 bombers from Hamilton Field, unarmed and low on fuel, arrived in Hawaii. Warned of the attack, the planes were diverted to other airfields and saved. (Courtesy Novato History Museum.)

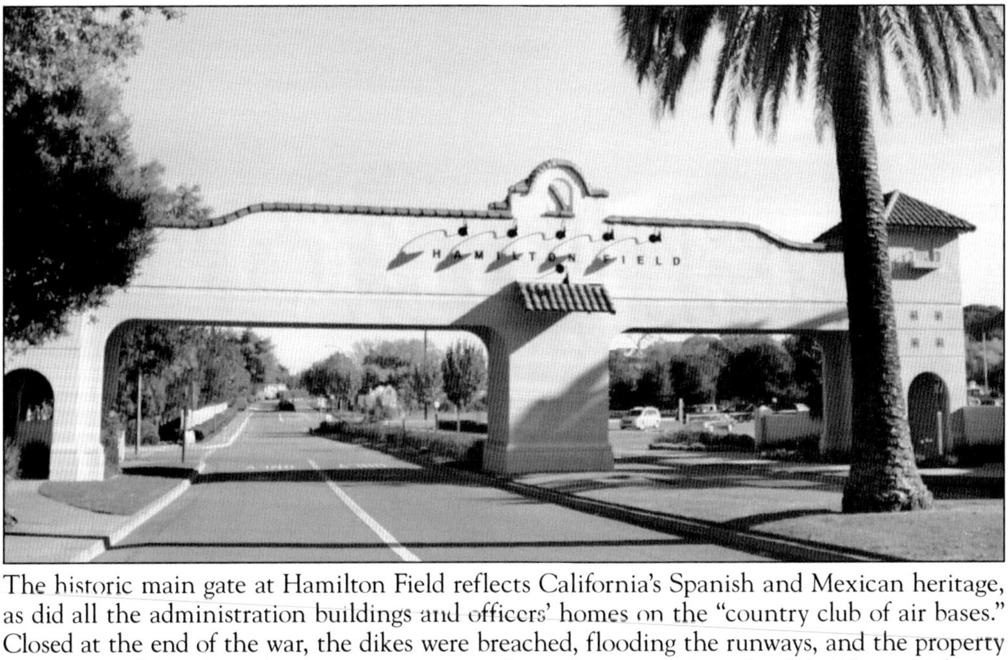

The historic main gate at Hamilton Field reflects California's Spanish and Mexican heritage, as did all the administration buildings and officers' homes on the "country club of air bases." Closed at the end of the war, the dikes were breached, flooding the runways, and the property was then sold. The huge hangers were converted to offices and a branch of the Novato Library. New housing has been built, augmenting the homes on officers' row.

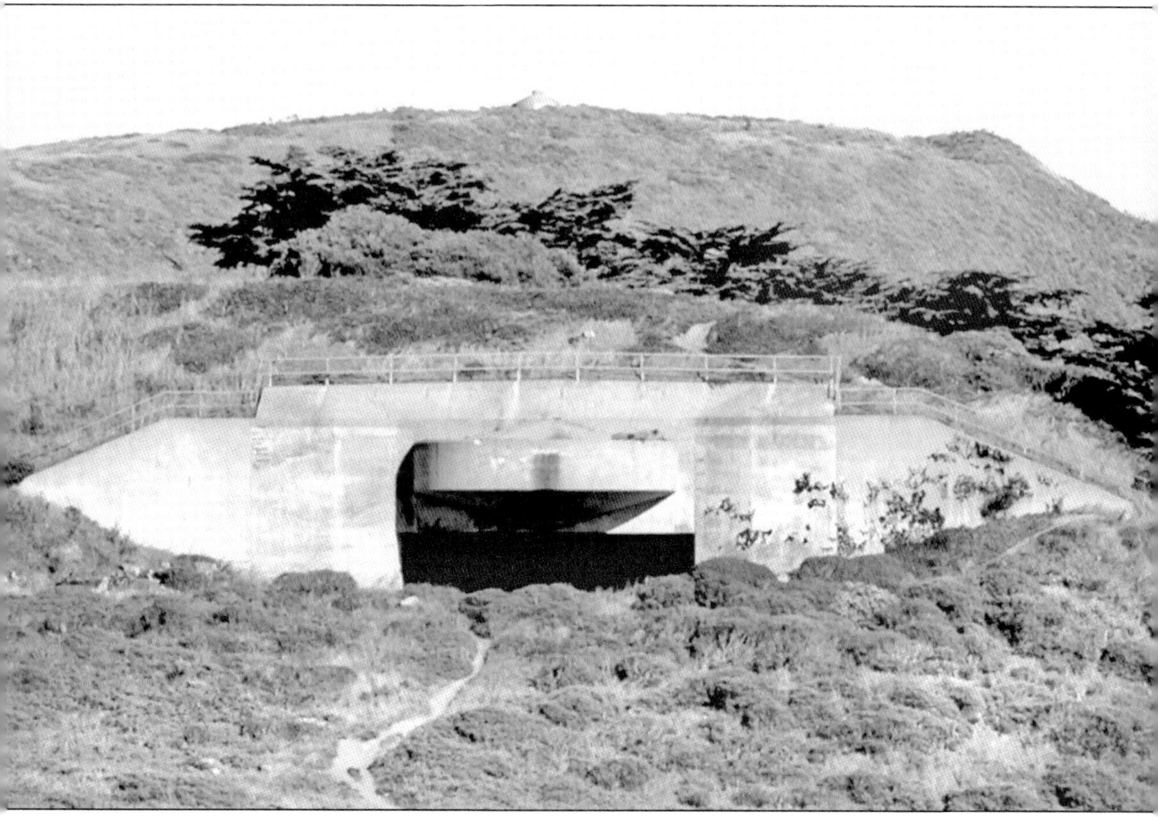

The original plan for the defense of San Francisco and the bay was to have a powerful fort on each side of the Golden Gate. By the time Fort Point, on the San Francisco side, was completed however, the concept changed; so military fortifications on the Marin side ranged from Civil War–era muzzle loaders to 16-inch naval rifles embedded in these massive concrete bunkers during World War II. The headlands are laced with the roads and tunnels built to service these fortifications.

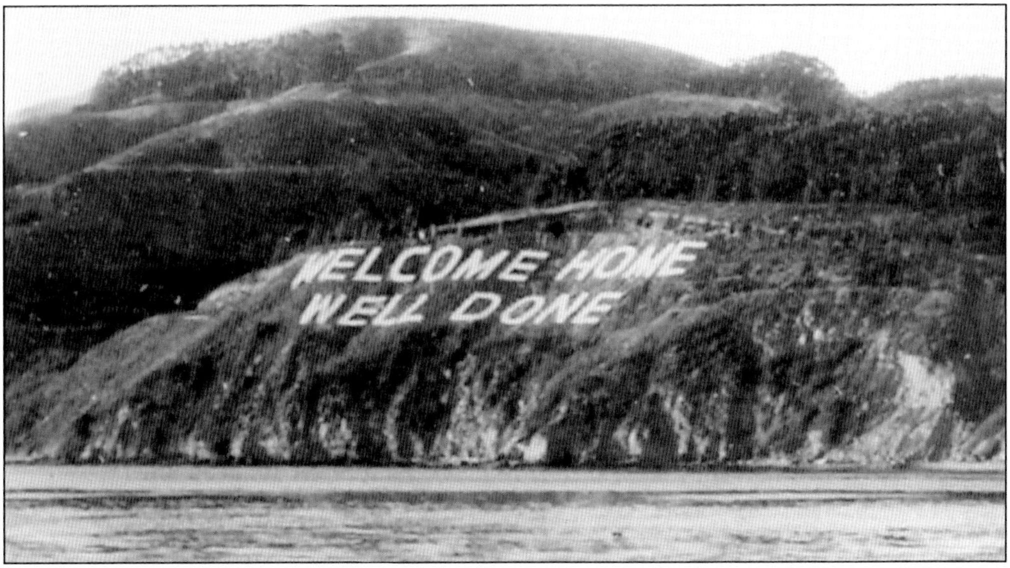

Even though World War II was over and the future of Angel Island was in doubt, it still had one more role to play. With the help of the Angel Island Italian Service Unit, these 60-foot-high letters welcomed home the troops who had fought the war in the Pacific theater.

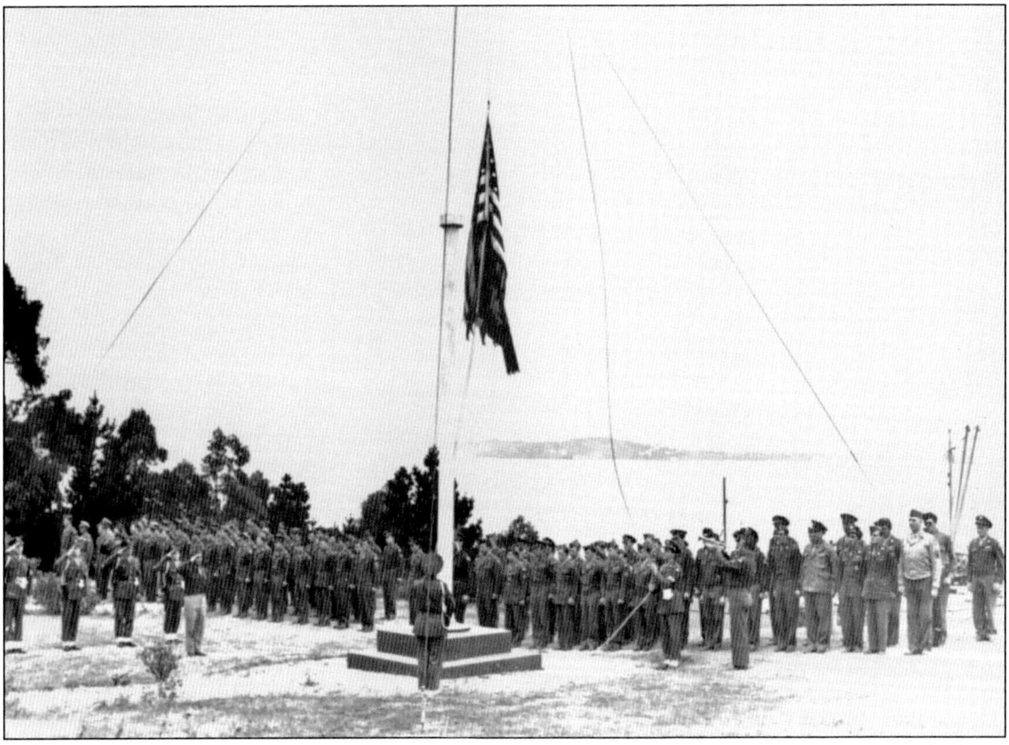

On August 28, 1946, in a ceremony at Fort McDowell, the remaining troops on Angel Island formed ranks and lowered the flag for the last time, or so they thought. The men who had served there could be proud of the part they had played in recruiting, training, and supporting at least one million soldiers during seven wars. However, the army did return to Angel Island for a decade in the 1950s and 1960s to man the Nike missile battery. (Courtesy California State Parks.)

The Nike system required the coordination of the missile, several radar stations, and computers. Once on the surface, the Nike missiles were wheeled into firing position and elevated to await orders from the radar and command stations on top of Angel Island and Mount Tamalpais. The last Nike missiles in Marin were not taken out of service until 1979.

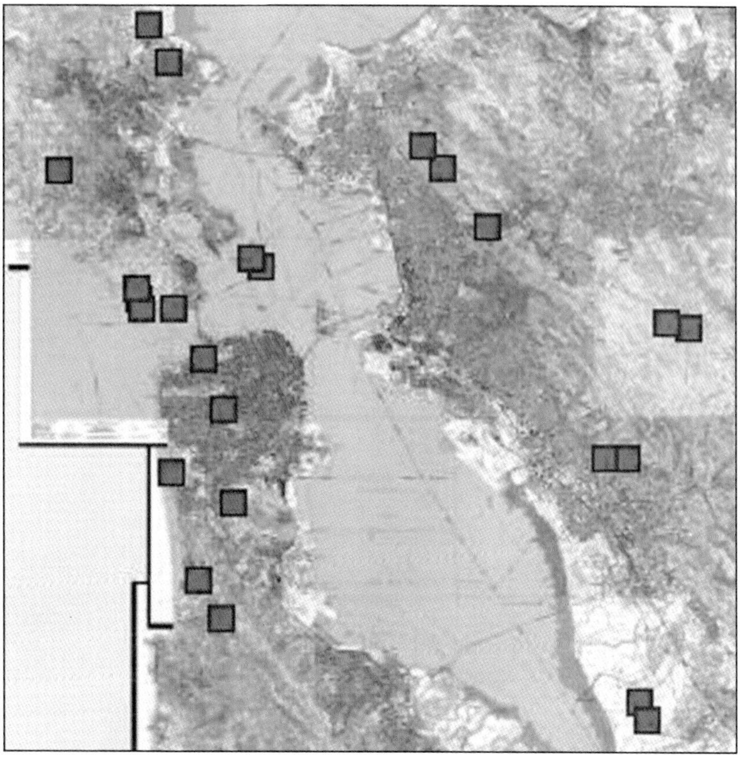

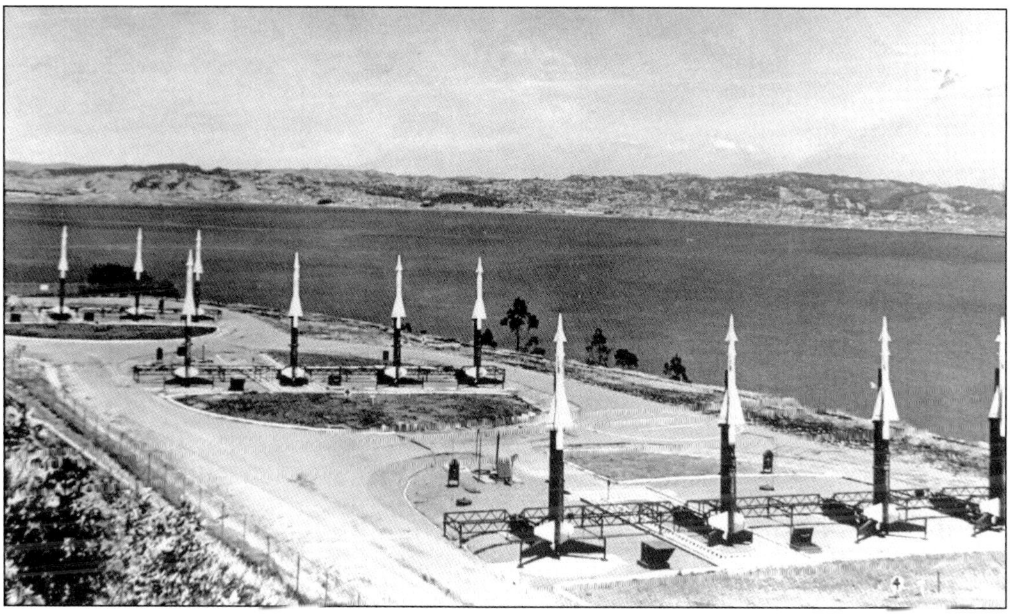

Primarily a defensive weapon, the Nike missile was never used in the United States. Nike missile bases were located throughout the Bay Area, with the largest installation on Angel Island. There, 36 missiles were stored in bombproof underground bunkers. Although army-operated, once launched, the main control of a missile passed to air force officers at the radar station on top of Mount Tamalpais. The long-range radars could look far out to sea and detect enemy bombers long before they reached a release point. (Courtesy Angel Island Association.)

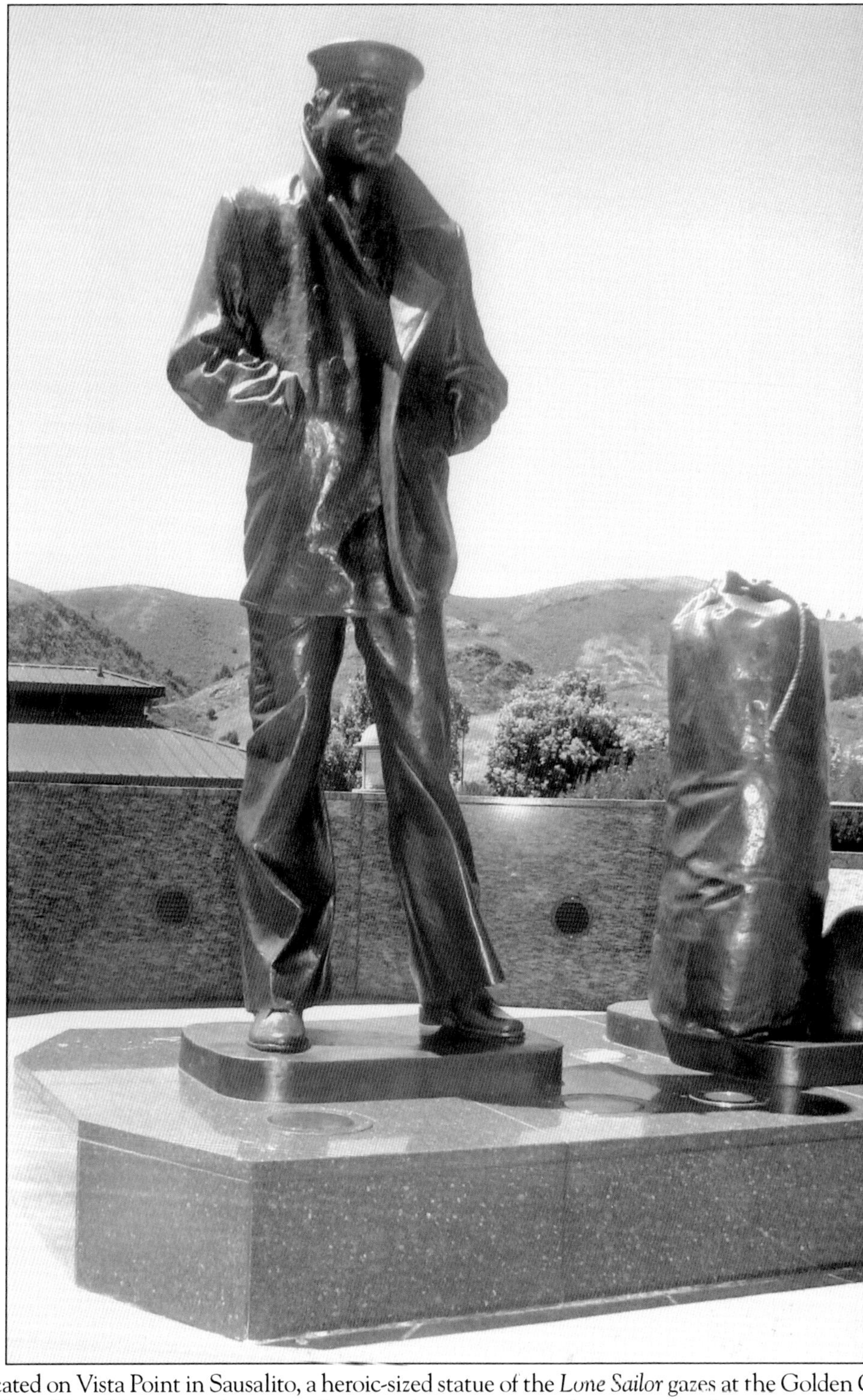

Located on Vista Point in Sausalito, a heroic-sized statue of the *Lone Sailor* gazes at the Golden Gate as if recalling shipmates—be they sailors, marines, coast guardsmen, or merchant seamen—who sailed through these dramatic portals, perhaps never to return.

Seven

More Than a Great Playground

Even the earliest ranchers loved to party. Soon after settling, the landed Californios began a round of rodeos and fiestas. The traditional hospitality of the ranch country meant that a stranger could travel throughout Marin and know that he had a bed and a meal waiting for him at the nearest ranch. As the Bay Area population grew and the cities became more crowded, Marin beaches and yacht clubs became popular destinations for holiday seekers. Hiking, or "tramping" as it was known locally, particularly on trails over Mount Tamalpais to the Pacific Coast, became popular. For a few dollars, it was possible to purchase a small lot at Willow Camp, the future Stinson Beach, and pitch a tent or build a small cabin and have a summer home. Loaded ferries brought hundreds of pleasure seekers to Sausalito, Tiburon, and San Rafael to swim, wade, or picnic, free from San Francisco hoodlums whose greatest joy was disrupting the pleasure of the "good people." In most waterfront towns, one could hire small rowing boats, and convenient bait shops provided all the fishing gear for a day on the water. So many large yachts manned by professional sailors crowded Marin's yacht clubs that a new club (the Corinthian) was formed that restricted membership to amateur boat owners. Boatbuilding and repair became, and still is, a major industry in Marin. Picnic grounds were replaced by waterfront restaurants and cafés. Bicycling did not appear until the 1970s, when paved trails started to wind along the shore of the bay. High-speed ferries still bring diners to Sausalito, Tiburon, and Larkspur to savor the latest catch while enjoying some of the grandest views in the world. By the 1950s, the "Save the Bay" movement grew to prevent more filling of the waters around Marin. The San Francisco Bay Conservation and Development Commission (BCDC) was created. A retired naval base became the Romberg Tiburon Center for Environmental Studies, and the Richardson Bay Audubon Center and Sanctuary now protects more than 1,000 acres of the bay.

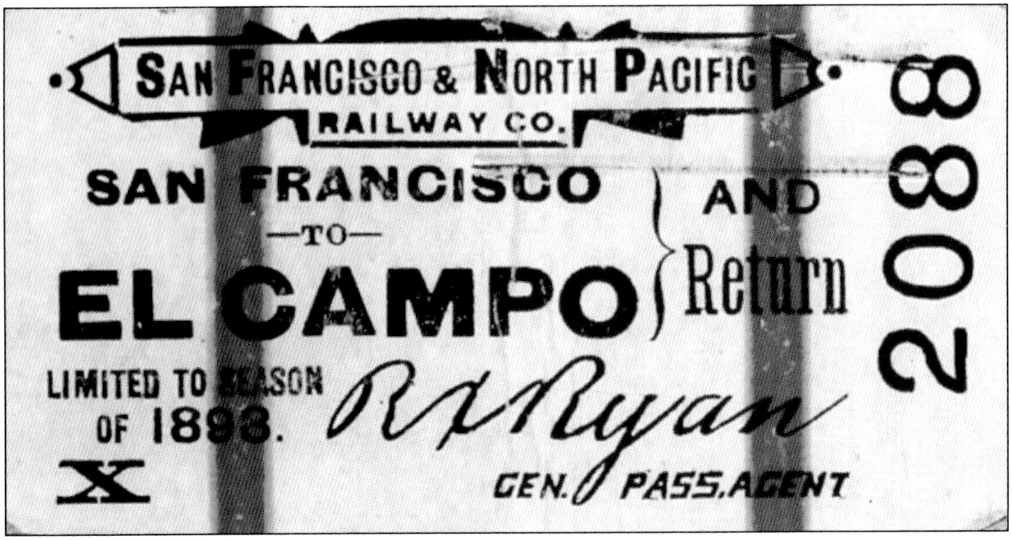

One of the first actions of the railroad line when it reached southern Marin was to create a picnic ground near where Paradise County Park is today. It was called El Campo, and one of reasons for its popularity was that it could only be reached via a ferry operated by the railroad. As many as 1,500 picnickers would line up to board the ferry in San Francisco, and railroad security made sure that only "nice people" boarded. (Courtesy the Morrison Family Collection.)

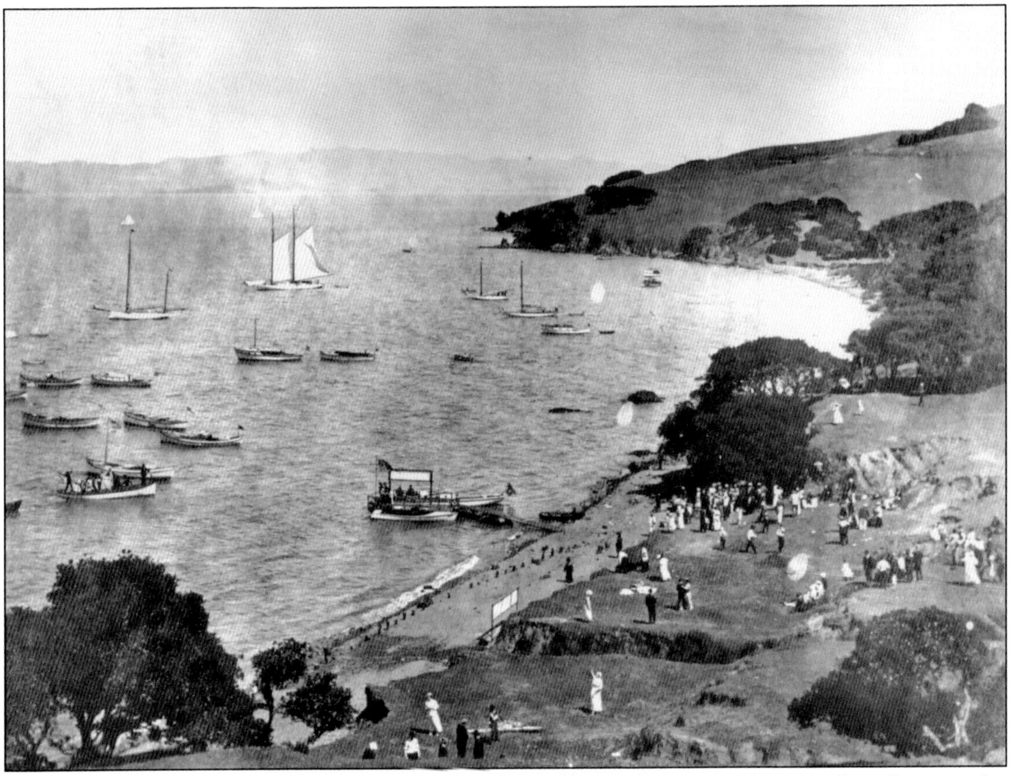

At El Campo, there were beach games, a bowling alley, a dance pavilion, and wading in the shallow water. To keep their skirts from getting wet, daring young ladies would raise them to their knees. Shocking! (Courtesy the Landmarks Society.)

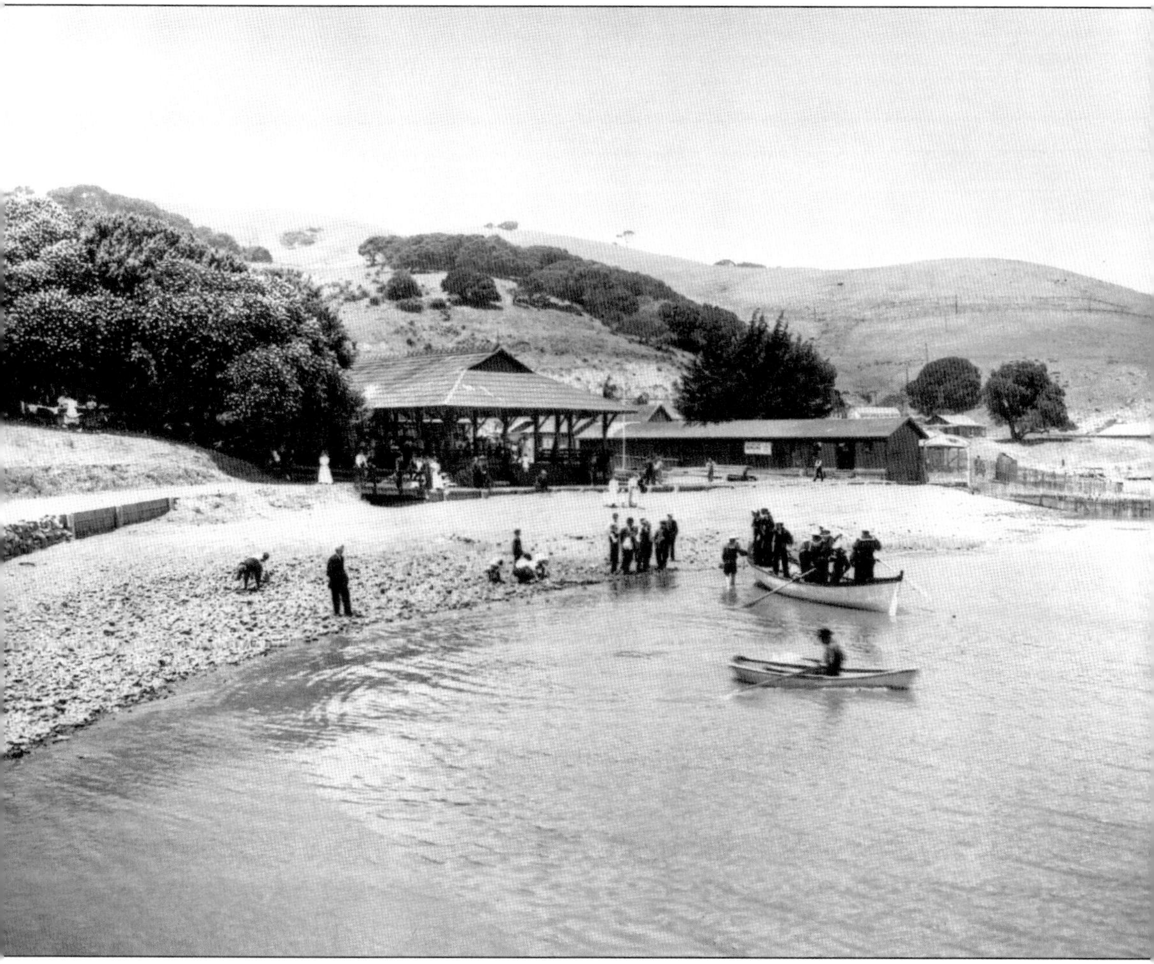

The cove at El Campo would also fill up with pleasure boats of all sizes on weekends. (Courtesy the Landmarks Society.)

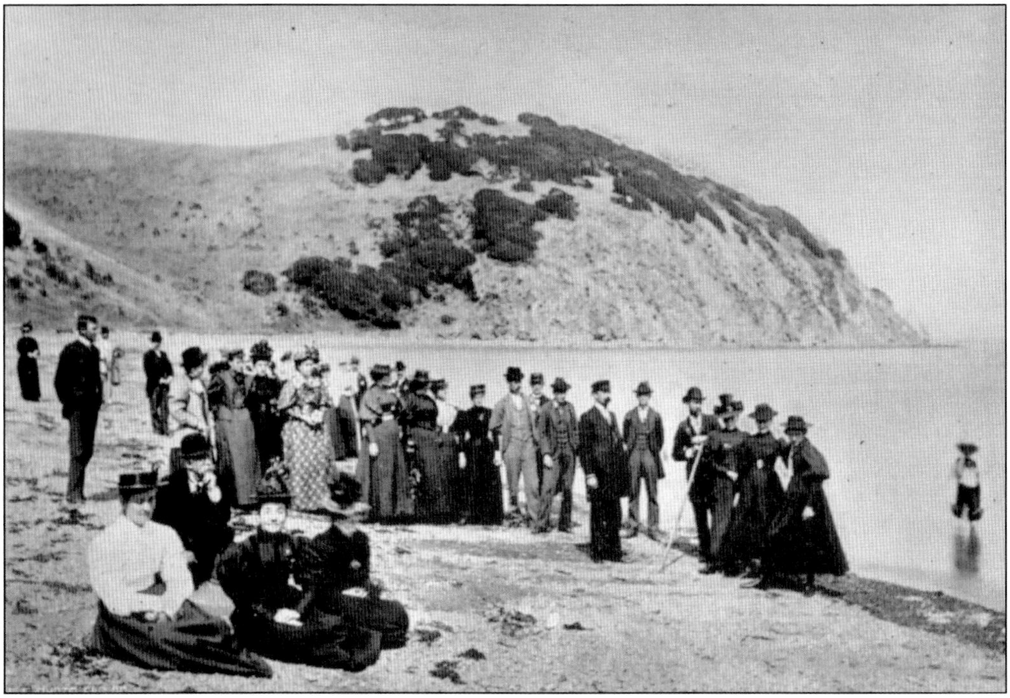

Within walking distance of the Tiburon ferry terminal was another picnic ground at what is now Keil Cove. (Courtesy the Landmarks Society.)

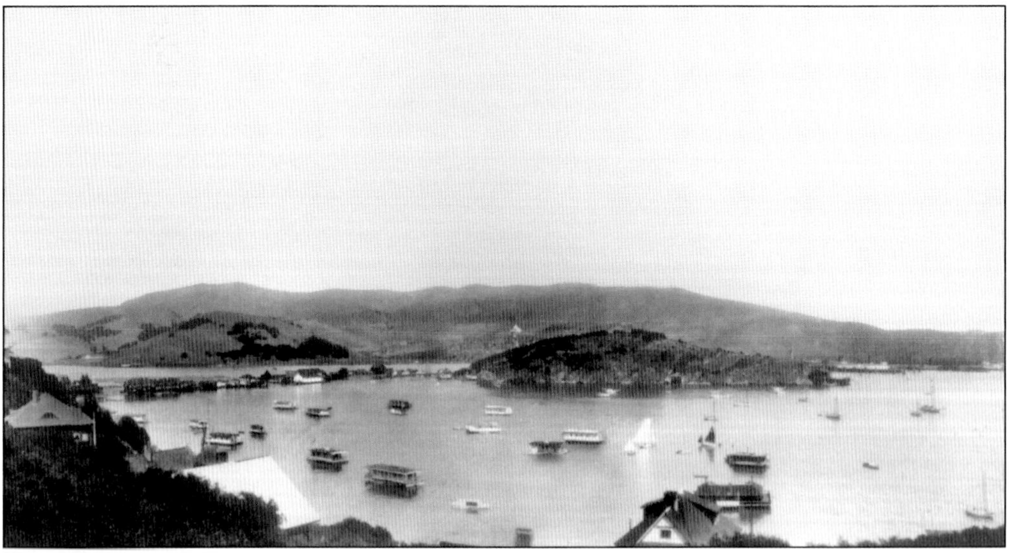

Belvedere Cove filled up with houseboats every summer. During the winter months, they were moved to the protected waters of the Tiburon Lagoon. The opening and closing of the drawbridge on Main Street to let the houseboats pass was the cause of a parade and celebration. (Courtesy the Landmarks Society.)

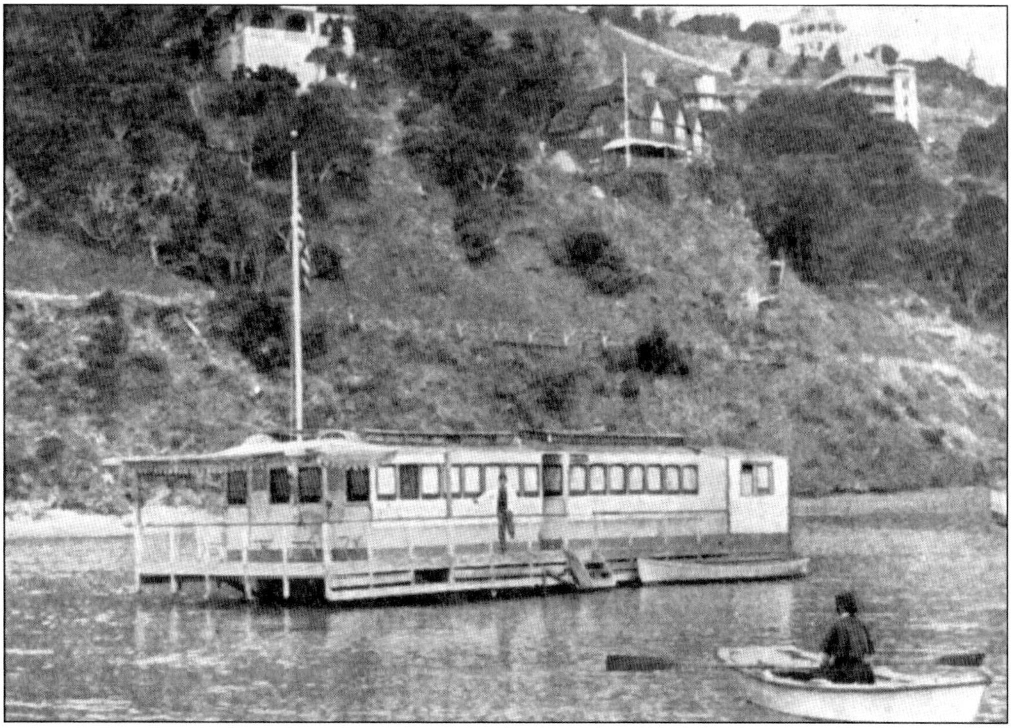

Houseboats in Marin were often elaborate affairs, such as this one made out of four San Francisco streetcars. Colorful parties were held, with revelers moving from houseboat to houseboat. (Courtesy the Landmark Society.)

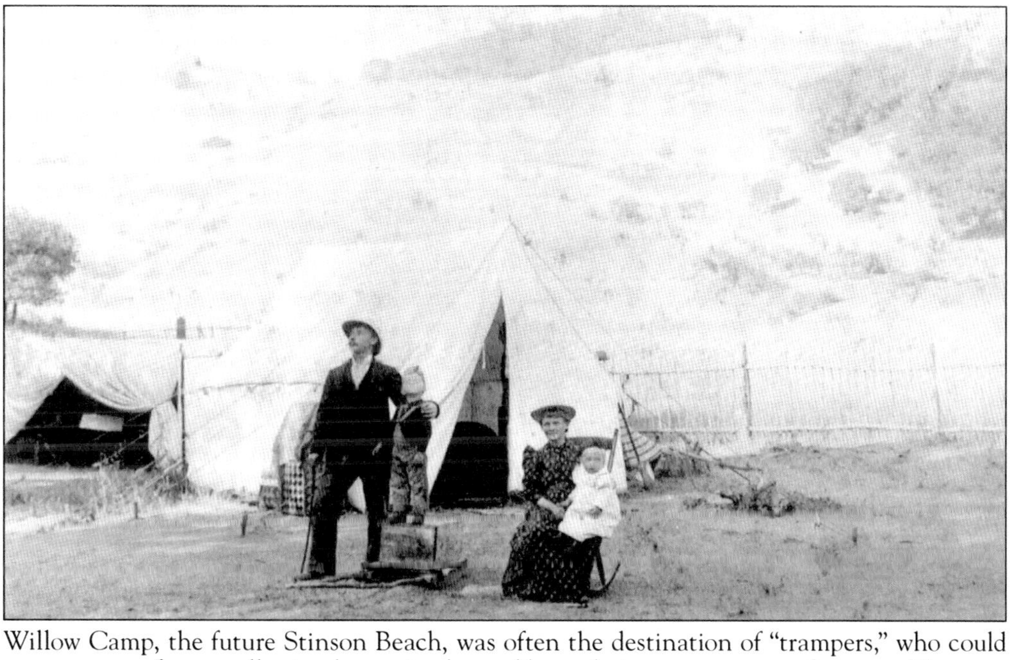

Willow Camp, the future Stinson Beach, was often the destination of "trampers," who could rent a tent or, for a small price, buy a tiny lot and have their own spot year after year. (Courtesy Marin History Museum.)

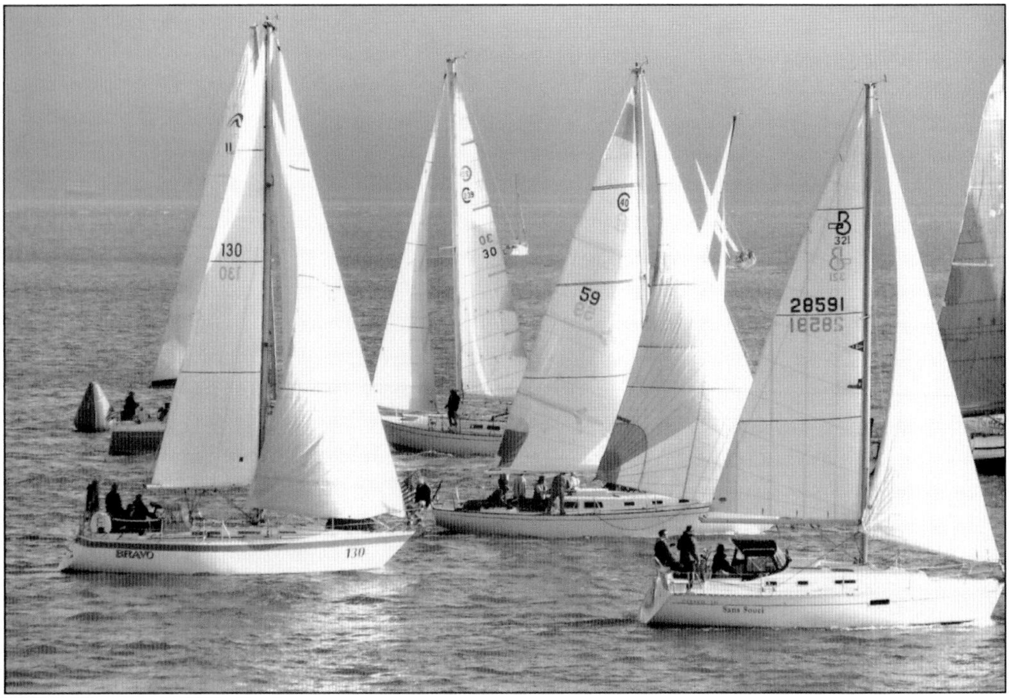

Sailboats from all over the bay converge on Marin during the yachting season for a continuous round of races. Even a midwinter regatta draws a crowd.

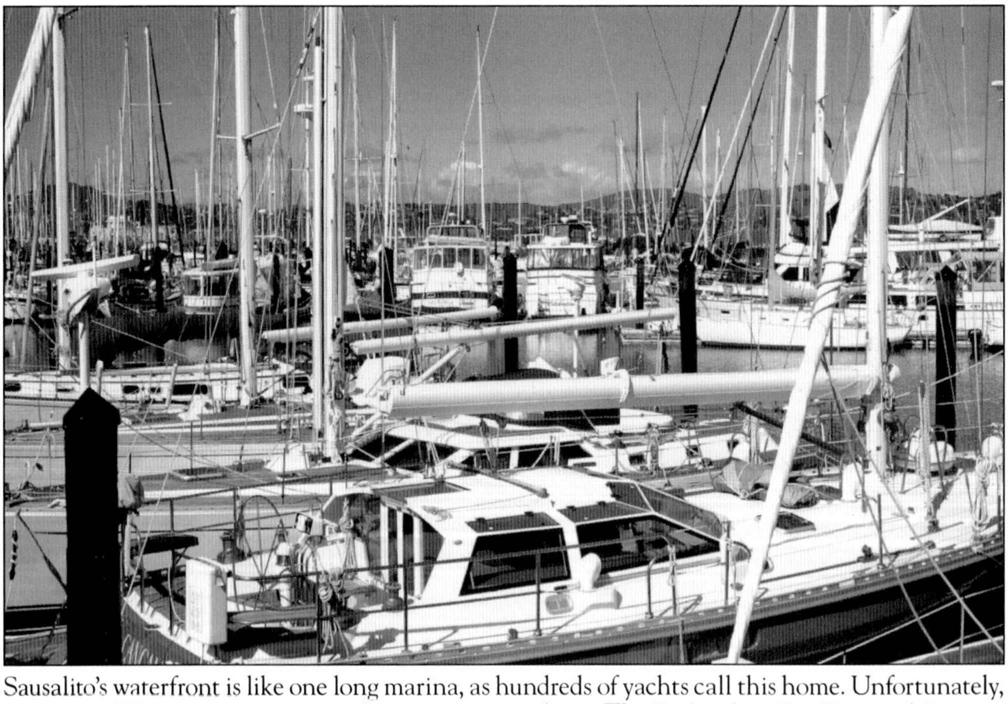

Sausalito's waterfront is like one long marina, as hundreds of yachts call this home. Unfortunately, too many, 100 or more, are occupied on a permanent basis. The Richardson Bay Regional Agency, made up of the towns of Mill Valley, Sausalito, Belvedere, and Tiburon, and the County of Marin, is trying to get a handle on the situation before being faced with another houseboat colony.

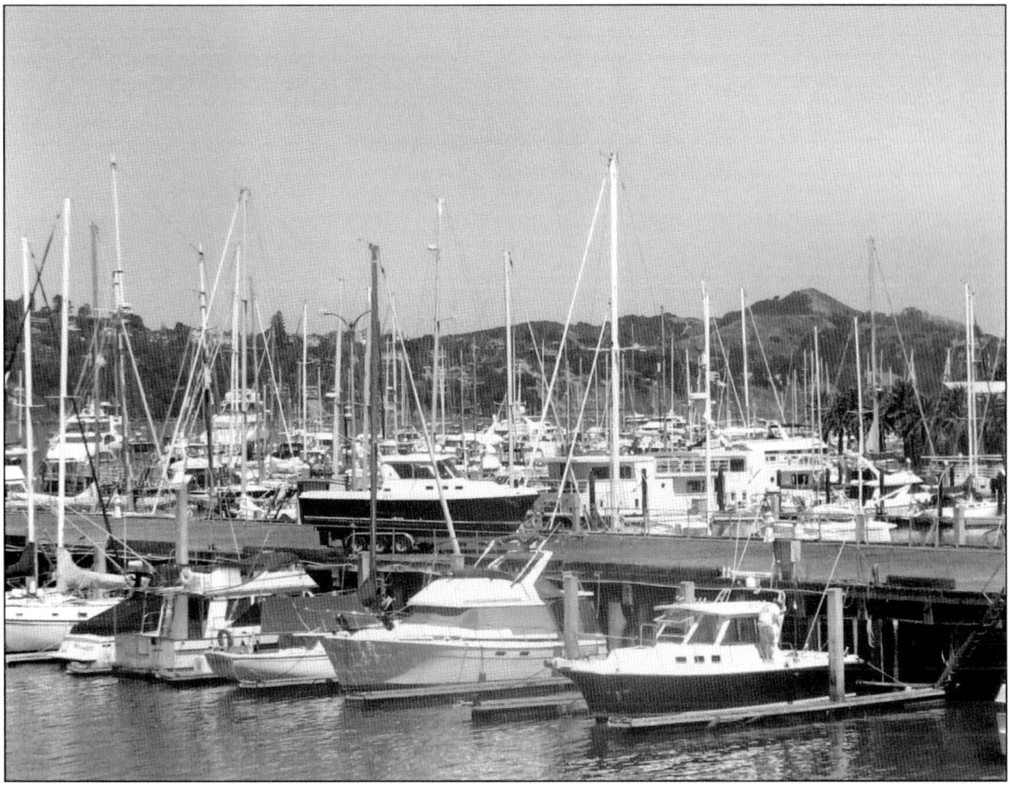

San Rafael has miles of boat storage, both indoor and outdoor, and small, boat maintenance facilities.

In 1854, the American clipper ship *Flying Cloud* sailed from New York to San Francisco in 89 days, a record that stood for 135 years. In 2008, the *Gitana 13*, a 110-foot-long catamaran, with a crew of 10 and flying the French flag, made it in 43 days. Both followed the 14,500-mile route around Cape Horn. After passing the Golden Gate, the *Gitana 13* dropped anchor in the harbor at the Corinthian Yacht Club in Tiburon.

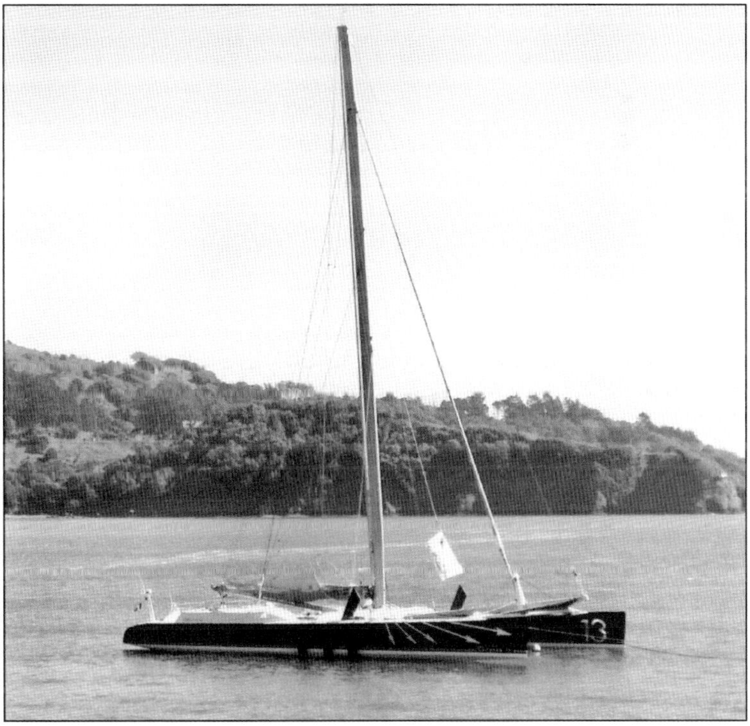

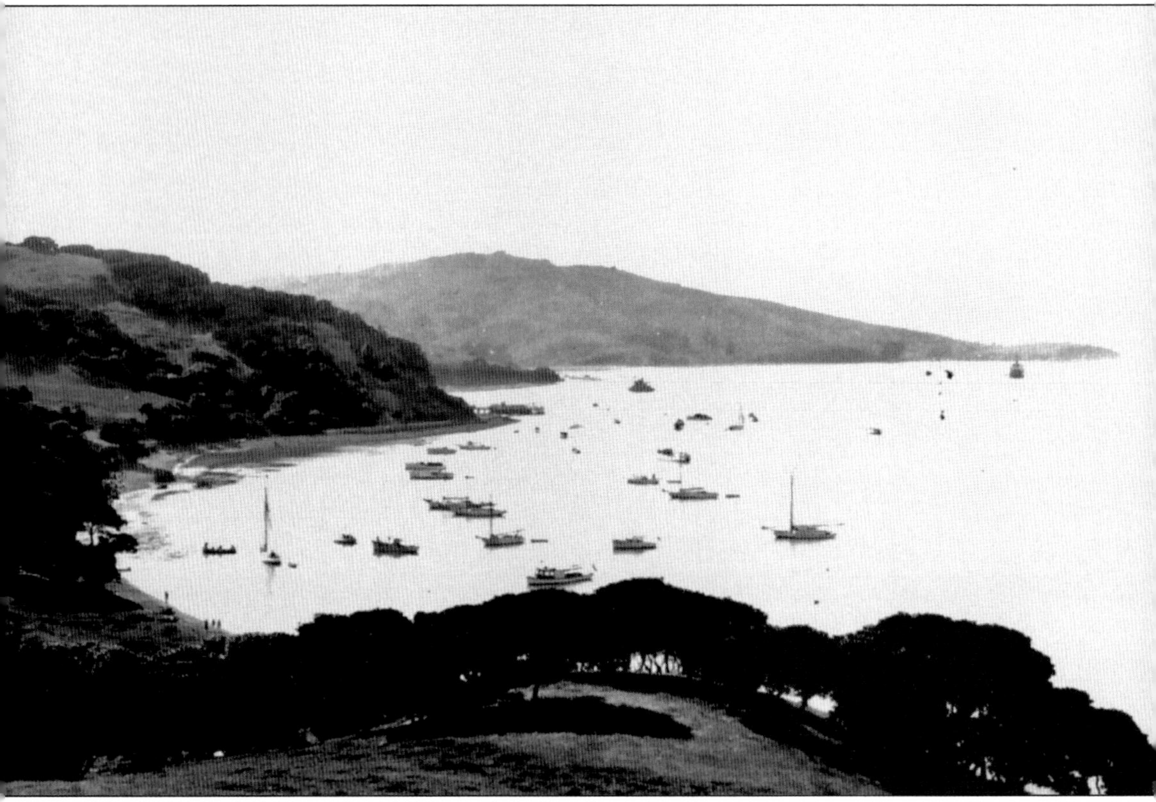

Many of the holiday seekers came in their own boats in the 1890s, just as they do today. Paradise Cove on Raccoon Strait was a popular destination. (Courtesy the Landmark Society.)

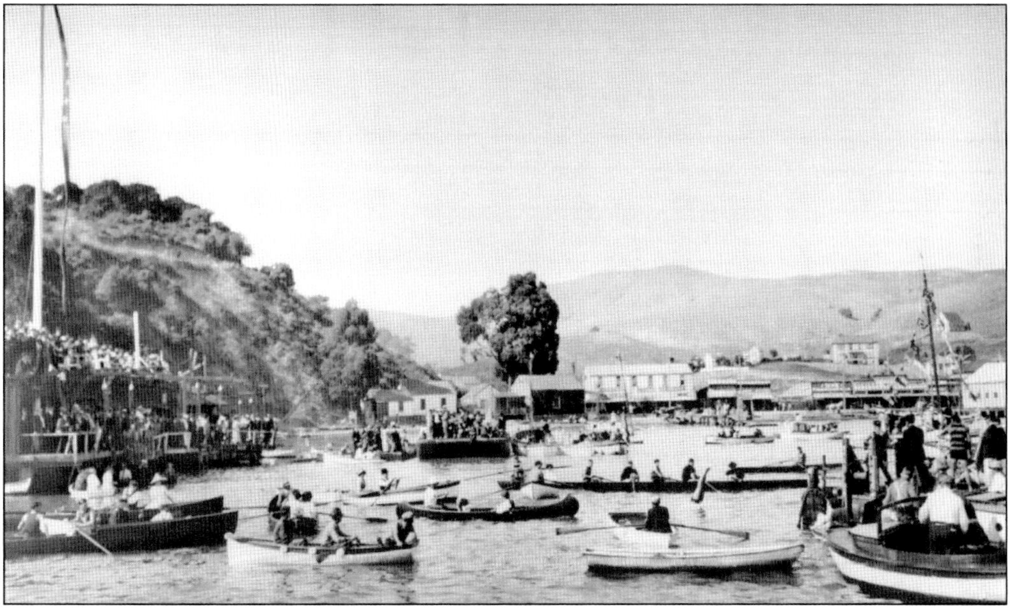

The first Corinthian Yacht Club, completed in 1887, burned down in 1910. The new, large, white building was built for $25,000. A grand "sail in" celebration was held for its opening. (Courtesy the Landmarks Society.)

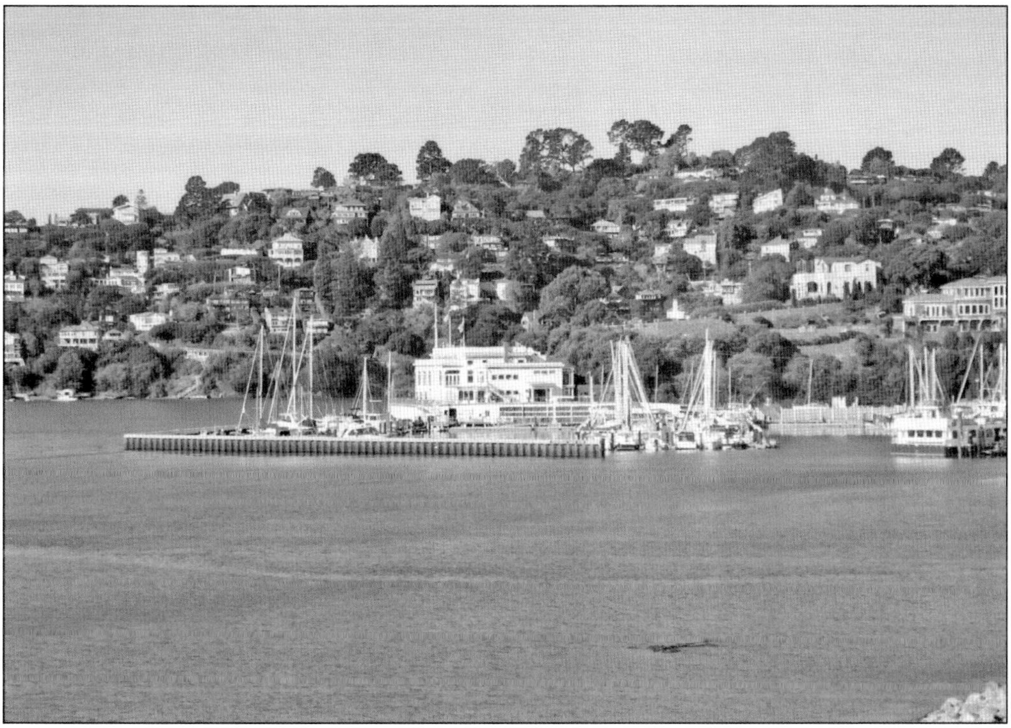

The new Corinthian Yacht Club opened in 1912 on the border between Belvedere and Tiburon. It is the landmark center of a busy harbor, with ferries to San Francisco and Angel Island arriving and departing, fleets of small craft bringing diners to waterfront restaurants, and the normal activities of a yacht club.

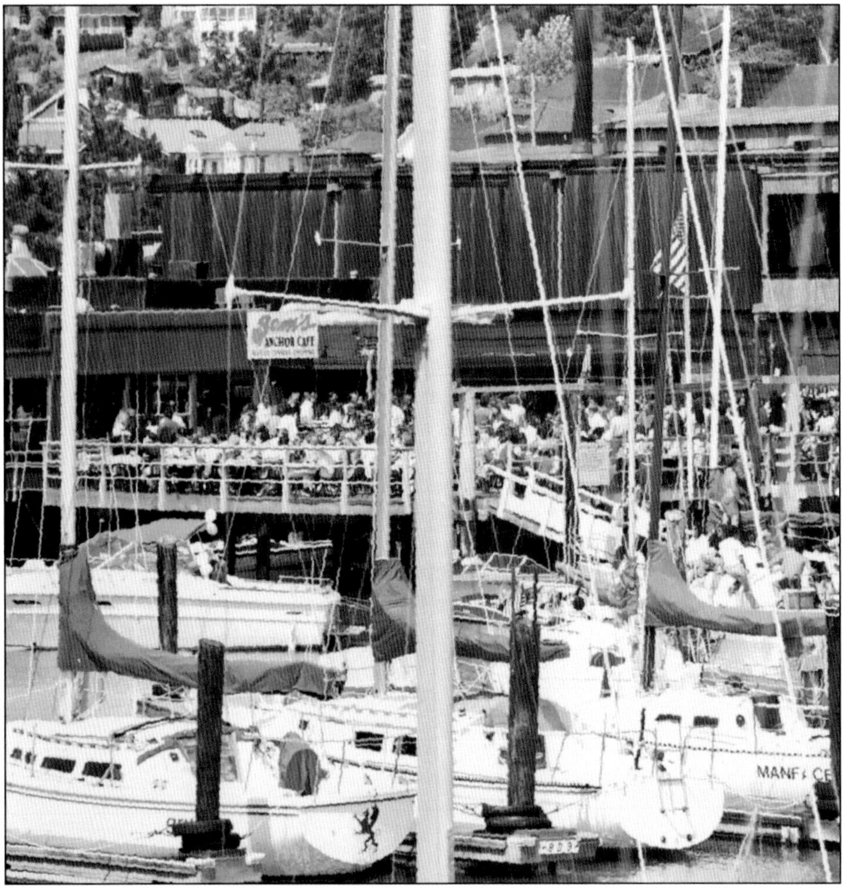

Waterfront restaurants in Sausalito, Tiburon, and San Rafael draw crowds of boaters whenever the weather cooperates.

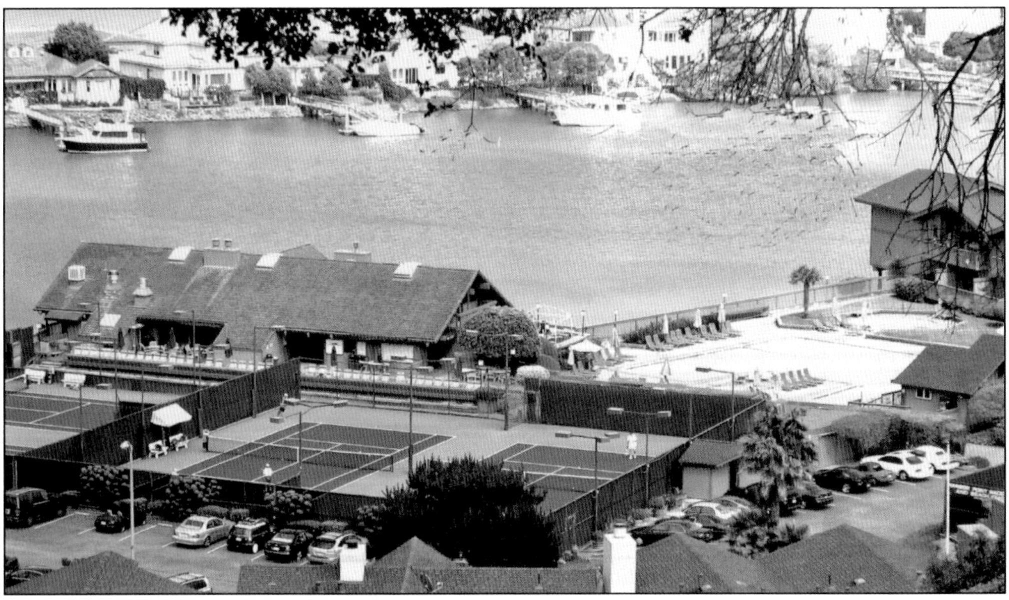

Yachting may not be the dominant sporting activity at the Harbor Point Tennis Club, but its waterfront location on the Strawberry peninsula allows its members a choice.

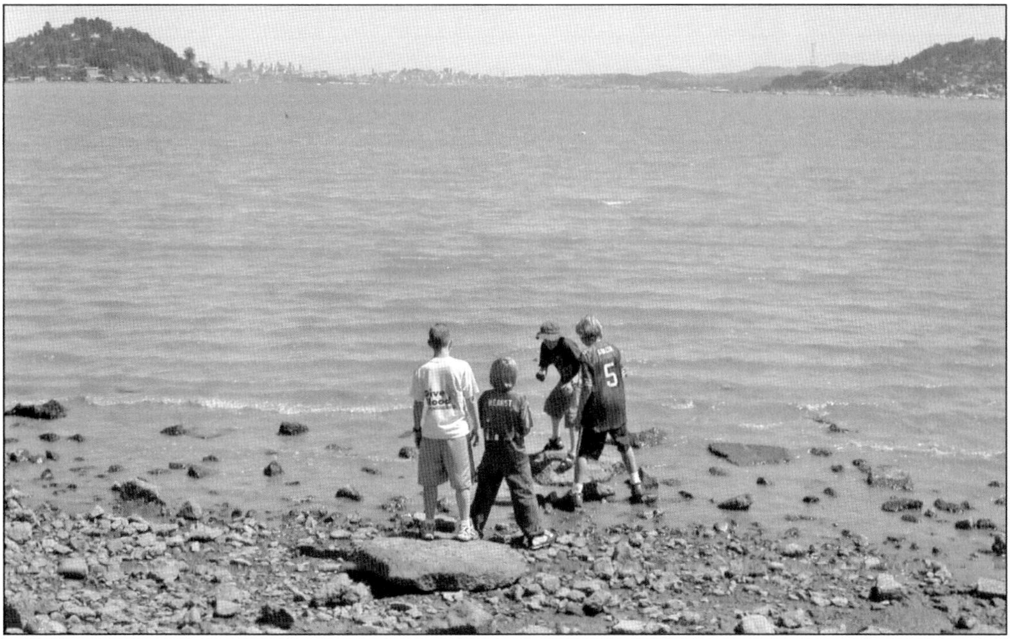

The joy of growing up by the bay includes deciding what adventures to pursue each day. These young lads have many choices: sailing, fishing, swimming, exploring, or taking one of many classes in marine ecology offered by the schools, parks, and research stations in Marin.

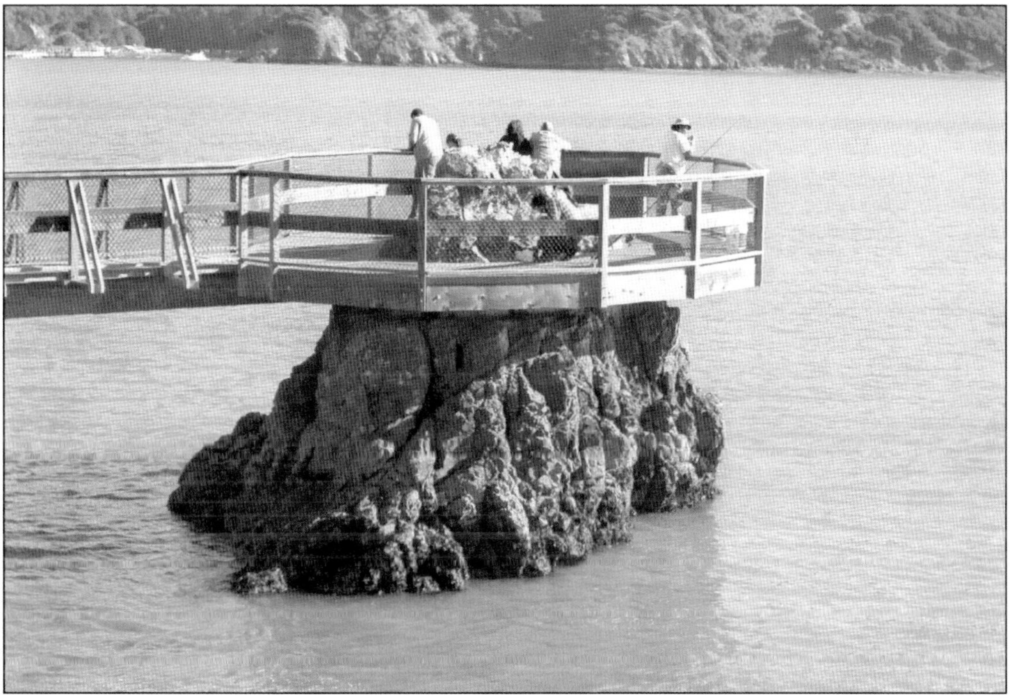

In 1961, a young Tiburon boy was drowned while fishing in Raccoon Strait. The Elephant Rock Fishing Pier was built by volunteers to provide a safe place for fishing for those under 16. By 1999, the cost of repairing and rebuilding the pier had risen to the point that public funds were required, so the age restrictions were dropped.

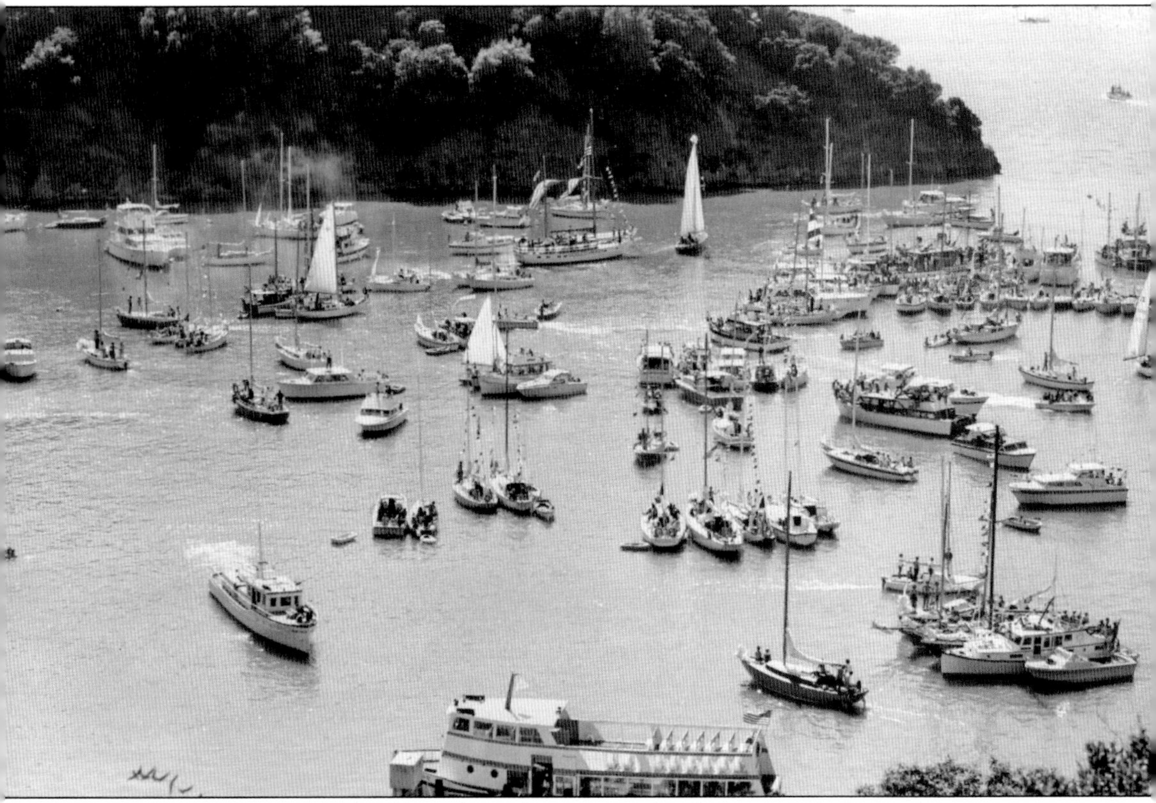

Ayala Cove on Angel Island has always been a popular destination for boats from communities all around the bay, although for about 50 years it was off limits to recreational boaters while it served as a quarantine station for the Public Health Service. To protect its citizens from diseases for which there were no cures, arriving passengers at San Francisco were held here until they were cleared. (Courtesy Angel Island Association.)

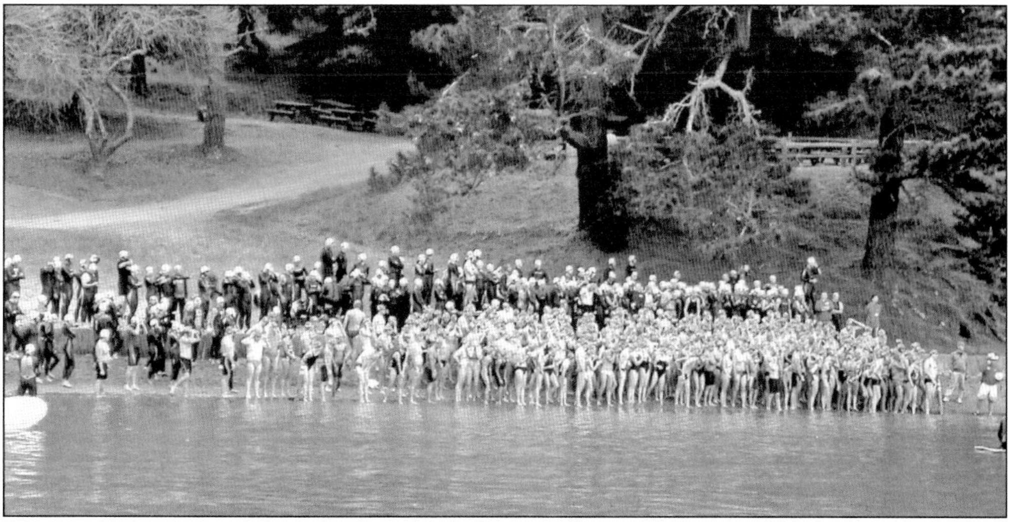

Once each year, about 800 to 900 swimmers compete in the Tiburon Mile, a race from Angel Island to the Corinthian Yacht Club.

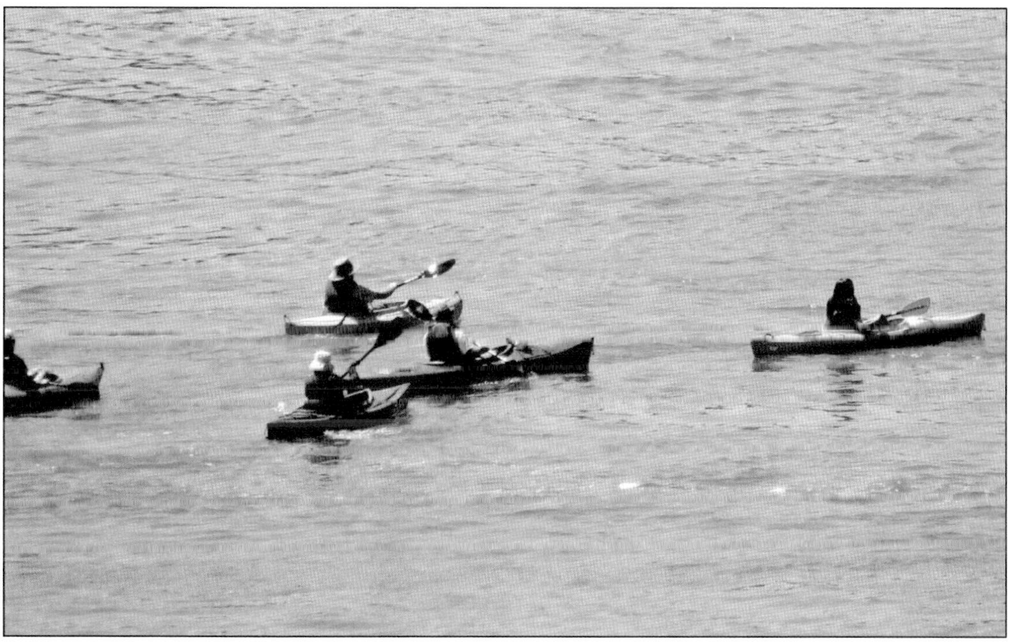

A sport gaining in popularity is kayaking. In rough weather or calm, the devotees of this strenuous activity are out on the bay.

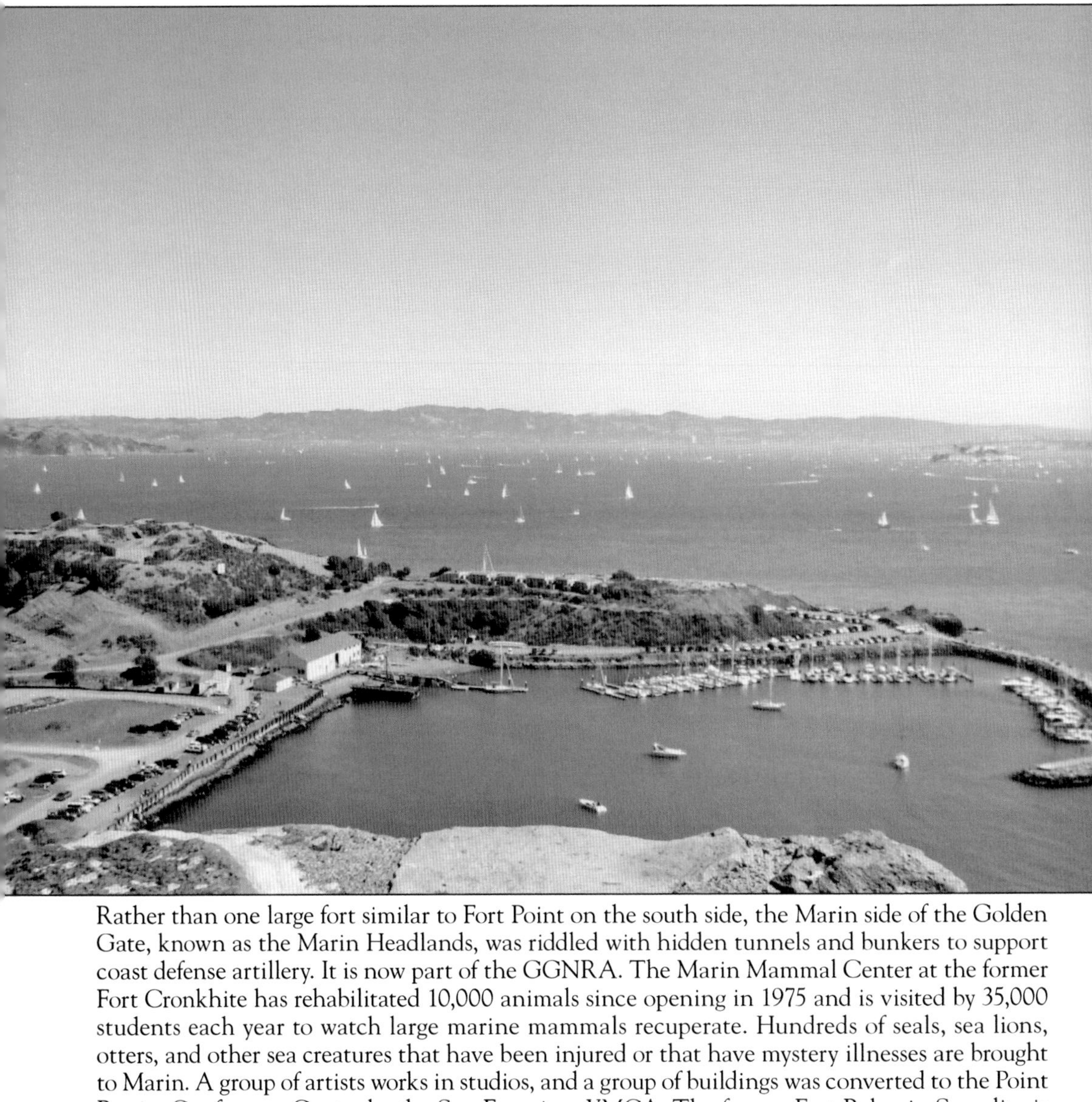

Rather than one large fort similar to Fort Point on the south side, the Marin side of the Golden Gate, known as the Marin Headlands, was riddled with hidden tunnels and bunkers to support coast defense artillery. It is now part of the GGNRA. The Marin Mammal Center at the former Fort Cronkhite has rehabilitated 10,000 animals since opening in 1975 and is visited by 35,000 students each year to watch large marine mammals recuperate. Hundreds of seals, sea lions, otters, and other sea creatures that have been injured or that have mystery illnesses are brought to Marin. A group of artists works in studios, and a group of buildings was converted to the Point Bonita Conference Center by the San Francisco YMCA. The former Fort Baker in Sausalito is being transformed into a conference center with a yacht harbor, as seen in this photograph from Vista Point.

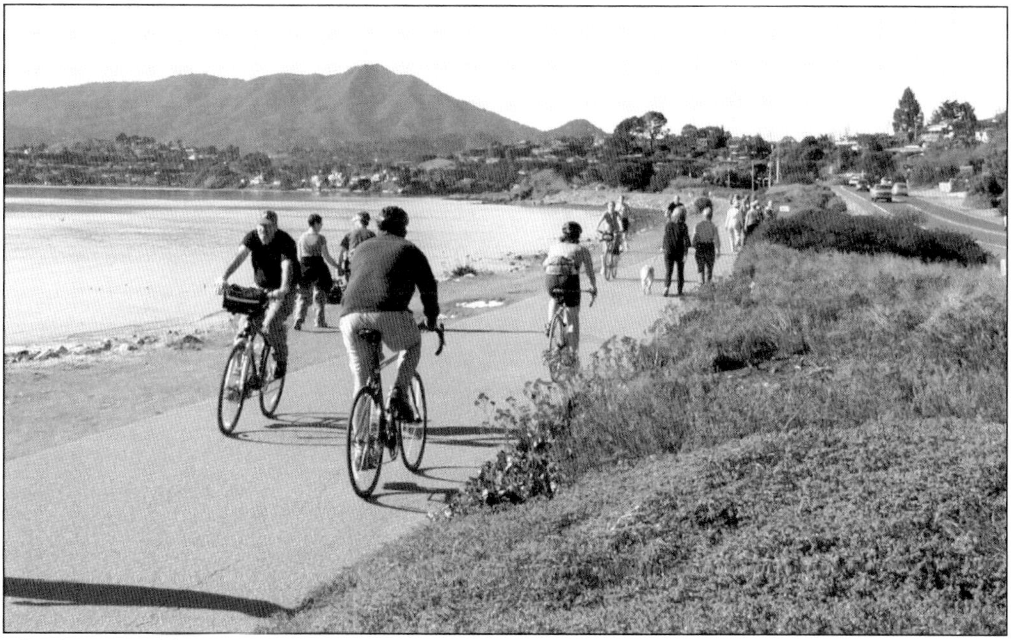

The first paved bicycle path was built along the shore of the Richardson Bay Audubon Center and Sanctuary on the former right-of-way of the Northwestern Pacific Railroad. It was soon followed by many more miles of paths, but much more needs to be done to get them connected to each other.

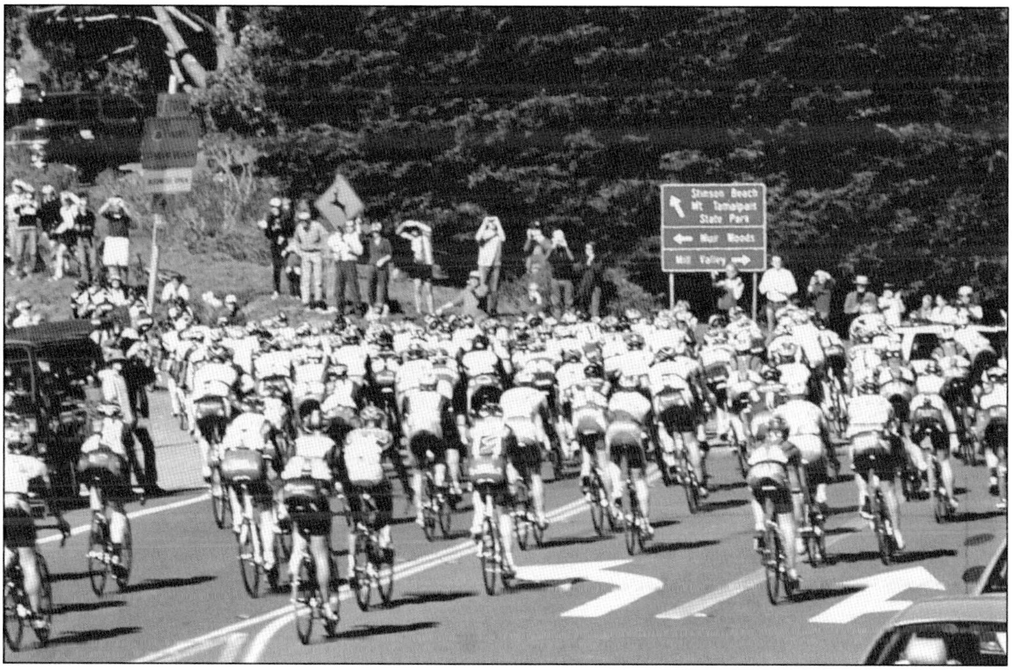

California's answer to the Tour de France is the Tour of California. It starts in Sausalito, grinds over the flanks of Mount Tamalpais, and then follows the Pacific Coast to the county line. It ends a week or so later in Southern California. The competitors form a peloton, or solid group of racers, as they dash through the coastal towns of Marin.

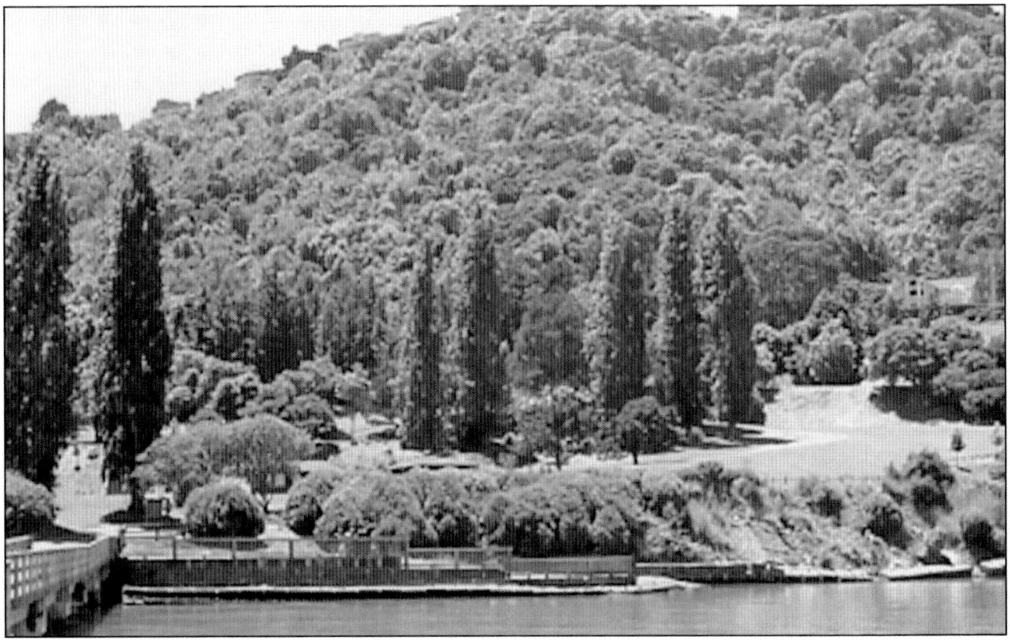

The lovely Paradise County Park was the former Floating Drydock Training Center during navy days. Now the pier is a favorite fishing spot.

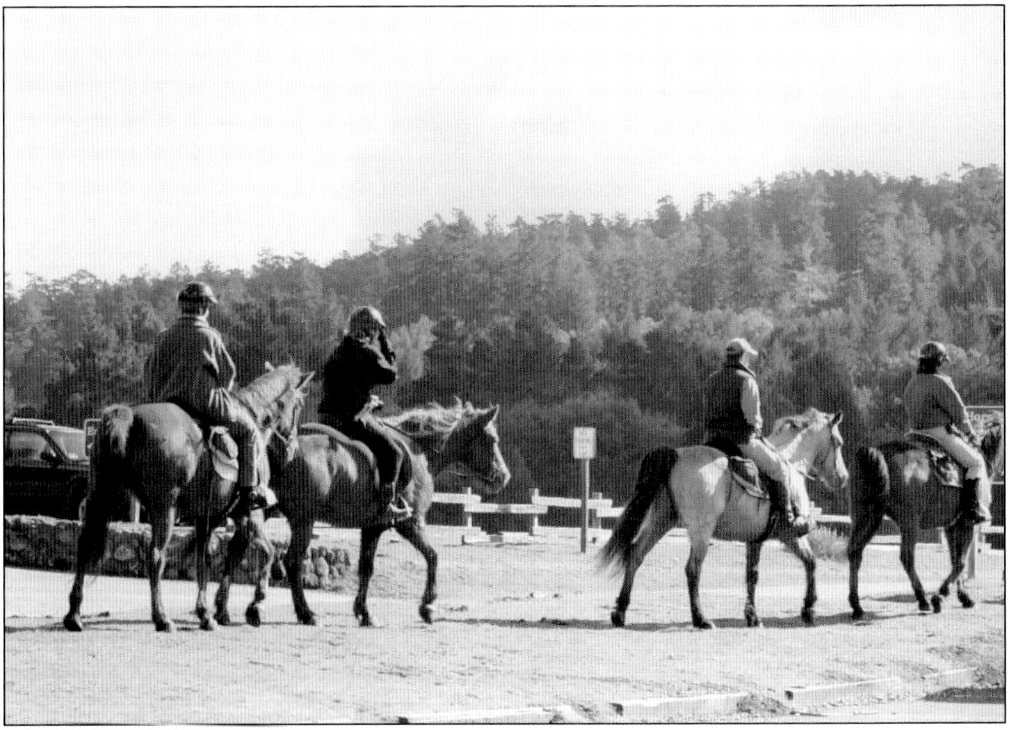

There are bridle paths through much of the GGNRA. Equestrians can bring their own mounts or rent them from riding stables in the area. Experienced horsemen are on call to form rescue teams when children or campers are lost in rugged country.

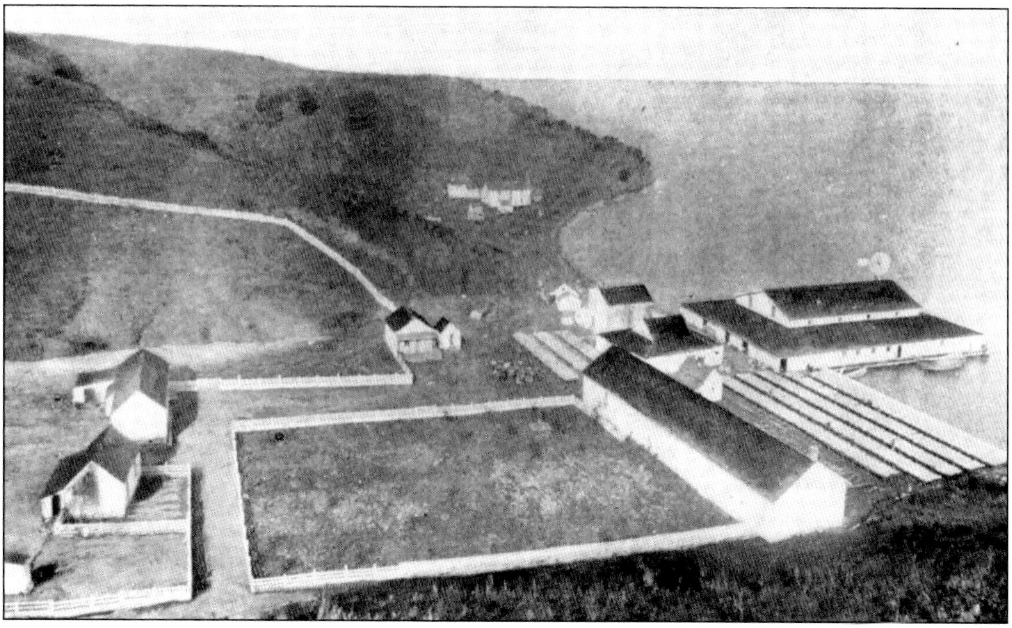

The first recorded use of the Paradise Drive site was in 1877 as a codfish-canning factory. A deepwater dock made it possible to unload cod caught in northern waters. The cod were washed to remove the salt used to preserve them on the long trip south, air dried on racks at the plant, and then packed for sale throughout the country. (Courtesy Romberg Tiburon Center.)

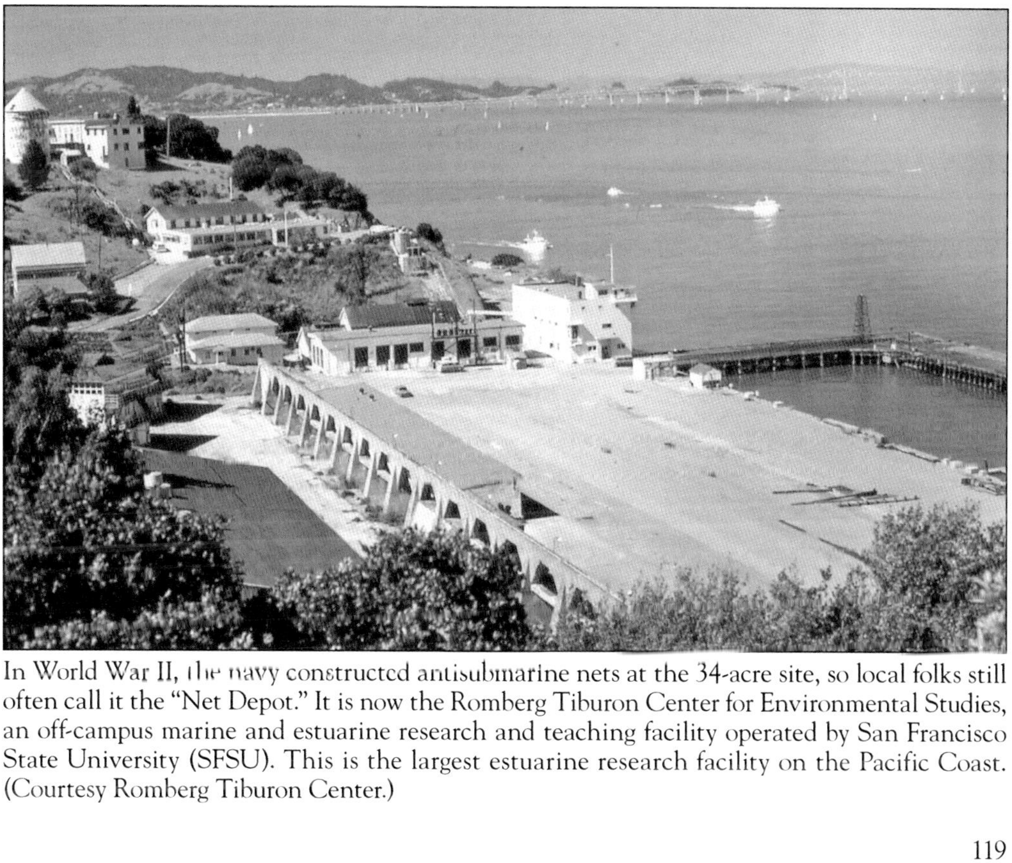

In World War II, the navy constructed antisubmarine nets at the 34-acre site, so local folks still often call it the "Net Depot." It is now the Romberg Tiburon Center for Environmental Studies, an off-campus marine and estuarine research and teaching facility operated by San Francisco State University (SFSU). This is the largest estuarine research facility on the Pacific Coast. (Courtesy Romberg Tiburon Center.)

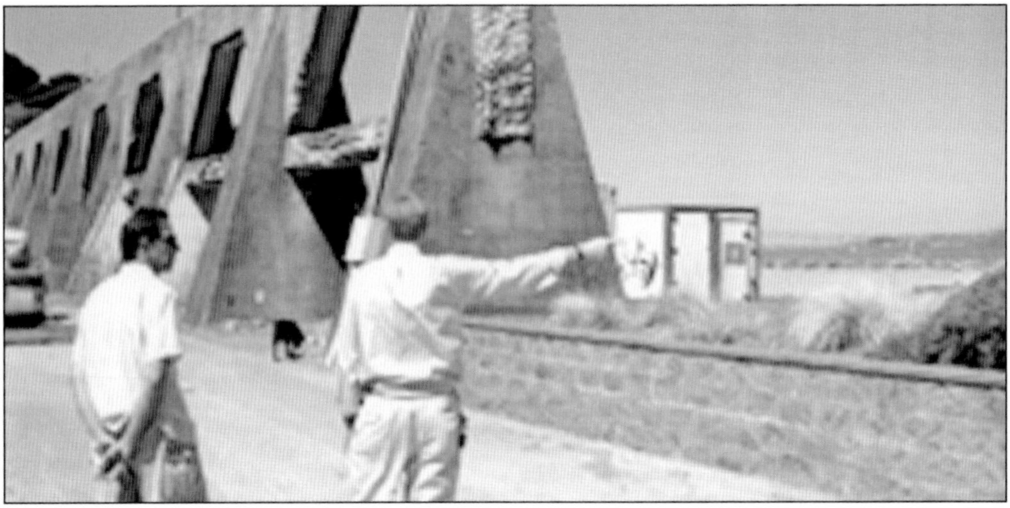

Dave Gotz (left), president of the Belvedere Tiburon Landmarks Society, and Toby Garfield, director of the Romberg Tiburon Center, inspect facilities left from the variety of uses during the center's naval career, which lasted more than a century. Since title passed from the navy to SFSU in 2007, the historical significance of its many structures must be researched before major changes are made.

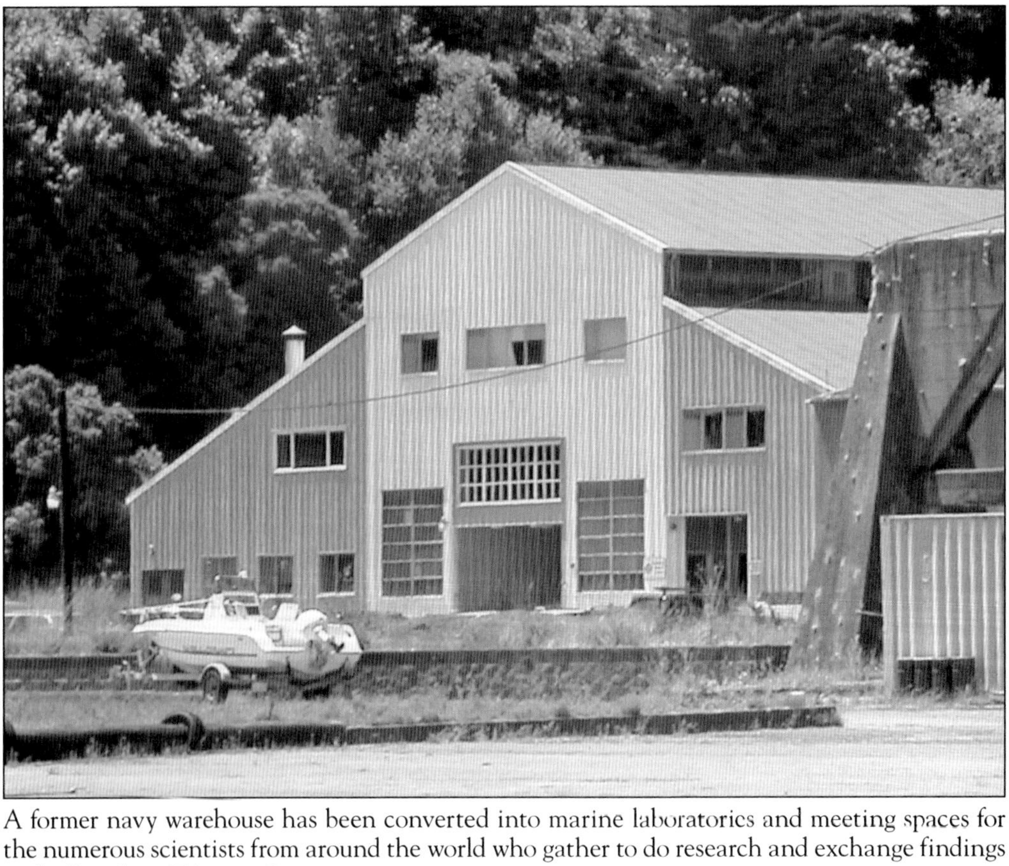

A former navy warehouse has been converted into marine laboratories and meeting spaces for the numerous scientists from around the world who gather to do research and exchange findings at the Romberg Tiburon Center.

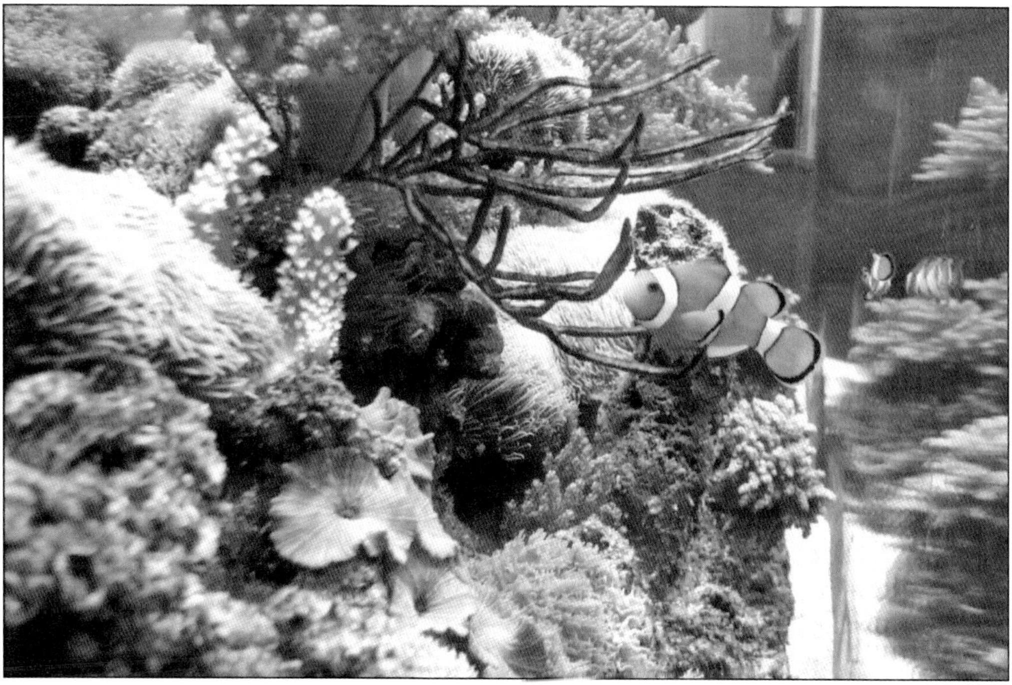

Scientists at the Romberg Tiburon Center (RTC) are making extensive studies of the effect of waterborne pollutants on coral reefs. Biological oceanography, ecosystems ecology, molecular marine ecology and evolution, and coastal processes are just a few of the studies carried on at the RTC.

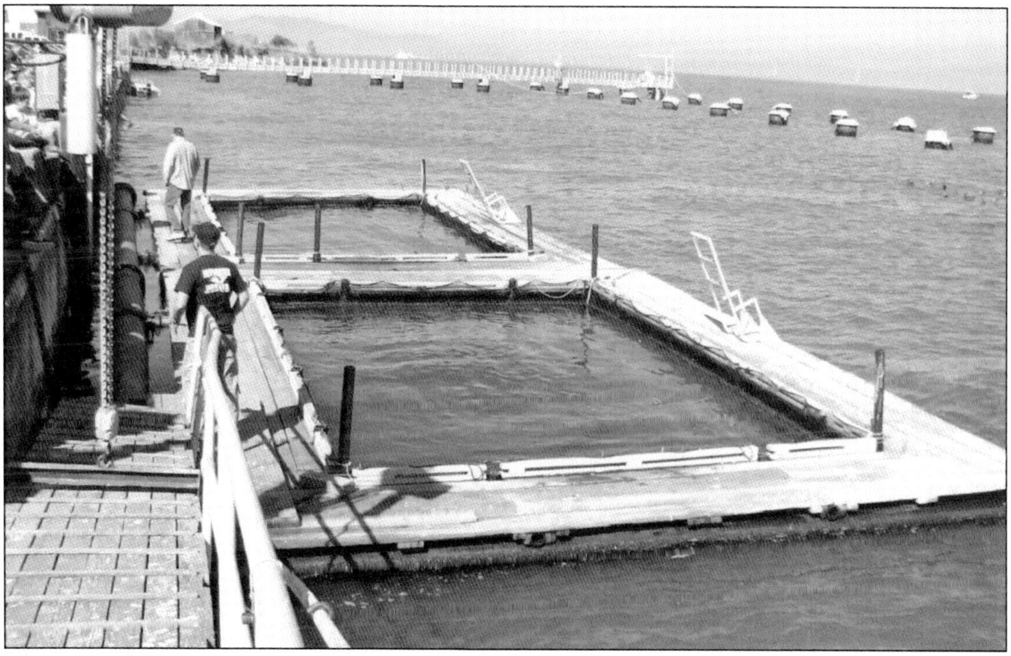

The Tyee Club operates a salmon recovery program at the Romberg Tiburon Center. From 50,000 to 70,000 juvenile salmon are released into the bay each year in the hope that they will return in four or five years to spawn and help perpetuate the species.

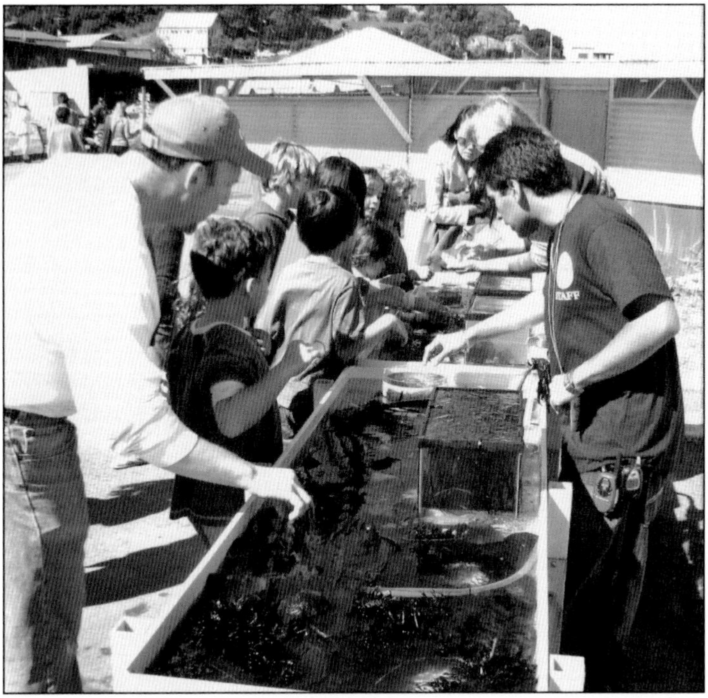

Students and guests examine marine life during one of the frequent open houses conducted at the RTC. The historic officers' club has been converted into the Bay Conference Center.

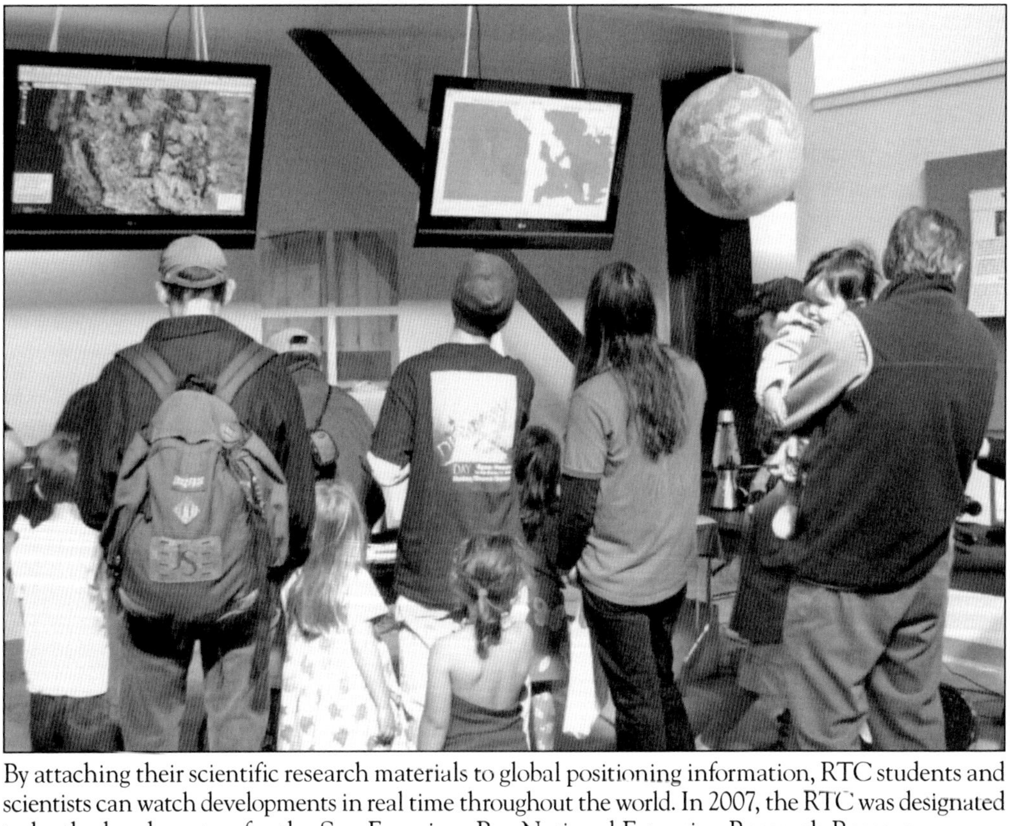

By attaching their scientific research materials to global positioning information, RTC students and scientists can watch developments in real time throughout the world. In 2007, the RTC was designated to be the headquarters for the San Francisco Bay National Estuarine Research Reserve.

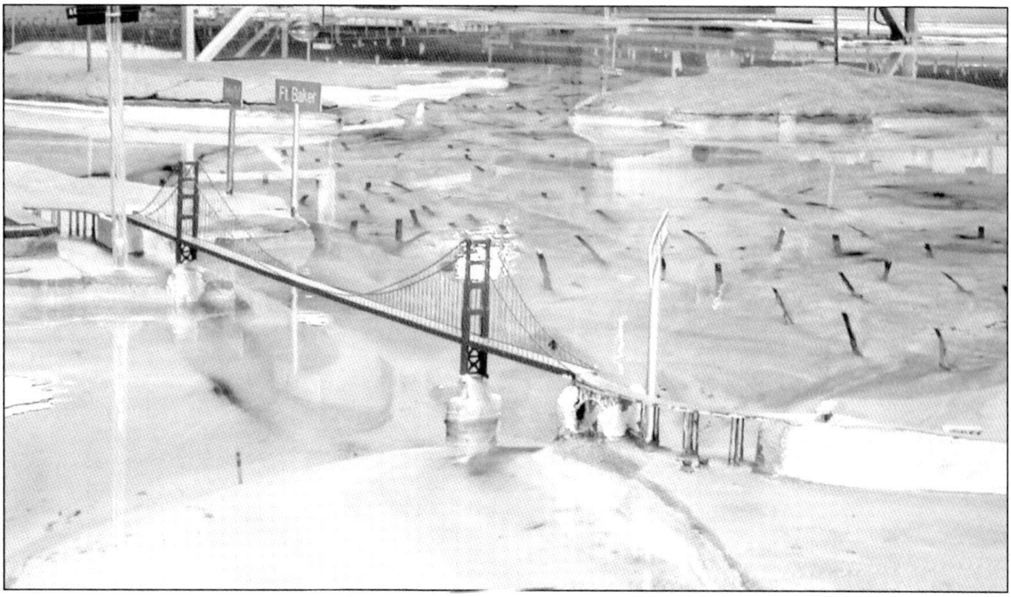

In order to study the long-term effects of the many changes that have been proposed for the San Francisco Bay Estuary, a working model was constructed by the U.S. Army Corps of Engineers in a former Marinship building in Sausalito. The model covers 1.5 acres and represents the complete estuary from outside the gate to Sacramento.

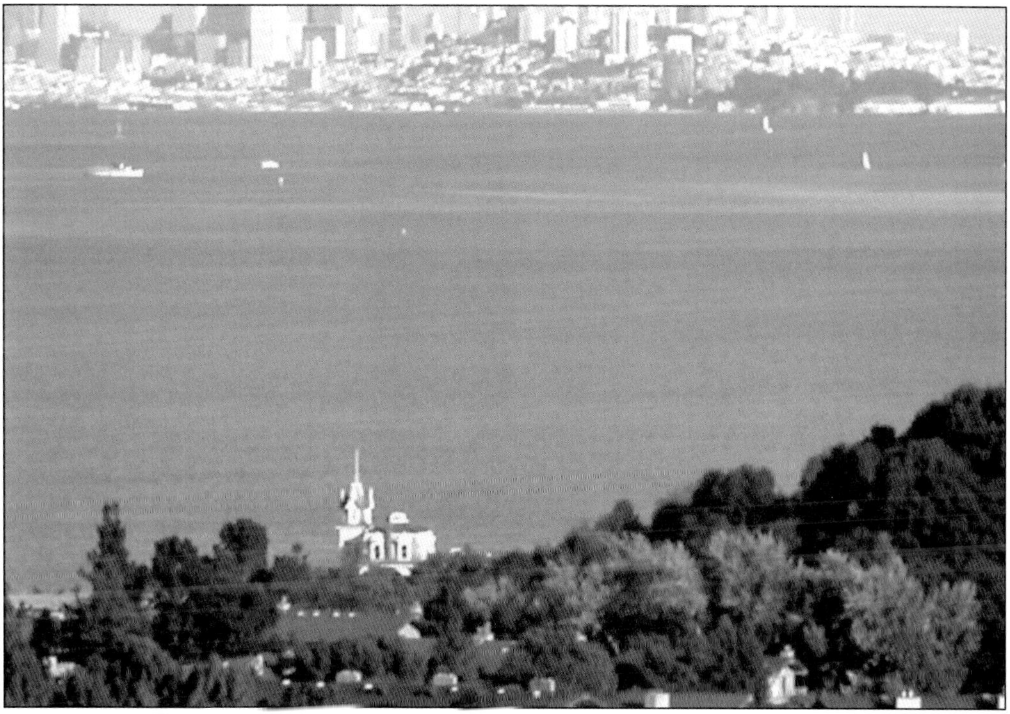

A plan to fill Richardson Bay and construct 2,000 homes spurred community activity in the 1950s to acquire the tidelands and preserve the land for future generations. The historic Lyford House, about to fall to the wrecker's ball, was successfully moved over from Strawberry Point to the Richardson Bay Audubon Center and Sanctuary.

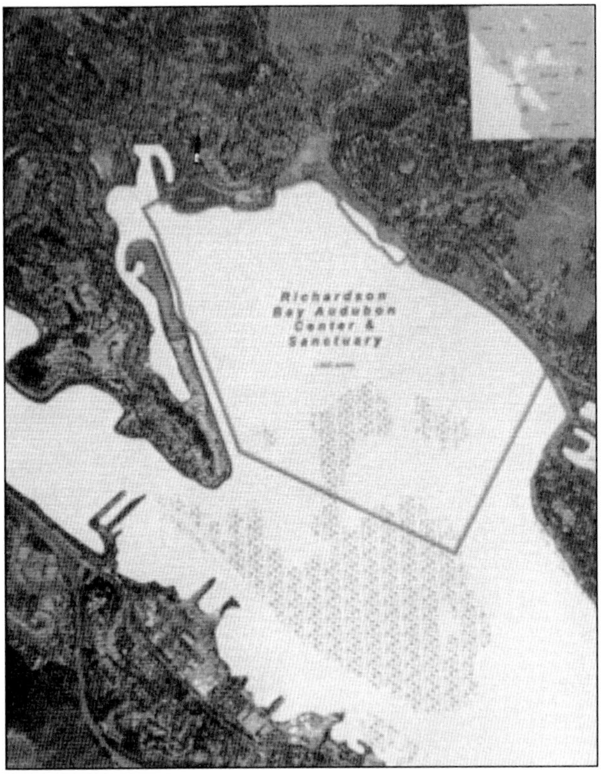

Comprised of 11 acres of uplands and 900 acres of submerged lands, the Richardson Bay Audubon Center and Sanctuary provides an important feeding stop for migrating birds on the Pacific flyway. Eighty thousand surf scooters, a diving duck, arrive each November to rest and feed in the bay. The sanctuary also involves community residents through education, conservation, and restoration programs that support a variety of ecosystems and make it a diverse and engaging outdoor classroom.

A hazardous materials team searches for oiled birds on the shores of Richardson Bay after a container ship struck a tower of the Bay Bridge. Thousands of birds were caught in the resultant oil spill. Hundreds were rescued, cleaned by sanctuary staff and volunteers, and returned to the wild. Thousands more did not make it.

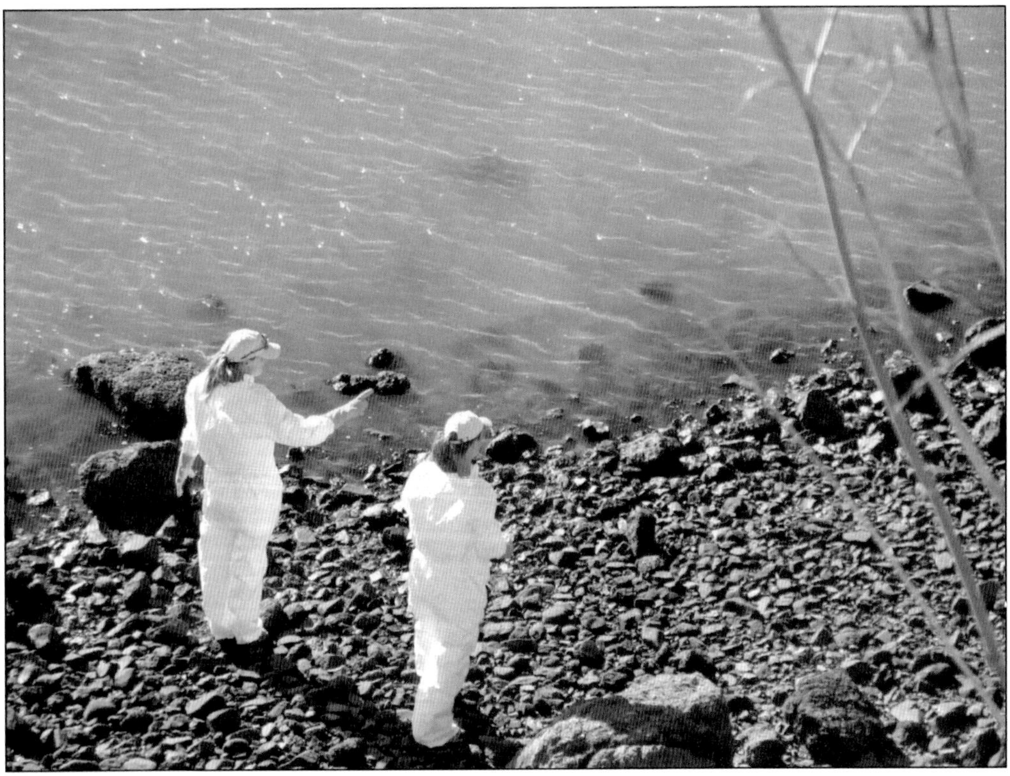

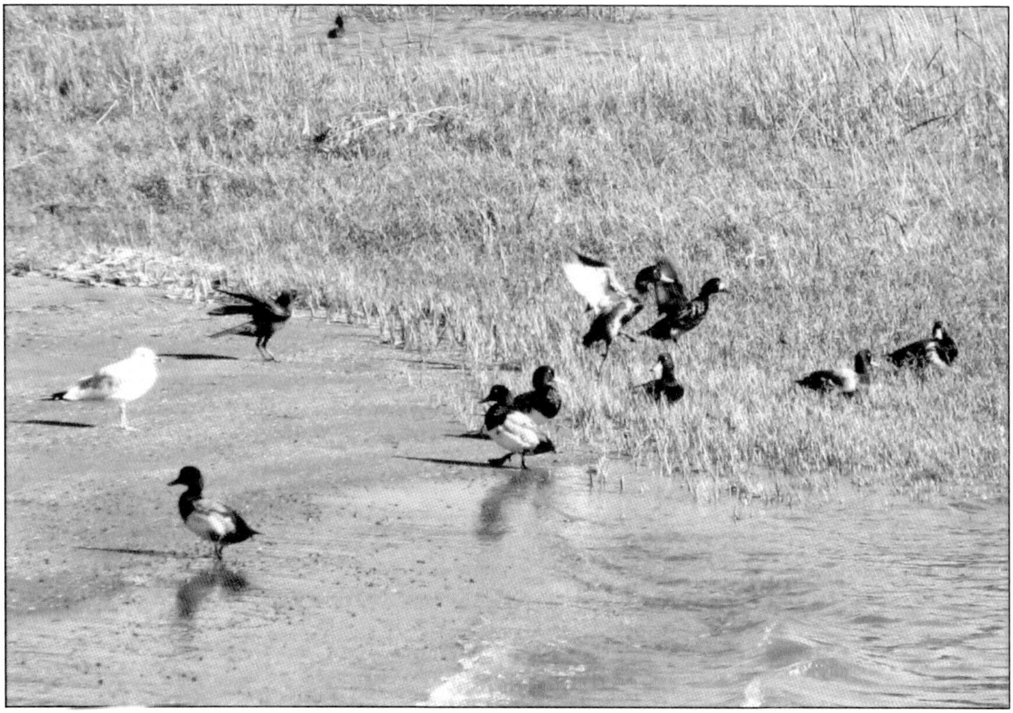

San Francisco Bay is an incredibly rich marine ecosystem that supports large populations of ducks and shore birds.

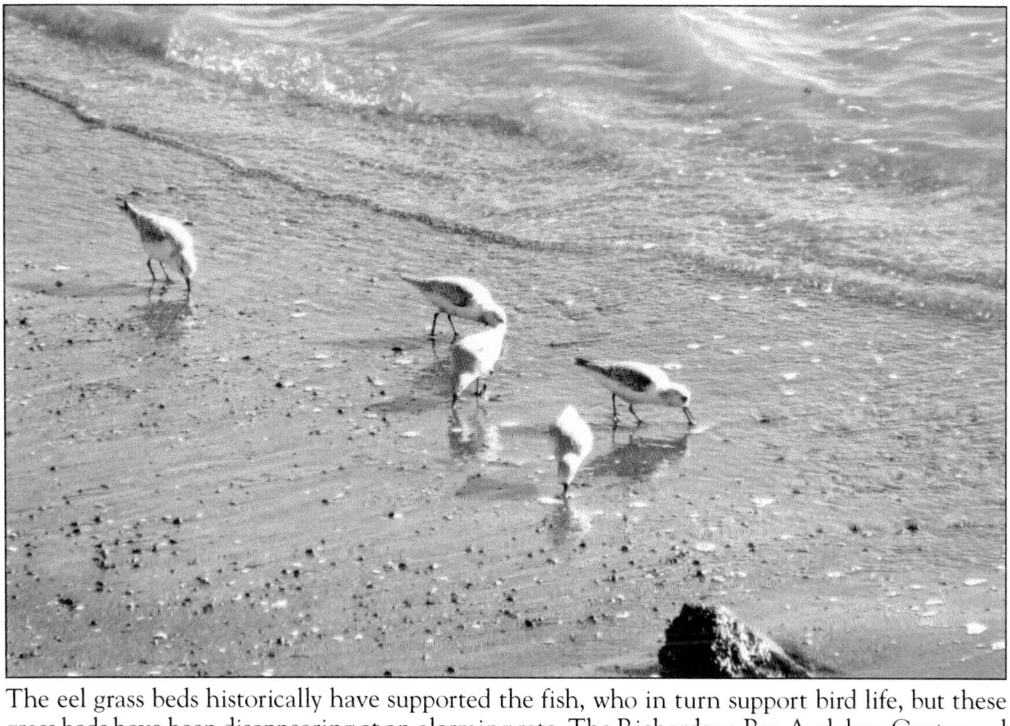

The eel grass beds historically have supported the fish, who in turn support bird life, but these grass beds have been disappearing at an alarming rate. The Richardson Bay Audubon Center and Sanctuary has instituted a program to reestablish eel grass in the restored wetlands of the bay.

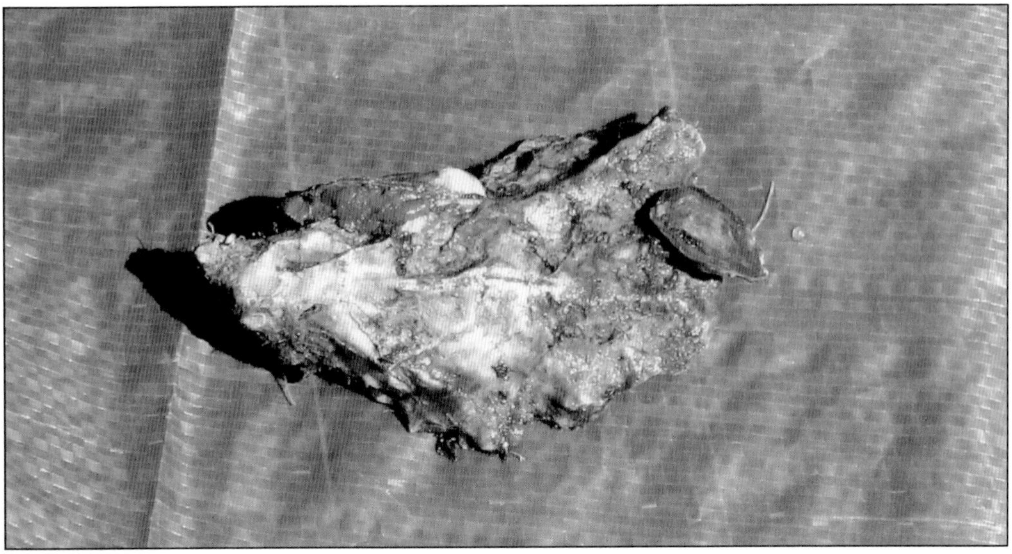

Oysters were a substantial part of the Miwok Indian diet but have all but disappeared from the bay. Large oysters from the Orient have been imported and are grown and harvested all along the Pacific Coast. A joint research project between the Romberg Tiburon Center and the Richardson Bay Audubon Center and Sanctuary has produced some results, as seen in this image. By placing bundles of large Pacific oyster shells in the bay, the small native oysters suddenly reappeared, clinging to the large shells.

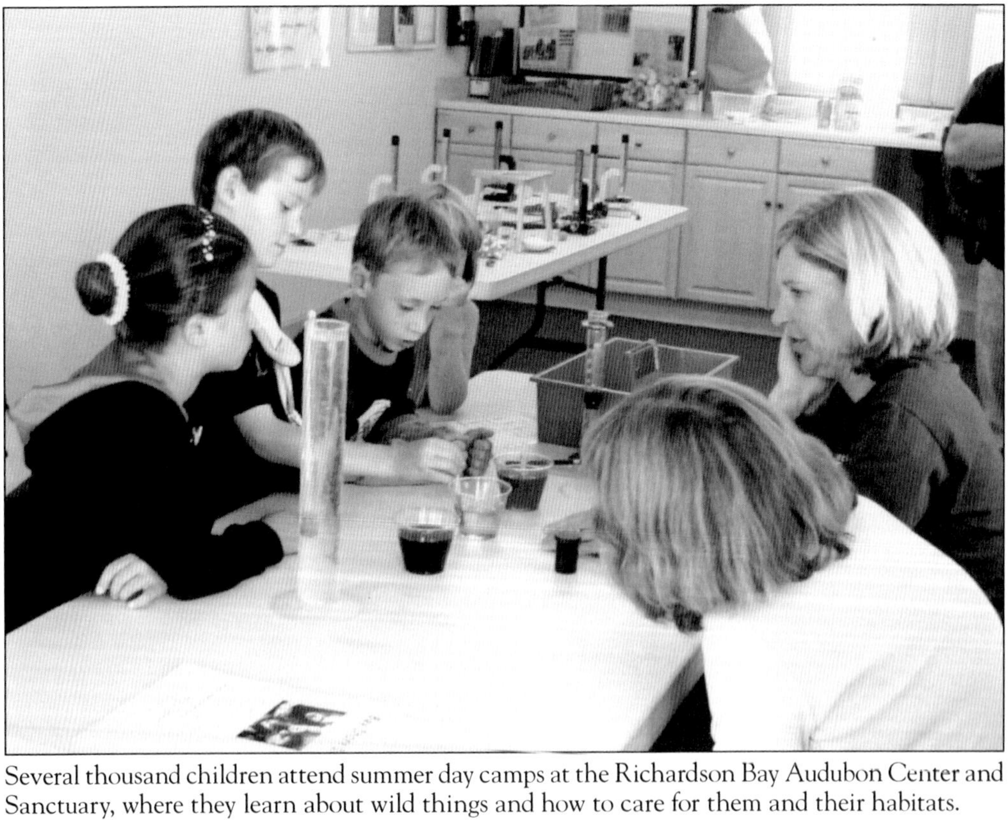

Several thousand children attend summer day camps at the Richardson Bay Audubon Center and Sanctuary, where they learn about wild things and how to care for them and their habitats.

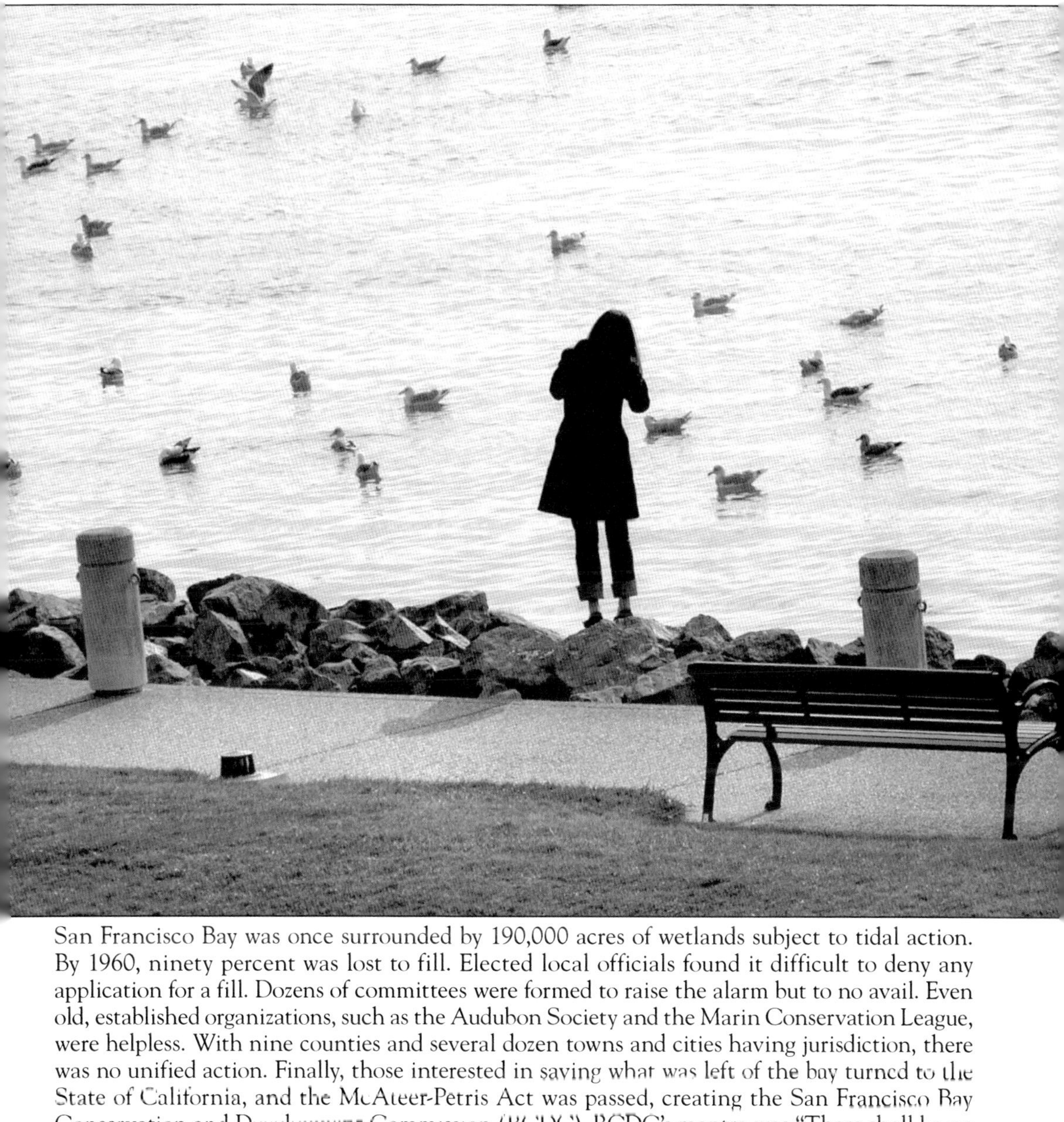

San Francisco Bay was once surrounded by 190,000 acres of wetlands subject to tidal action. By 1960, ninety percent was lost to fill. Elected local officials found it difficult to deny any application for a fill. Dozens of committees were formed to raise the alarm but to no avail. Even old, established organizations, such as the Audubon Society and the Marin Conservation League, were helpless. With nine counties and several dozen towns and cities having jurisdiction, there was no unified action. Finally, those interested in saving what was left of the bay turned to the State of California, and the McAteer-Petris Act was passed, creating the San Francisco Bay Conservation and Development Commission (BCDC). BCDC's mantra was "There shall be no use of the bay for which an alternative upland location is available." It worked. The bay is larger today than it was in 1969 when BCDC began its work.